The Transitional Age

The Transitional Age

British Literature

1880 - 1920

by

Edward S. Lauterbach

and

W. Eugene Davis

The Whitston Publishing Company
Incorporated
Troy, New York
1973

Library of Congress Catalog Card Number 72-87110

ISBN 0-87875-036-3

Printed in the United States of America

For
KAREN
and
SHIRLEY

PREFACE

This book is a concise guide to British literature between 1880 and 1920, a span of literary history now generally called the transitional age. Part I consists of four essays which survey significant developments in the fiction, poetry, drama and non-fictional prose of the era. Part II consists of selective bibliographies of more than 170 authors, each with a list of primary and secondary works and a brief assessment of the author's place in the period. (An explanation of the organization of Part II appears on pages 77-78.) The two parts of the book are meant to complement each other; the essays trace themes and concerns common to works within each major genre, while the individual entries indicate the importance of each author's work.

As a guide to transitional English literature, the book may be used in a variety of ways. Persons interested in a general outline of the period will find Part I helpful. Readers interested in determining the more relevant primary works of the period will be directed to them in Parts I and II. Students engaged in detailed study of individual authors of the period will find the selective bibliographies especially useful.

This book includes all authors of major importance who published their most significant books during the transitional years. We also cover a number of minor authors whose work is of historical importance though no longer recognized for its intrinsic literary worth. For example, we include Grant Allen, a very minor novelist, because *The Woman Who Did* is important today as a mirror of late-Victorian attitudes toward extra-marital sex.

We established two criteria for inclusion: dates of publication of the author's work, and the presence in it of themes, ideas and forms characteristic of transitional literature. If most of an author's works, or his most characteristic works, were published between 1880 and 1920, he is listed. But in the case of a few late Victorian and a few post-transitional authors, inclusion on this basis was not justified. For example, about half of George Meredith's publications appeared after 1880, as did many of William Morris' important prose romances. But both Meredith and Morris belong in spirit to the Victorian age and they are excluded. Similarly we exclude James Joyce, although both *Portrait of the Artist as a Young Man* and *Dubliners* were published before 1920, since his later and more characteristic work is definitely not transitional.

At both ends of the period, however, we treat as transitional a few authors whose works, by strict chronological limits, lie mainly outside the 1880-1920 period. For example, Walter Pater's *Studies in the History of the Renaissance* (1873), a seminal influence on the aesthetic and decadent movements, had to be included. We represent such later authors as W. B. Yeats, D. H. Lawrence, George Bernard Shaw, W. Somerset Maugham and E. M. Forster; even though some of their work may be termed post-transitional or "modern," their pre-1920 writings are the literary culmination of the transitional period.

iii

The authority for all dates and titles has been: (1) *British Museum General Catalogue of Printed Books* and its supplements; (2) *A Catalog of Books Represented by the Library of Congress* and its supplements; (3) specialized, single-author bibliographies (listed in the entries for individual authors). Though some titles are shortened, every effort has been made to list them accurately.

For books, the publication date is that of the first edition. In a few instances, we used the date of the first appearance of an edition for the general public even though an earlier edition had been issued in limited quantities for private distribution. With few exceptions a work's importance stems from wide distribution to the reading public, not from limited circulation among an author's friends. When a title was published in the United States before initial British publication, the earlier date is given. Dates of first publication in the British Museum and Library of Congress catalogs and in single-author bibliographies do not always agree, although such discrepancies are comparatively rare. We list what seems to be the initial appearance of a book.

For plays, the date given is that of first performance, when it was possible to determine it, since public performance is usually more important than publication for tracing a play's influence. Furthermore, many plays of the early part of the transitional period were not published until several years after the year of first performance because of lack of copyright law and the fear of piracy, especially on the American stage. In one or two instances, first performance of a play was in America, and this date is listed.

Every effort has been made to check dates. Those of first performances of plays have been the most difficult to confirm since records for much of the dramatic history of this period are inaccurate or not yet published. We are responsible for all titles and dates listed here and would like to have errors called to our attention.

We wish to acknowledge the help and encouragement of Professor Helmut E. Gerber, who was present at the inception of this book. As all students of 1880-1920 literature are aware, Professor Gerber has helped reassess the literary achievement of the era in individual essays and books, in the compilation of numerous bibliographies and in his editorship of *English Literature in Transition.* Thanks are due Professor Morton Cohen and Professor J. Randolph Cox for help concerning specific authors. We wish to thank the librarians of the Lincoln Center of Performing Arts and the British Drama League. Special thanks must go to Katherine Butts Robinson, Interlibrary Loan Librarian, Purdue University. We also wish to thank our research assistant Gaylin Cassidy, who worked so untiringly for us, and Betty Welt, Carmen Smith, Nancy Clark and Janet Reed, who typed various drafts of the manuscript. Thanks must be given to the Purdue Research Foundation, which provided summer grants for the completion of this book. Last of all, thanks to our wives who suffered patiently through many revisions and who provided encouragement for what seemed, at times, an endless task.

Edward S. Lauterbach
W. Eugene Davis

Purdue University
June, 1972

CONTENTS

Preface i

PART I: IMPORTANT TRENDS IN THE PRINCIPAL GENRES OF TRANSITIONAL LITERATURE

Fiction

The Novel 1

The Short Story 17

Entertainment 24

Poetry 29

Drama 45

Prose 59

PART II: INDIVIDUAL AUTHORS AND TERMS

Selective Bibliographies of British Authors 1880-1920 and Definitions of Some Literary Terms 77

Index 315

PART I: IMPORTANT TRENDS IN THE PRINCIPAL GENRES OF TRANSITIONAL LITERATURE

FICTION:

THE NOVEL

By 1880, writers of English fiction had begun a conspicuous revolt against Victorianism. In part their quarrel was with many of the ideals of Victorian society. They showed keen dissatisfaction with Religion, Education and Progress by revealing hypocritical piety in churchmen and laymen, by showing how ill-prepared for life high-born, "educated" young men often were, and by describing the horrors of contemporary slum life. In the approach to reform, however, the major difference between transitional and Victorian fiction is one of degree, not kind. Dickens and Thackeray had criticized society in their novels, but later novelists were more blunt, at times savage, in their attacks and generally more pessimistic about the possibility of righting society's wrongs.

Transitional fictionists also objected to the rules or established conventions which seemed to govern the choice and treatment of subject matter in the Victorian novel. Novelists earlier in the century, for the most part, avoided depicting the subjects of sex and reproduction, often treated characters of society's lower classes with humor or sentimentality and preferred to conclude their novels by reaffirming man's essential goodness and triumph through faith. The work of later fiction writers showed that a dramatic shift in artistic ideals occurred in the transitional period. They wrote of hopeless poverty with stark realism, treated sex as a violent, destructive force, saw religion not as man's Great Comforter but as a profoundly disturbing, alienating force and usually allowed their stories to end according to inner logic.

The desire of transitional novelists to experiment with narrative forms is also an indication of their break with Victorianism. With the disappearance of Victorian part publication, three-decker novels and the repressive influence of lending libraries, authors were freer to experiment with fiction as a serious art form.

Instead of the plot-centered Victorian novel, with its clearly defined beginning, middle and end, which laid stress on the coherence of life and man's experience, transitional authors often preferred less structured forms. They began experimenting with the use of multiple points of view and stream-of-consciousness and achieved a degree of authorial aloofness unknown in earlier fiction. Transitional fiction, therefore, often has a kind of random, unfinished quality unlike the logical, four-square world of Victorian fiction. Of course few novels of the 1880-1920 period incorporated all the new developments in both subject matter and technique. Older traditions of plotting, use of coincidence, indulgence in sentimentality or reticence about sex appear in conjunction with experimentation in content and form. Thus, the fiction of the period is truly transitional.

The level of achievement in transitional fiction is high. Fiction was clearly in the ascendancy over poetry, at least in terms of the number of talented men and women who wrote it. The dominant tendencies among serious fiction writers were to be realistic, to experiment with new modes of expression and to put self-realization before pleasing the public.

Samuel Butler, Thomas Hardy and William Hale White ("Mark Rutherford") portray men and women whose attitudes and beliefs are unlike those typical of characters in earlier fiction. As early as 1872, Samuel Butler had expressed the younger generation's mistrust of Victorian institutions in his satiric novel *Erewhon*. Butler cleverly pilloried Victorian respectability, religion and educational systems in his depiction of the inhabitants of a hidden Utopia, Erewhon, who worship a goddess named Ydgrun (i.e., Mrs. Grundy), participate in Musical Banks which, like Victorian respectability, mask the true basis of Erewhonian society and receive education at Colleges of Unreason.

Butler is less amusing and more blunt in his attack on society in his realistic novel *Ernest Pontifex or the Way of All Flesh*. Highly autobiographical, the novel is a bitter analysis of the wrongs done to innocent young men by shortsighted, pious parents, the church and the educational system. Ernest's problem in achieving maturity is to harmonize the conflicting demands put on him by his parents and society with his instinct—the pattern of expectations and desires inherited from his forebears. When *The Way of All Flesh* appeared, it influenced the thinking of many social reformers like George Bernard Shaw, despite the fact that much of the book had been written thirty years earlier. Butler had withheld publication of the novel until after his death, presumably because it was too personal a testament of his quarrels with society and his own family.

Like Butler, Thomas Hardy disagreed with several basic principles of Victorian life. He rejected the idea of a Benevolent Deity; he saw the psychic and physical suffering created in the name of Progress; he differed with the notion that women were passive instruments for the use and pleasure of man; his view of life was anything but confident or optimistic. Despite such basic quarrels with its prevailing ideals, early in his career Hardy was at best a circumspect and reticent critic of society. *Far From the Madding Crowd* established his reputation. Neither the flatness of characterization (the eternally faithful Gabriel Oak, the melodramatic scoundrel Sergeant Troy), the heavy sentimentality with which Hardy described the death of Fanny Robin, nor the clumsily constructed plot bothered readers who were pleased by the novel's descriptions, sentiment and happy ending when faithful Oak marries the reformed coquette Bathsheba Everdene. *The Return of the Native* also ends on a relatively happy note, although there is ample gloom earlier in the novel: Eustacia Vye, a *femme fatale*, lures Wildeve to his death, the "native," Clym Yeobright, endures an unhappy marriage and nearly goes blind. The wedding of Diggory Venn and Thomasin at the end was added at the suggestion of Hardy's friends. Neither book overtly challenged society's beliefs.

After the mid-1880's, the book versions of Hardy's fiction gradually became more candid in representing problems arising from sexual indiscretions and more direct in criticizing society. In the serial versions of the same novels, however, Hardy's artistic development remained frozen. In the serial version of *The Mayor of Casterbridge*, as published in *The Graphic*, Henchard, in the long years between the sale of his first wife and her reappearance, has married Lucetta in Jersey. In the book version of *The Mayor*, however, Henchard has had an affair with Lucetta, a much more probable outcome of their brief, passionate encounter. Differences between the serial and book versions of *Tess of the d'Urbervilles* are even more marked. In the serial, the later complications of Tess' life are based on a mock marriage with

Alec; in the book, Tess presumably lives with Alec for a period of "some few weeks" as his mistress.

Tess is also Hardy's most severe portrayal of religion's inadequacy to help puzzled young men find their way in life. Angel Clare was destined by his father for the ministry. When he sought another occupation, his clergyman father failed to respond with love and understanding. Ironically, Angel, too, fails to respond with love and understanding when Tess confesses her affair with Alec. Hardy's final novel, *Jude the Obscure*, was Hardy's most blunt depiction of sex and marriage and his bitterest attack on society. Jude's failure to obtain the education he desires at Christminster is largely due to society's insensitivity to the needs of men like Jude.

Publication of *Jude* brought about sharp disagreement among reviewers. Havelock Ellis and a few other critics praised Hardy for his candor, but many critics were horrified by Hardy's frankness. Hardy's relations with the public prior to *Tess* and *Jude* had been generally cordial, but the stormy reception of these books by critics and the general public caused a crisis in Hardy's life. His response was twofold. Henceforth he would write no more novels, and he would devote himself to writing poetry, a freer, less public genre.

While Hardy rarely dealt at length with late nineteenth-century religious problems, they are central to the work of the minor novelist William Hale White ("Mark Rutherford"). White knew the hopes and optimism, the doubts and despair of the Victorian age at first hand. He had been destined for the dissenting ministry, but was expelled from college over a matter of faith. In *The Autobiography of Mark Rutherford* and *Mark Rutherford's Deliverance*, White described crucial phases in his own life, veiled by alterations of names and situations. Both books are gloomy because of White's preoccupation with his own and modern man's loss of religious faith and with the miseries of poverty. White's dissent from the guiding religious principles of Victorian society was far quieter than that of Hardy or Butler, but it was unmistakable. The Church, through its intolerance, lack of intellectual curiosity and insularity, in White's view, had lost touch with its people. Even the dissenters, once a vital force in the religious life of England, had lost all vitality. White was not so much a novelist as a man impelled to comment upon life through fiction; nevertheless his novels remain important documents of religious inquiry.

A number of transitional writers of fiction were influenced by the naturalistic impulse which had come to prominence in France somewhat earlier in the nineteenth century. Naturalism strove for a factual, literal rendering of lower-class life. In France, the pioneer was Honoré de Balzac, whose vast *Comédie Humaine* (1829-1846) inspired later naturalistic fiction such as Gustave Flaubert's *Madame Bovary* (1857), the Goncourt brothers' *Germinie Lacerteux* (1865) and Émile Zola's *L'Assommoir* (1877). As Zola stated in *Le Roman Expérimental* (1880), the naturalistic novelist must be a scientist with no loyalty to particular systems of morality or art. He will seek to show "what a certain 'passion,' aroused under certain circumstances and in a certain environment will result in as regards the individual and society."

French naturalism was introduced to England after 1880 largely through the publication of translations of the novels of the Goncourts and Zola, through the appearance of notices and critical articles in periodicals and through the writings of certain English travelers and students of French literature. The English critical and popular reception of this French fiction was no more coolly rational than that granted to the production of Henrik Ibsen's plays. The courageous publisher, Henry Vizetelly, for example, was prosecuted and finally jailed for issuing translations of French novels.

The sudden rise in England of fiction which denied the right of constituted authority to govern man, emphasized sex as man's major driving force and concentrated on faithful rendering of lower-class life can be traced to the example of French naturalistic fiction. Among the first English writers to respond were George Gissing and George Moore.

Few novelists of the early transitional era lived a life of such open revolt from traditional standards of civilized English life as did George Gissing. Although he had inclined toward an academic career, his hopes were ruined by imprisonment for petty theft, his marriage to a prostitute and a subsequent life of dire poverty and humiliation. Gissing drew upon this personal agony for his novels, many of which chronicle the physical misery of the destitute and the psychological misery of people forced to live like the poor despite education and aspirations. In his vivid, candid depiction of the life of the lower strata of society, Gissing obviously had much in common with French naturalists. *Workers in the Dawn* relates the sordid story of a young man's marriage to an immoral woman. *The Nether World* mirrors the gloom and misery of the Clerkenwell slums of the 1880's.

A major theme in Gissing's fiction is spiritual exile: the denial of a person's rightful place in society or the ruining of a character's "expectations" of success, fame or security by forces partly beyond his control. In *New Grub Street*, his finest novel, the talented, sensitive Edwin Reardon sees marriage, authorship and life itself lose meaning because of poverty and his inability to compromise himself by doing the kind of work that would bring him success. The novel, as its title suggests, is an anatomy of the literary world with which Gissing was intimately familiar. In this new Grub Street of the 1880's, Gissing shows that men like Jasper Milvain will succeed through sheer adaptability and industry, while old-fashioned idealists like Reardon are doomed. Hence Reardon's expectations of fame and financial security, based on a successful early novel and a happy marriage, bring only separation from his wife, crushing poverty and oblivion. Reardon seems a helpless pawn of fate, but Gissing knew that spiritual exile could also be traced to a man's faulty judgment. In *Born in Exile*, Godwin Peake resolves to take holy orders to achieve his goal of worldly success although he knows that in doing so he is going against his deepest convictions. By compromising himself in this way, Peake brings about his own tragedy.

Although Gissing's predilection for various forms of misery is reminiscent of Zola, as novelist and short story writer he remained English and somewhat Victorian. His vision of life was not invariably gloomy. In *New Grub Street*, Jasper Milvain achieves success and, presumably, happiness. And the story "The House of Cobwebs" shows the happy result of a writer's determination to see a manuscript through to completion. The symbolic meanings that cling to the decaying, Dickensian house which Goldthorpe shares with Mr. Spicer also suggest Gissing's debt to earlier nineteenth-century writers.

George Moore's early novels similarly reveal the modified form French naturalism assumed when assimilated by English novelists. While living in France in the 1870's, ostensibly to study painting, Moore came into close contact with French culture, notably contemporary literature. He later recounted his experiences and opinions of his French years in *Confessions of a Young Man*, a book influential in generating interest in French painting and literature. When he wrote fiction, he revealed what deep imprints the subjects and method of the French novel had made on his eclectic nature. *A Modern Lover,* which derives directly from Moore's French experience, tells of an artist's rise to fame—made possible by women rather than by talent. Although the novel portrays "nice" people, it resembles naturalistic fiction in that Moore allows the hero several discreet love affairs without meting out the punishment for promiscuous sexual experience typical in Victorian fiction. Innocuous as *A Modern Lover* may seem in the twentieth century, it embroiled Moore in a fight with Mudie's circulating libraries, which withdrew him from their approved list. Moore fought back by writing "Literature at Nurse, or, Circulating Morals," an attack on the censorship power of lending libraries and the publication of fiction in three-volume form, and he convinced Henry Vizetelly to issue his next novel in one-volume form. *A Mummer's Wife* was more shockingly naturalistic than *A Modern Lover.* Kate Ede leaves her invalid husband for a new lover, Dick Lennox, manager of an *opéra bouffe* company. She suffers wild fits of jealousy, and Moore faithfully depicts her long, pitiful degradation through drink.

Moore's finest early novel, *Esther Waters,* concerns Esther's struggle to raise her illegitimate son. The detailed description of Willie's birth and the period immediately following, during which Esther struggles heroically to save herself from the workhouse and her son from certain death at a baby-farm, are the most overtly naturalistic sections of the novel. But some of Moore's tendencies and interests ran counter to naturalism. As evidenced by the pastoral interlude when Esther goes to visit Fred Parson's parents, Moore had a humanitarian, almost a sentimental side. He also had a reformer's desire to blame the upper classes for causing, or doing nothing to remedy the sufferings of the poor. Much of the novel is concerned with horse racing, a sport which destroys lower- and middle-class people for the pleasure of the rich.

In 1901, Moore's London years ended, as did his naturalistic tendencies in fiction. He moved to Ireland and plunged into the Irish literary movement as a playwright. The volume of Irish stories he wrote at this time, *The Untilled Field,* indicates a further softening of the harsh naturalism of his earlier novels. After 1905, Moore turned to biblical and historical subjects for inspiration. *The Brook Kerith,* a fictional retelling of the origins of Christianity, and *Héloïse and Abélard* are, however, logical developments of the streak of religious mysticism present in earlier works like *Evelyn Innes* and *Sister Teresa.* In his later fiction, Moore put the perfection of style ahead of any other consideration.

Naturalistic influence is also apparent in *Liza of Lambeth,* Somerset Maugham's first novel. Liza, a factory worker, rejects a good lad and makes love to Jim, a married man. The results are a bloody fight between Liza and Jim's wife and a drunken celebration that leads to the death of Liza, pregnant with Jim's child. The material, as well as Maugham's freedom from stereotyped attitudes toward sex, is reminiscent of Zola or earlier English naturalists like Gissing, yet the naturalistic edge of the book is blunted by Maugham's English humor. The scenes of good-hearted play and the comic touches in characterization and dialogue suggest that Maugham's view of "mean street life" was not totally gloomy. And Maugham clearly had no intention of reforming the slums. The barrister who does his duty to the barmaid he seduced in *The Merry-Go-Round* only makes himself miserable and drives her to suicide. A far better plan, Maugham hints, would have been for the barrister to remain free, thereby salvaging his own, and possibly her happiness.

A remarkable quality of Maugham's fiction is his objectivity or coldness. In *Of Human Bondage,* Maugham's most autobiographical novel, he draws characters and situations which must have struck deep responses in himself without betraying either malice for the boys who ridicule Phillip's clubfoot or pity for the protagonist. In his later fiction, written after 1915, Maugham struck out in other directions, such as the *romans à clef* like *The Moon and Sixpence,* based on the career of Gauguin, and *Cakes and Ale,* which may have been based on gossip concerning Thomas Hardy, but he produced no more novels of note.

Social realists like Arnold Bennett, John Galsworthy and H. G. Wells wrote of the conflict and tension found in higher levels of society than those usually depicted by the naturalists. They described the attempts of persons from a lower class to gain acceptance in a higher, the struggles between people of different social levels and the difficulties caused an individual because of the expectations of his particular class. Though their stories are usually too quiet or uneventful and the problems their characters face too tame for their fiction to be considered as continuing the naturalistic tradition, these authors do show the influence of the naturalistic mode in their concern for minute depiction of suffering and strife.

Arnold Bennett was thoroughly familiar with provincial

middle-class life, the stratum of society which provided the characters and problems of all his novels. In his delight at recording the ordinariness of life by the accumulation of detail, Bennett shows the influence of the reportorial aspects of French naturalism. His best fiction, which appeared mainly before World War I, was set in the industrial midlands of England. His first novel, *A Man from the North,* is a study of frustration. Richard Larch leaves the provincial life of the Five Towns district to go to London, but his ambitions to become an author are destroyed by his promise to marry a lower-class city girl. Frustration is also the central theme of *Anna of the Five Towns.* Anna, though she becomes an heiress and therefore can be her own mistress, marries a man she does not love because she has been conditioned to obey her father without question. Bennett's masterpiece, *The Old Wives' Tale,* chronicles the rather ordinary lives of two sisters, Constance and Sophia Baines. Bennett's main theme, the process of change and decay in their lives, is reinforced by the gradual modernization of life in their village. Even the life of Sophia, who elopes with a lover to Paris, becomes as routine and unexciting as that of Constance, who remains at home.

Similarly, the effects of frustration and the passing of time are important in the three novels of the Clayhanger family, which concern two ordinary people living in the Five Towns district. *Clayhanger* records Edwin Clayhanger's fight against parental tyranny, his escape after the death of his father and his love for Hilda Lessways. *Hilda Lessways* retells many of the events of *Clayhanger* from a woman's point of view. In the process, Hilda loses the romantic aura Edwin has thrown over her. *These Twain* describes the unhappy marriage of Edwin and Hilda.

Unlike other social realists, John Galsworthy carried his study of a family and its problems far beyond the covers of a single novel or trilogy. The history of the Forsytes begins with *The Man of Property,* a self-sufficient novel in which a basic conflict develops between Property, represented by Soames Forsyte, and Beauty or Art, represented by his wife Irene and the architect Bosinney. Irene's efforts to free herself from Soames' unjust claims on her cause the accidental death of her lover Bosinney. As the many later volumes of the series appeared, Galsworthy carried his story into the twentieth century and beyond World War I. As time passed, Galsworthy's view of propertied classes mellowed, and even the epitome of this class, Soames, eventually seemed to his creator an attractive old curmudgeon, a somewhat nostalgic holdover from late Victorianism. In his non-Forsyte novels, Galsworthy sometimes looked into classes and problems he did not fully understand, as in *Fraternity,* which concerns the world of poverty, and *The Dark Flower,* which depicts a man's three love affairs with a real, if over-indulged emotion.

Galsworthy's investigation and mild criticism of society lacked bite because of his limited knowledge of more than one stratum of society. His well-bred tranquillity was also a considerable handicap. Like Bennett, Galsworthy was intrigued by the effects of time on the struggle of human life, but he failed to discover a technique to enable him to make dramatic use of this awareness. Instead, his novels seem hurried and confused because of frequent and whimsical shifts of time and point of view.

Since H. G. Wells rose from the ranks of the hardworking, lower middle class, he understood the struggle of the self-made man. Wells saw both heartbreak and humor in the struggle of individuals to find places in the fluid late nineteenth-century social order and depicted his characters with sympathy. His middle-class heroes—Hoopdriver, Kipps and Polly—all wish to break out of the confines of their futile lives. In *The Wheels of Chance,* Hoopdriver innocently seeks a few days' escape from the dull routine of his life, but Wells' other heroes want a more radical departure from the *status quo.* In *Kipps,* a young assistant in a draper's shop attempts to become a gentleman when he inherits money. The result is the clash between Kipps' instinct to do right and the hypocrisy imposed on him by wealth. His marriage with a girl of the lower class is marred by bickering. The middle-aged protagonist of *The History of Mr. Polly* searches the English countryside for an intangible "something" that will transform his dull, prosaic life and allow him to escape his monotonous existence.

The humor in *Tono-Bungay,* Wells' best novel, is less prominent than his discussion of social structure. Here he achieves a panorama of a decaying English society which clings to Victorian concepts of life. Again Wells shows the efforts of a lower middle-class man, Edward Ponderevo, to rise in society. Lacking the idealism of a Hoopdriver, Uncle Edward uses chicanery in the patent medicine business. Metaphors of rise, fall and decay give the novel symbolic unity, and George's description of the decaying landmarks along the Thames at the novel's end is an effective declaration of change in English society and of the passing of outdated Victorian institutions. After *Tono-Bungay,* Wells' satire became more bitter, his discussions more earnest, his journalistic voice more strident. For example, *Ann Veronica* depicts a girl, suffocated by Victorian parents, trying to find her place in society; *The New Machiavelli* satirizes education, marriage, politics. With each succeeding book, Wells moved further away from writing novels.

In the first two decades of the transitional era, the revolt in fiction against Victorianism found expression chiefly in subject matter. By 1900, however, much of the heat of battle between the younger, seemingly radical writers and the older, more conservative traditionalists had been dissipated, largely because the goals of the younger men had been achieved. English novelists could write quite frankly about many topics and situations which Victorian writers had been forced either to avoid or treat very gingerly. Though the novel retained its importance in the struggle for social reform, novelists of the latter part of the transitional era tended to experiment not so much with content as with narrative form, point of view and time-sequence.

The novels of Joseph Conrad testify to the restless curiosity of their creator, even though he began his literary career when he was past 35. Conrad went through a rather conventional early phase in which he felt his way toward the techniques best suited to his subjects and attitudes. *Almayer's Folly* and *An Outcast of the Islands* show Conrad's uncertainty with several aspects of the novelist's art. His prose is heavy and consciously literary and his characters are not fully realized. *The Nigger of the "Narcissus,"* despite occasional flaws of characterization and style, shows a considerable improvement in technique. The novel is typical of Conrad's mature fiction in its representation of the mysterious James Wait (is he really ill, or simply malingering?), the symbolic overtones of the voyage and the descriptive powers it evinces. But the narrative method of the novel is conventional. Conrad used the omniscient point of view, structured his story chronologically and described most of his characters in a straightforward manner.

In the "Preface" to *Nigger,* Conrad wrote that "My task... is, by the power of the written word to make you hear, to make you feel–it is, before all, to make you *see.*" As he developed in the next few years, he discovered new means of achieving these ends. One device was the repeated use of Marlow, a garrulous old seaman, as narrator. In *Heart of Darkness,* Marlow gives the history of Kurtz, an ivory trader in the Congo who was seduced by primitive culture into abandoning the saving restraints of civilization; in *Lord Jim,* he tells of an idealistic young seaman who abandoned a ship and ruined his career. Marlow is initially drawn to both men and later relates his experiences with them, without, however, coming to any conclusion about how their catastrophes might have been avoided.

In terms of structure, *Lord Jim* is the less conventional. While *Heart of Darkness* is basically a chronological record of Marlow's journey into Africa, his encounter with Kurtz and his return to Europe, no such traditional beginning, middle and end can be used to describe the fragmentary, episodic *Lord Jim.* Marlow assembles evidence he has gathered from knowing Jim and talking with others who did, repeating each separate encounter, letter and discussion in an order uniquely his own, one not ruled by clock and calendar. The result is the slow accretion of detail in a portrait of a gifted young man betrayed by his idealistic nature. In his later novels, Conrad often dispensed with Marlow but continued his experimentation with narrative form. While he used the omniscient point of view in *Nostromo,* he once again presented evidence in the form of dramatic incidents reinforced by the testimony and recollections of various participants, with no attempt to assemble such evidence into a more coherent, but infinitely narrower version of this panoramic story.

Conrad's importance to English fiction is not, however, limited to his experimentation with narrative form. As readers in his own time perceived, Conrad was bitterly, if obliquely, critical of imperialism in several of his novels. Soon after its publication, for example, *Heart of Darkness* was widely interpreted as an anti-Belgian or anti-colonial tract. While such an interpretation unquestionably narrows the full significance of the book, the novel is obviously critical of white men who mask their materialistic motives for exploiting primitive countries with rhetorical statements about the need to "protect" and "Christianize" the natives. *Nostromo* makes essentially the same point. In this novel, the challenge to the Englishman Charles Gould is twofold: to make a success of the Costaguana silver mine and to assure domestic tranquillity in a turbulent Latin American country. He succeeds in both, but at a terrible price. As his wife knows, he has become a living machine, incapable of love or sympathy, controlled by the distant financier Holroyd. Conrad's point in these novels is clear: there are terrible dangers to man's freedom and individuality in making himself a servant of material interests.

In certain respects, Ford Madox Ford (F. M. Hueffer) was a follower of Joseph Conrad. Early in Conrad's career the men were close personal friends and collaborated on *Romance* and *The Inheritors*, two indifferent novels. After a quarrel, the literary careers of the two developed separately, but in view of Ford's later growth as novelist, it is possible that Conrad's narrative innovations impressed the younger man. In *The Good Soldier*, Ford tells the story of Edward Ashburnham from the point of view of John Dowell who, like Marlow in *Heart of Darkness*, is both part of and distinct from the protagonist's life history. Like Conrad and other late transitional writers, Ford used the novel as a vehicle for psychological explorations. As Dowell unfolds his tale, it becomes clear that he prefers illusion or appearance to reality. His own marriage is an illusion, in that it was never consummated, and in large part, Dowell's life was only a vicarious existence made possible by his more venturesome, daring friend and alter ego Ashburnham. Ford's development as a psychological novelist culminated in *Some Do Not, No More Parades, A Man Could Stand Up* and *Last Post*, a tetralogy known in the United States as *Parade's End*. Ford worked toward freer, more plastic narrative modes, such as the series of linked interior monologues in *Last Post* which resemble stream-of-consciousness narration.

Another ardent devotée of this narrative method was Dorothy Richardson. Instead of presenting finished stories by ordering carefully selected details of characters and events in a traditional chronological framework, she presented the raw material for stories by centering her fiction in the mind of the protagonist. Attempting to describe a woman's search for her unique feminine identity, Miss Richardson evolved, beginning with *Pointed Roofs*, the nervous, subjective mode characteristic of the twelve novels which comprise *Pilgrimage*. She may have been indebted to the fictional experiments of Conrad or Ford, but she transcended their example in her vast experimental saga. Its peculiar curse, however, is dullness, a result perhaps of her undisciplined subjectivism. Her heroine is herself, her subject matter her own rather colorless, drab life. As one commentator put it, she reduced the stream of consciousness to a trickle.

By 1920, D. H. Lawrence was already recognized as a major English novelist. Although he wrote capably, sometimes brilliantly, in other literary genres, his reputation rested primarily on his novels—serious, thoughtful considerations of human relationships, the plight of sensitive men and women in crassly modern, industrial society. As a novelist Lawrence changed radically between *The White Peacock* of 1911 and *Women in Love* of 1920. As with other fictionists, the change is partly attributable to the shedding of the influence of earlier writers. But in Lawrence's case, it was also due to his strong urge to explore the new fictional possibilities opened up by investigations into psychology. The ample and rather amorphous form he had inherited from nineteenth-century novelists gave him almost unlimited, and potentially dangerous freedom to experiment with these new psychological concepts and approaches to fiction. In the finest novels of his first creative decade, however, the desire to experiment was restrained by a strong realistic tendency to stay close to the facts of scene, local custom and character. *The White Peacock* is interesting as an indication of Lawrence's considerable debt to earlier novelists. His own description of the book as "a novel of sentiment...all about love—and rhapsodies of Spring scattered here and there—heroines galore—no plot...." suggests that he regarded it as rather conventional and derivative. His "rhapsodies of Spring," for example, are reminiscent of nature passages in Hardy's novels. In *The White Peacock,* Lawrence describes both the idyllic beauty of the Nottinghamshire and Derbyshire countryside and the damage caused by industrial expansion to produce an image of corrupted pastoralism similar to that in *Tess of the d'Urbervilles*. The plot also seems Hardyean. As in *The Woodlanders,* the failure of Lettie and George to discover their need for one another leads ultimately to unhappiness. George is too sluggish and Lettie too proud to overstep the differences of class and education which separate them.

Lawrence was much more his own master in *Sons and Lovers,* his most autobiographical novel. Early as the book stands in Lawrence's canon, it shows the tension between his desires to experiment with new material for fiction and to be faithful to a way of life he knew intimately. Lawrence used the conventional novel-of-education format for his story of Paul Morel's struggle toward manhood. Paul's education is hampered by twisted love within his home; he despises his rude, untaught father and grows into a substitute lover for his sensitive, educated mother. In the usual novel of education, many of the protagonist's difficulties are solved simply by his maturation, but Paul's are, instead, dramatically intensified. Because of his Oedipal attachment to his mother, Paul cannot love another woman, as his disastrous affair with Miriam proves. Even the death of his mother cannot free him from this enslavement. For all its psychology, however, the novel is a triumphant artistic re-creation of a way of life. Although the novel is set in the same region as *The White Peacock,* the balance has shifted from idyllic beauty to the real ugliness wrought in town and countryside by mining—the railways, the pit-heads, the dreary sameness of the miners' homes.

Lawrence's development was rapid and dramatic. The publication of *The Rainbow* marks such a sharp break both with Lawrence's earlier works and that of other English fiction writers that it may be regarded as a landmark in twentieth-century fiction. Lawrence himself considered it something new, a novel which, as he wrote, "hasn't got hard outlines." Rather than study the progress of an individual in a world severely limited in time and space, Lawrence here presents three generations of Brangwens: Tom and Lydia, Will and Anna, Ursula and Anton Skrebensky. The novel has no story. The struggles of each generation parallel those of the others, but there is no single plot problem. In its last stage, the central concern becomes Ursula who, unlike her female forebears, fails to experience a satisfactory love affair and marriage. The novel also marks a development in Lawrence's technique with its intricate, elaborate symbolism. Its title comes to seem appropriate to the reader as he sees the various "rainbows" in the novel, which symbolize connections, aspirations and links between diverse human beings.

The story of Ursula's quest for love is continued in *Women in Love*. This novel, perhaps Lawrence's most artistically controlled, is both a study of the attempts of Ursula and her sister Gudrun to find satisfaction in love and an anatomy of modern urban life. After 1920, Lawrence went on to write a very wide variety of fiction. Unfortunately, his desires to experiment and to lecture mankind detract from many of his later novels such as *Lady Chatterley's Lover* and *Kangaroo.*

Although E. M. Forster has been a most influential innovator in his use of imagery and symbolism, his debt to earlier fiction is great. Rather than search for new formal means of narrating his stories as Conrad and Lawrence did, Forster often preferred the mode of social comedy, as in *Where Angels Fear to Tread.* Furthermore, the quantity of authorial comments in novels like *A Room with a View* is reminiscent of Thackeray. In the two great novels of his maturity, however, Forster outgrew Victorian propensities for chatty, coincidental social comedy. The matter of *Howards End* and *A Passage to India* is both serious and significant for modern man. The most striking feature of these books is Forster's power of creating symbolic detail, like the wasp in *Passage to India,* a leitmotif which links very different characters, or the circumstances surrounding the death of Leonard Bast in *Howards End.* Leonard dies after Charles Wilcox strikes him with an old sword (symbolic of the Wilcoxes as materialistic conquerors of England) and is "buried" by a flood of books (symbolic of the Schlegels' culture) from a bookcase he pulls over as he falls. Both novels have much resonance, moreover, because of Forster's skill in harmonizing details of imagery into large chords of significance. *Howards End,* for example, is dominated by the house of that name, by its possessor, the elderly Mrs. Wilcox, and by the vanishing way of life it embodies, all of which meld with events that take place there. This same symbolic interaction of scene, character and incident makes the Marabar Caves section of *Passage to India* impressive. The reader has no clear idea of what happens, but the descent of Adela Quested into the Caves, the noises she hears there and her apparent hallucination create the impression that she has had a religious experience, one beyond normal human limits.

The leading idea of Forster's fiction is expressed by the verb "connect." "Only connect," Margaret Schlegel tells the obtuse Henry Wilcox, "the prose and the passion and both will be exalted, and human love will be seen at its height." The central problem is the existence of barriers so formidable that individuals are seldom able to create the all-important connections. Mankind is sundered by many differences: national, like the English and Indians in *Passage;* financial, like the rich and poor classes in *Howards End;* and cultural, like the materialistic Wilcoxes and idealistic Schlegels. In Forster's fiction, even marriage, good will or well-intentioned, cultured liberalism usually do not lead to connection but to a further delineation of the differences. This inability to connect or communicate was to become a major theme in twentieth-century fiction after 1920.

FICTION:

THE SHORT STORY

The emergence of the short story was an important development in transitional fiction. This is not surprising since the emphasis of the period was on experiment in form and revolt against Victorian cultural and artistic conventions. With its brevity, the short story lent itself to experimentation, and as a relatively new form, it was unfettered by literary traditions. Many of the forces that shaped transitional novels had important effects on the short story. In the short fiction of Hubert Crackanthorpe, one can chart the influence of French naturalism; D. H. Lawrence's stories show the profound effect the study of psychology had on fiction; and Katherine Mansfield's narrative technique demonstrates that impressionism was as suitable to shorter fictional forms as to longer. Yet the history of the short story between 1880 and 1920 is not so much one of basic trends or influences as of individual figures.

In his short stories as in his essays, Robert Louis Stevenson was concerned not only with his immediate subject matter but also with its inherent moral implications. *New Arabian Nights*, Stevenson's first collection of stories, shows an interesting blend of tradition and innovation. Although the stories may now seem old-fashioned because of his free use of mystery and other romantic materials, Stevenson was surprisingly modern in technique. He achieved the concentration and intensity characteristic of effective short stories by limiting himself to a single situation and by creating an atmosphere that exactly suited his tales of evil and mystery. In "A Lodging for the Night," Stevenson turned the rather conventional material of nineteenth-century romance into something new, an intense analysis of man's moral nature.

Villon assists at a murder, flees through fifteenth-century Paris and argues until dawn with the Sire de Brisetout about the difference between thievery and war. The conflict between the poet-rascal and the old warrior resolves finally into a moral debate: is there any essential difference between war and crime, between doing great crimes nobly and small crimes meanly? "The Sire de Maletroit's Door" is another example of Stevenson's turning romantic material to moralistic use. Denis de Beaulieu, accidentally caught in a trap laid for another man, is forced by the Sire de Maletroit to marry the Sire's niece and ward, Blanche. The story transcends the trite Gothic situation—villainous uncle forces innocent maiden to marry against her will—in a scene in which the two young people face the moral issue (should a man marry to save his life?) and find a way to obey the Sire without sacrificing either their lives or principles.

Though Stevenson occasionally dealt with more realistic matters in his stories, the results were rarely as impressive or atmospheric as his more romantic stories. "The Beach of Falesá," for example, is superficially reminiscent of the Eastern fiction of Conrad or Maugham in its depiction of a white man's struggle to come to terms with a foreign culture, but Stevenson's rather narrow English propriety kept him from seeing deeply into the real nature of the situation created when whites invade an alien culture for reasons of "trade." Far more impressive and characteristic is *Dr. Jekyll and Mr. Hyde,* a long horror tale of such power that it has become Stevenson's best-known story. Stevenson was intrigued by the concept of the split personality, especially in the way it could illuminate the existence of great capacities for good and evil in one person. By drinking a modern-day witch's-brew, a potion scientifically prepared by Dr. Jekyll, the peace-loving and rational doctor liberates his buried self in the interest of science. But when the dark self eventually gains command, the only hope for the tragically split personality of Jekyll-Hyde is death. Stevenson made a substantial contribution to the development of the English short story by using traditionally romantic material as a basis for moral and philosophical comment and by subordinating all aspects of his stories to the creation of highly intense, unified narratives.

Although Stevenson continued the tradition of fictional romance, another group of transitional short story writers moved in an opposite direction. The new realists or naturalists preferred to use stories to remind readers of the pain inherent in life and of the misery conferred on hapless men and women by illness, madness and poverty. A major impetus behind the rapid growth of this kind of fiction was the French naturalistic story as written by Balzac and de Maupassant. This movement among short story writers of the 1880's and 1890's was a counterpart of the novelists' revolt against Victorianism.

Hubert Crackanthorpe, a leader among the English realists, contributed experimental, naturalistic fiction to such brilliant but ephemeral periodicals as *The Yellow Book* and *The Savoy*. Crackanthorpe demonstrated that poverty and psychic suffering could be dealt with immediately and honestly in the short story. His first collection, *Wreckage*, contains stories which depict brutal degradation and squalor. In "Profiles," a girl of unstable will becomes a "fallen woman" but, unlike her Victorian forebears, she chooses to go on falling and becomes a streetwalker. "The Struggle for Life" is so blunt in its picture of suffering begotten of poverty, infidelity and drink that it almost seems a translation of Zola or the Goncourts.

Unfortunately for the struggling author, *Wreckage* aroused little notice, perhaps because the stories lacked the artistry which might have attracted serious readers. But Crackanthorpe's talent developed rapidly, and by the time he published *Sentimental Studies*, he was in far greater command of his literary technique. One of his most successful stories, "Anthony Garstin's Courtship," tells of Garstin's relentless determination to wed Rosa Blencarn, even after he discovers she is pregnant with another man's child. Garstin succeeds, but his triumph is muted by the lies he adopts to win his mother's consent to the marriage; he tells her that Rosa's unborn child is his. Crackanthorpe's plain, homely style is the ideal medium to capture the pathetic situations in which his simple characters have become entangled. The full maturation of an unusually promising talent was cut off by Crackanthorpe's tragic early death.

Rudyard Kipling's early training as a short story writer took place in India, where he wrote stories for English-language newspapers in the 1880's, later printed in England as *Plain Tales from the Hills*. He frequently chose bizarre, romantic material for his stories and occasionally showed a predilection for brutality suggestive of French naturalism. But Kipling's artistic practices cannot be explained by suggesting his debt to any school or movement. This popular, successful and influential exponent of the short story evolved a method which was uniquely his own. Regardless of the length of narrative he selected, Kipling was primarily a teller of tales, one who put the creation of intriguing characters and surprising stories ahead of analysis of character or the subtle probing of a character's mind.

Although Kipling's early stories are largely realistic short narratives of actual life, his technique makes his fiction basically different from that of contemporary English realists. Rather than absenting himself from his fiction by creating narrators unlike himself (as Conrad did) or writing with cool objectivity and detachment (as Crackanthorpe did), Kipling made no pretense of keeping his opinions to himself. In his many Indian stories, for instance, Kipling-as-narrator saw India from the point of view of the white ruling minority who imposed some law and discipline on a sprawling, chaotic, utterly primitive land. *Plain Tales* suffers from this cocksureness, the narrator's pose of knowing everything about a foreign culture and about the odd forces that drive men to do bizarre things. Later, Kipling mellowed somewhat and changed from an omniscient lecturer to a more sympathetic observer. In "Without Benefit of Clergy," Kipling does not damn the Englishman for marrying across the color line or imply, as he might have done earlier, that even though such marriages lead to suffering, Englishmen *will* go on forming unhappy alliances. Instead, he records the marriage of Ameera and Holden with tenderness and comparative objectivity.

Kipling's later development as a short story writer defies generalization because of his ever-widening political, social and artistic interests. He traveled widely and became a kind of spokesman for Empire. An early interest which is evident in a number of his later stories is the supernatural. While in *Plain Tales* and other early volumes Kipling dealt bluntly with superstition and magic, later stories are more subtly mysterious and refined. For example, this development is seen in "The Wish House" where an unselfish lover assumes the curse of a fatal disease through white magic. Sometimes Kipling achieved a rare blend of psychology and the supernatural, as in "The Gardener." In its magic climax—a mysterious gardener offers to show the spinster Helen Turrell where her son lies in a vast graveyard of war dead—Kipling reveals what the reader may have suspected all along: in calling the boy her nephew, Helen Turrell has cruelly deceived the boy about his parentage. Although Helen has so long and so movingly lied to her son that she has blinded herself to the truth, her contact with the God-like gardener restores her sight. Throughout his career, Kipling stayed aloof from particular schools of short fiction. He remained a creator of good stories artfully told.

D. H. Lawrence's prose study *Psychoanalysis and the Unconscious* indicates his interest in psychological research, and his stories show the profound effect the study of psychology had on the development of short fiction. His stories are based not so much on a person who acts as on a psychological entity who apprehends, responds to or changes as a result of the situation disclosed in the story. For example, "The Odour of Chrysanthemums" concerns the mind of Elizabeth Bates and the revelation brought about by the death of her husband. Lawrence's main characters are often peculiar or abnormal in some respects. They are usually sensitive, introverted, passionate or, as in "The Rocking Horse Winner," clairvoyant. In this tale, Lawrence attacks the modern obsession that "there must be more money." The exploitation of the boy's unusual mental gift, learning the names of winning horses by riding his hobby horse, leads not to the love and security he craves but to ever greater demands for money, and ultimately to his death.

Lawrence's characters are often victims of compulsion. They are driven by powerful forces, usually related to sex, that often run counter to the laws or demands of society. Either a character acts in accordance with the compulsive force or he attempts to subdue or evade it. Lawrence usually saw the former alternative as natural, therefore healthy. "The Horse Dealer's Daughter" is typical. After Dr. Fergusson saves Mabel from drowning herself, she makes emotional demands on him. He capitulates to them, despite his fear of sexual experience, because of the compulsive force Mabel arouses in him. Hence compulsion may help man overcome fears which prohibit his fullest self-realization. But relatively few of Lawrence's characters yield to their compulsions. When they do not, the result may be physical or mental destruction. "The Prussian Officer" is a clear if extreme example. The officer, held in the army's rigid class and rank system, dares not express his love for his orderly. His bottling-up of a socially taboo but powerful emotion leads to the officer's killing of the man he loves and to his own death.

Lawrence did not theorize to any significant extent about the short story, but his achievement in the form was impressive. He had an unusual gift for projecting meaning from common objects and rituals. In "The Horse Dealer's Daughter," for example, Dr. Fergusson's immersion in a murky pond which is repulsive to him is a counterpart of his later yielding to Mabel's sexual demands. "The Fox," one of Lawrence's most perfect achievements in shorter fiction, is rich in symbolism. The fox, whom March fears to kill, is symbolic of the aggressive masculinity embodied in Henry, who finally wins March away from her unnatural relationship with Banford. In his psychological exploration and his employment of symbolism, Lawrence was a seminal influence in the development of the short story.

Unlike other important practitioners of the transitional short story, Katherine Mansfield found the form so congenial that except for a relatively small amount of criticism and poetry she wrote in it exclusively. She felt her way toward an impressionistic narrative method unlike that of any of her English predecessors. The impetus for her first volume of short stories, *In a German Pension,* was a trip to Bavaria in 1909. The stories show how a very proper, rather sensitive English girl was alternately offended and amused by the remarks, manners and general behavior of boorish Germans. They also show, in choice and treatment of subject, the influence of Anton Chekhov. "The-Child-Who-Was-Tired" closely resembles Chekhov's "Spat Khochetsia," and even in the many stories which give no evidence of direct borrowing, recurrent touches of comedy create a rather sardonic, Chekhovian tone. In "The Germans at Meat," for instance, she depicts the crudity of German table manners in a witty and amusing fashion.

In her later volumes, Katherine Mansfield largely outgrew Chekhov's influence by turning from omniscient, aloof narration to intimate presentation of character and event. Her mature narrative technique is impressionistic. Instead of presenting characters ready-made, as she did in *In a German Pension,* she learned to let her characters create themselves by recording how they spoke, what they perceived and how they behaved. "Bliss" concerns a woman who struggles desperately—if unconsciously—to deceive herself about her marriage. Because the story is told through her own mind, Bertha conveys by her words, gestures and hysterical laughter both the true pathos of her life (she loves her husband but is afraid of sex) and her losing struggle to conceal the truth from herself and other people. This impressionistic technique allowed Katherine Mansfield to present both faces of the self-deceived character—the one he shows to his neighbors and the one he tries desperately to conceal from him-self—without passing judgment on which is the "real" person. Her detached, objective narrative technique was certainly in-fluential in the development of the short story in the twentieth century. [1]

While such anti-realistic elements as fantasy, magic and the supernatural are on the periphery of E. M. Forster's novels, they are central to his short fiction. Several of his stories study the alienation which results from a person's unusual sensitivity or range of experience. In "The Celestial Omnibus," the boy protagonist discovers a road to a heaven where ideals of art and literature are actualities. The boy can exist there because he believes in these ideals, but Mr. Bons, the unbeliever, is hurled to his death. In "The Story of a Panic," Eustace has a vision of Pan which both frees him from the moral restraints of ordinary social life and sets him apart from the rest of humanity. Similarly, Mr. Lucas, an aged man with clear parallels to King Oedipus, has a vision in "The Road to Colonus." Inside a hollow tree, a shrine to a deity, he finds that all of the world's constituent parts have symbolic meaning. Again, transcendent experience cannot be shared, and the possessor of it suffers alienation.

Romance, realism, psychology, fantasy: these interests and tendencies hardly exhaust the many cross-currents that had important influences on the wayward but brilliant development of the short story in the transitional period. But they do allow one to make the generalization that writers of short fiction were interested in experimentation, in using the new, supple form to express their own visions of man and his problems.

---

[1] The work of James Joyce belongs, in large part, to the modern period. *Dubliners* (begun 1905, published 1914), however, has many parallels with the fiction of Mansfield, Lawrence and Forster. Joyce's stories study the spiritual paralysis of Dublin life as seen in the failure of will, lack of moral courage and mind-less following of custom common to his characters. His stories are told with utmost economy and with objectivity so perfect it is difficult to draw conclusions about his characters. Like his English contemporaries, Joyce, at this time, aimed at producing faithful impressions of life and conveying his insights through images rather than direct comment.

FICTION:

ENTERTAINMENT

Some writers were not seriously affected by the stirrings of realism and the experiments with form that altered fiction so greatly between 1880 and 1920. Though these writers concerned themselves primarily with entertainment, their skill as story tellers and their style often rivaled that of more serious writers of fiction. The writers of entertainment did not form a specific movement, though their subjects and treatment of themes often ran counter to the increasing use of realism. They focused on high adventure, supernatural horror, mystery and detection and science fiction. Few writers made sharp distinctions between serious fiction and entertainments. Such a distinction, however, is a way of grouping fictional narratives that fall outside the main developments of the novel and the short story but still deserve attention.

Robert Louis Stevenson was a blend of the entertainer and the serious artist. In late works like *The Master of Ballantrae,* which also contained elements of high adventure and the supernatural, and in the unfinished *Weir of Hermiston,* he wrote with a serious purpose. However, Stevenson's most memorable fiction is predominantly entertainment.

Stevenson was fascinated with high adventure, perhaps because he found in it tonic for his own frail body. His great achievements are *Treasure Island* and *Kidnapped* in which he made piracy of the eighteenth century colorful and the intrigue of the Jacobites in Scotland fascinating. His emphasis in these two books was on the excitement of buried treasure, narrow escape from peril and hunt-and-chase. Although Stevenson wrote these books primarily for boys, he created believable protagonists beset by danger that seemed more romantic than terrifying. In these novels, Stevenson established a pattern for almost all subsequent stories of high adventure.

H. Rider Haggard, a writer whose style and sense of structure were inferior to Stevenson's, continued the tradition of high adventure on a wager that he could write a book as good as *Treasure Island.* The result was *King Solomon's Mines,* a story of African adventure, hidden treasure and a lost race. *She* related an even more exotic African adventure dealing with a woman who remained eternally beautiful, though thousands of years old. Fantastic as they were, his tales seemed contemporary as actual Englishmen continued to explore remote parts of the world, encountered little-known tribes and discovered mineral wealth in the form of new gold and new diamond mines. Haggard wrote an almost endless series of adventures involving exploration and discovery of lost races, but the more he wrote the less readable his stories became.

Other writers created notable stories of high adventure, usually meant for juvenile readers, but so well written that an adult could easily succumb to the romantic excitement and the color of strange lands or historical periods. J. Meade Falkner returned to Stevenson's eighteenth-century England in *Moonfleet,* a tale of a boy involved with smugglers. Though Falkner could not equal Stevenson's style, *Moonfleet* is filled with mystery, suspense, hunt-and-chase and hidden treasure. In *Kim,* Rudyard Kipling drew adventure against a rich panorama of India. Kipling was skillful in underplaying the element of intrigue, but suspense and interest arise from the fact that Kim is trained by the Indian secret police. *The White Company,* by Sir Arthur Conan Doyle, combines chivalry with adventure in a story of fourteenth-century France and Spain.

Following the lead of Haggard, John Buchan repeated the motifs of secret treasure and native rebellion in Africa in *Prester John* . But Buchan also saw the possibilities of placing high adventure in his own time. *The Thirty-Nine Steps* was set in modern Great Britain, with the hunt-and-chase occurring across the Scottish moors. In this story, Buchan developed the espionage element earlier introduced into English fiction by Erskine Childers in *The Riddle of the Sands.* After *The Thirty-Nine Steps,* the spy story became a separate genre of entertainment emphasizing espionage as much as adventure. *The Riddle of the Sands* and *The Thirty-Nine Steps* were written to entertain adults, and such stories were soon to be called "thrillers," a label that indicated they were not meant to be read as serious fiction.

Supernatural tales, popular in the Victorian era, continued to flourish in the 1880-1920 period, and there was no clear break with the tradition of Edgar Allan Poe and J. Sheridan Le Fanu. M. R. James was influenced directly by Le Fanu, and many of his stories have a distinctly Victorian flavor. Supernatural creatures appear when evil men pry into matters that do not concern them ("The Treasure of Abbot Thomas") or try to manipulate supernatural forces for their own purposes ("Casting the Runes"). There is an old-fashioned poetic justice when such characters are destroyed by the malignant supernatural forces they have uncovered. Though M. R. James' style is plain and at times dry, his ghosts and demonological horrors are still terrifying.

Arthur Machen used an elaborate, ornate style in creating horrors which often stem from man's primordial past. Degenerate hidden races, evolution in reverse and mysterious drugs are some of his motifs. Unlike M. R. James, Machen also interwove psychological problems with horrible supernatural events. The main character of "The Great God Pan" has absolute evil revealed to her, and the girl in "The White People" slowly goes insane as a result of her contact with supreme supernatural evil.

Robert Louis Stevenson also had combined supernatural horror with psychological study. That he possessed both greater insight into human nature and greater artistic powers than James or Machen, *Dr. Jekyll and Mr. Hyde* demonstrates. "Markheim" also shows Stevenson's abiding interest in the human psyche and his willingness to go beyond the bounds of actuality to dramatize his insights.

Few novel-length horror stories of distinction were published in the 1880-1920 period. An exception is J. Meade Falkner's *The Lost Stradivarius*, in which the supernatural develops slowly and quietly. Through the power of a mysterious violin, Falkner's eighteenth-century hero eventually uncovers signs of human debasement and supernatural orgies in a villa in Italy. His hints of horror are often as potent as Machen's more explicit descriptions.

The most famous horror novel of the period, Bram Stoker's *Dracula*, is poorly written and filled with wooden characters who speak impossible dialects of American and Dutch. The early part of the story, Jonathan Harker's journal, is the most effective, but Stoker could not sustain the pace. Only the symbolic value of the vampire, a force strong enough to overwhelm and pervert men's souls, makes Stoker's story of the least interest. The turgid style of Stoker's other supernatural novels, such as *The Lair of the White Worm,* makes them incredibly bad.

With the advent of Sherlock Holmes in *A Study in Scarlet,* by Sir Arthur Conan Doyle, the detective story became important as a distinct type of entertainment. Its immediate forebear was the mystery story, in which interest was maintained by the existence of an unknown quantity which was sure to be revealed by the end of the tale. To this pattern, the detective story added a figure who could solve the mystery by intellection. Both Edgar Allan Poe and Wilkie Collins had written detective stories in the earlier decades of the nineteenth century, but it was Holmes, the amateur detective of extreme and eccentric intelligence, who captured the reading public's imagination. Though Doyle devoted four novels to Holmes, only *The Hound of the Baskervilles* proved an unqualified success. His best work was the short detective story, found in collections like *The Adventures of Sherlock Holmes* and *The Memoirs of Sherlock Holmes,* where the eccentric detective outwitted the criminal and often baffled the official police with the ingenuity of his deductions. The pattern of Holmes with his faithful follower Dr. Watson as narrator became the prototype for countless pairs of sleuths. Sherlock Holmes has become something of a modern myth.

In the early 1900's there were numerous fictional rivals of Sherlock Holmes. The most original was G. K. Chesterton's Father Brown, a somewhat eccentric priest who used intuitive methods almost exclusively. Father Brown was, of course, concerned with spiritual matters that did not interest Holmes. Chesterton's detective-in-clergyman's-collar was popular but lacked the appeal of Sherlock Holmes.

Though Jules Verne had shown that qualities of high adventure were inherent in scientific investigation and mechanical invention, H. G. Wells was the first to write notable scientific romances. In both novels and short stories, he described wonderful places in the far future, strange life on other planets and extraordinary experiences on earth. His fantasies seemed plausible because they were based on scientific rather than supernatural phenomena. Though Wells described purely imaginary scenes or creatures, he used such convincingly realistic detail that fantastic beings like Martians, selenites and invisible men became believable.

In contrast to the other entertainers of the transitional period, Wells usually included some social comment in his science fiction. *The Time Machine* shows the evolution of humanity into two distinct groups, workers and dilettantes; finally, as the time traveler sweeps into the distant future, he sees mankind completely extinct. Dr. Moreau, in *The Island of Doctor Moreau,* becomes so absorbed in surgical experimentation that he grows more beastly than the monstrosities created in his image. Invisibility seems to give unlimited power in *The Invisible Man,* but such power leads to disregard for social and moral restrictions and is not invincible. Always fascinated by evolution, Wells suggests, in *The War of the Worlds,* that the human race could be destroyed by organisms evolving on another planet. And the last part of *The First Men in the Moon* draws a satiric picture of over-specialized life forms, for though Wells was an apostle of scientific progress, he saw the limitations of science. Eventually Wells' predilection for social comment became dominant in scientific romances like *When the Sleeper Wakes* and *The Food of the Gods,* two of his least successful entertainments.

With his Professor Challenger stories, Sir Arthur Conan Doyle followed Wells' lead, but made no attempt at social comment. In *The Lost World,* he combined something of Haggard's lost race stories with Wells' science fiction. Professor Challenger and his companions discover a plateau teeming with prehistoric life and, incidentally, hidden treasure.

The 1880-1920 period, significant for the development of the serious novel and the short story, also produced fiction which, although written purely to entertain, was of a high quality. Though of minor literary importance, these works of high adventure, supernatural horror, detection and science fiction established or, as in the case of the supernatural story, continued as genres the forms upon which are based almost all twentieth-century popular fiction. And to capture the human imagination as Stevenson, Doyle and Wells did is no small achievement.

POETRY

Like the novelists, poets of the transitional era often disagreed with Victorian ideals and sometimes used their verse to attack such widely held concepts as man's need of faith or the need to subordinate sexual desire to society's demands. But the amount of poetry which directly criticized society for such failings was small. The basic cause for the sharp alteration in poetic ideals during the transitional era was not any clearly defined ideological quarrel with the Victorians but the changed concept of the poet as artist.

The idea that art should serve life by making it richer, more various and more moral was widely held by Victorian poets and critics. In "The Palace of Art" (1832), Alfred Lord Tennyson allegorically suggested that it was heresy for a poet to live apart from humanity, oblivious to the moral needs of man, in order to serve his own artistic ends. Tennyson's belief that an artist needed close contact with man both for reasons of self- and artistic-fulfillment is strikingly similar to Robert Browning's in "Sordello" (1840) and Matthew Arnold's in his criticism and poetry. This ruling principle of Victorian poetic theory and practice did not go unchallenged after 1850, however. The first issue of the Pre-Raphaelite periodical *The Germ* (1850) contained Dante Gabriel Rossetti's sensuous "The Blessed Damozel." Edward Fitzgerald's *The Rubáiyát of Omar Khayyám* (1859) celebrated indulgence in such earthly joys as wine, women and song without worrying about transgressing any of society's principles. And Algernon Charles Swinburne caused a scandal with the publication of *Poems and Ballads* (1866) by his obvious preference for pagan delights over Christian virtue. Rossetti and Fitzgerald still adhered to some vestiges of "respectability," however, and Swinburne was persuaded to omit the more objectionable erotic passages from his later poetry.

By 1880, these three poets may have seemed exceptions to the Victorian ideal of "art for life's sake," but they did not constitute a movement or a unified rebellion against Victorianism. The balance shifted as the next two decades passed without a new major poetic talent appearing to carry on the great Victorian tradition. Between 1880 and 1920, several new poets and new movements appeared on the literary scene. But despite the efforts of various poets to band together, it is impossible to see them as parts of a single movement. Rather, the transitional era is a period of many small poetic movements, such as aestheticism and decadence, the Georgian Poets and the Trench Poets. Furthermore, the fact that writers drifted from one group to another makes it difficult to define the limits of one group and causes such groups to seem, in terms of membership and poetic ideals, amorphous. The formation and dissolution of these "movements" indicate the restlessness and flux characteristic of English poetry of the era.

It is difficult to see the transitional period as a time of renewal in English poetry, although an effort to break with Victorian poetry and renew English prosody were exactly what several movements attempted. Although in many ways the transitional period was experimental and innovative, it was also, in terms of actual poetic achievement, a time of decline from the high level of the major Victorian poets. One critic has aptly described these years as a crisis in English poetry. It may have occurred because the young rebels found no satisfying, widely accepted ideals to substitute for those they rejected.

Many of the English poets who published their first important volumes in the 1880's and 1890's are commonly called aesthetes or decadents. The terms are almost interchangeable. Ideally, an aesthetic poet can be differentiated from a decadent by the relative morality or at least amorality of his verse. An aesthete may not feel bound by society's rules regarding love, for example, but neither does he seem interested in flagrant violations of them, as the decadent often was. However, the decadent poet often justified his personal actions and poetic sentiments as expressions of increased aesthetic pleasure. The distinction between aesthete and decadent is easily confused. The terms have this in common: they describe an artist who puts the realization of his own ideals before the expression of any of society's ideals. Both aesthetes and decadents, to put it differently, believe firmly in art for art's sake.

The art for art's sake movement which flourished in the 1880's and 1890's is in many ways a counterpart of the naturalistic movement in English fiction. Both arose in imitation of French examples, and both placed high value on the employment of subject matter which ordinary men found shocking, vulgar or horrible. The key French models for English decadence were volumes of poetry such as Theophile Gautier's *Albertus* (1832) and Charles Baudelaire's *Les Fleurs du Mal* (1855) and novels like Gautier's *Mademoiselle de Maupin* (1855) and Joris Karl Huysmans' *A Rebours* (1884). All stand in opposition to the Victorian concept of useful moral art. English aesthetes and decadents tried to imitate the immorality and perverse psychological experience they discovered in these books.

Swinburne is the Victorian step-father of the English art for art's sake movement. He knew contemporary French literature well, and his *Poems and Ballads* drew inspiration from that source. An English critic who gave the movement impetus was Walter Pater, whose *Studies in the History of the Renaissance* was itself basically art for art's sake in its approach to criticism. The book also seemed to encourage a hedonistic approach to life in its "Conclusion," which urged readers to burn with hard, gemlike flames and maintain ecstacy.

The example of Oscar Wilde suggests that Pater's fears of corrupting the impressionable young, which led him to suppress the "Conclusion" in a second edition of *The Renaissance*, were well founded. Wilde brought out his *Poems* while riding the crest of a wave of notoriety caused by his flamboyant dress and witty, iconoclastic attitude toward society's conventions. Unfortunately, the qualities that made Wilde a social success—his wit, audacity and humor—are absent from his early poems. But he did occasionally reveal a streak of world-weariness and youthful exhaustion, which became a common theme in decadent poetry. In "Hélas!" Wilde sighs, "To drift with every passion till my soul/Is a stringed lute on which all winds can play,/Is it for this that I have given away/Mine ancient wisdom, and austere control?" The collection also gives occasional glimpses into Wilde's artistic credo. In "Theoretikos," he laments that the British Empire "hath but feet of clay" and urges his soul to turn from contemplation of it, for "It mars my calm: wherefore in dreams of Art/And loftiest culture I would stand apart,/Neither for God nor for his enemies.'' However, the "dreams of Art'' which Wilde reveals in *Poems* are unsatisfying as poetry. No more eclectic volume of verse was written in the era. Wilde unashamedly wrote Wordsworthian sonnets, Keatsian odes and Byronic laments and freely stole ideas and images from scores of earlier poems. The best and perhaps most original poems in the book are simple poetic sketches like "Impression du Matin.''

Wilde's great creative decade was 1885-1895, but his most impressive works in these years were his plays, fiction and a few essays. In "The Sphinx,'' he bestowed baroque splendor on exotic subject matter, repeated the note of world-weariness and gave hints of lascivious evil to produce a characteristic decadent poem. After his trial and conviction, he wrote his most personal poem, "The Ballad of Reading Gaol,'' which uses vivid descriptions of the terrors of prison life to further an exercise in cultivated self-pity. Despite Wilde's announcement in *Poems* that he would stand apart from the world, he was in reality a showman, and very much a part of London social life of the 1890's.

While Wilde loudly proclaimed art for art's sake and the pleasure of decadence, the members of The Rhymers' Club were somewhat ambivalent in their attitudes toward these trends. Founded in 1891 by Ernest Rhys, T. W. Rolleston and that indefatigable founder of movements W. B. Yeats, the group met at the Cheshire Cheese, a London restaurant, to hear and comment upon each other's verse. The club soon attracted other poets, including Ernest Dowson, Lionel Johnson, Arthur Symons and Theodore Wratislaw. Members contributed poetry and prose to *The Yellow Book, The Savoy* and other *fin de siècle* periodicals and collaborated on *The Book of the Rhymers' Club* (1892) and a *Second Book* (1894).

The Rhymers' Club was a rather amorphous group without clearly defined objectives. Some members, like Dowson, were strongly influenced by the aesthetic-decadent movement, others, like Yeats, were almost unmarked by it, and most fell somewhere between these two extremes. Some of the Rhymers, like many of the decadents, were attracted to Catholicism and other philosophical systems which emphasized a mystical acceptance of the Divinity, rather than the kind of rational religion which had gained popularity throughout the nineteenth century. Their treatment of religious themes at times produced rather incongruous poems with clearly audible overtones of world-weariness and decay. The movement waned in the closing years of the century, but during its brief existence it encouraged young poets to cultivate their gifts. The Rhymers regarded three men as the leading poets of their group: Dowson, Johnson and Yeats.

Ernest Dowson wrote perhaps the best known decadent poem of the period, "Non sum qualis eram bonae sub regno Cynarae" ("I am not what once I was in kind Cynara's day"). The narrator is in despair that, although "the kisses of her bought red mouth were sweet," his pleasure is spoiled by remembrance of his earlier love, Cynara. Not even "madder music" and "stronger wine" can provide the forgetfulness he craves. The poem is typically decadent, not only for its depiction of forbidden pleasures, but because these pleasures fail to provide the world-weary narrator with the ecstacy, the loss of self, he desires. Dowson had genuine poetic talent and in a few poems memorably captured the moods and values of decadence. He also wrote some religious poetry. "Nuns of the Perpetual Adoration" suggests why the cloistered life appealed to Dowson. The poem praises the "calm, sad, secure" life of the nuns in preference to the "wild and passionate" world outside. Here too is the "escape from life" theme that sounds so often in art for art's sake poetry: "Surely their choice of vigil is the best?/Yea! for our roses fade, the world is wild;/But there, beside the altar, there, is rest."

In some of his poems, Lionel Johnson struck typical notes of decadence: sexual indulgence, world-weariness, despair. In "Nihilism," he looks beyond his sadly imperfect life to "the slow approach of perfect death." In the aptly titled "The Decadent's Lyric," he writes with uncharacteristic boldness, "Sometimes, in very joy of shame,/Our flesh becomes one living flame." Johnson was especially committed to two causes: Ireland and religion. Both concerns are evident in a number of his poems. Ireland attracted him because of its suffering at the hands of the English, the dreamy mysticism of its legends and its religion. "Ireland," which provided the title for his 1897 volume of poetry, prays that "The Isle of Sorrows" may triumph over its unnamed enemy. In "Ninety Eight," Johnson refuses to take "old defeat" for final doom and sees "in visions of the night,/A nation arming for the right."

Religious mysticism is prominent in Johnson's poetry. In "The Church of a Dream," Johnson does little more than sketch a picture of a lone priest celebrating mass in "the weatherworn, gray church, low down the vale." "To a Passionist" contrasts the way of the secluded celibate to that of the world. Perhaps his finest poem is the personal, immediate "The Dark Angel," in which Johnson sees himself opposed and his life ruined by a "dark Paraclete," an anti-Christ who changes joys to sorrows, delights to sinful indulgence. Like Dowson, Johnson should not be considered primarily a religious poet. He was a scholarly aesthete, whose work was colored by the decadent themes of loss, death, hopelessness of life.

If the Rhymers' Club did nothing more than nurture the development of William Butler Yeats, it would repay close study. From the beginning, however, Yeats stood somewhat apart from the others because of his conspicuous Irishness. He was instrumental in founding an Irish literary society in London and worked assiduously later in the 1890's, to help an Irish theater movement get underway. In *The Countess Kathleen,* Yeats used several figures of Irish history or legend such as Cuchulain and Fergus as subjects. However, two of the poems in *The Countess Kathleen,* "The Lake Isle of Innisfree" and "When You Are Old," show that Yeats was already capable of turning personal experience into memorable poetry. These two poems also sound a note of world-weariness, although neither can be considered decadent.

The Wind Among the Reeds contains several poems Yeats wrote while a member of the Rhymers' Club. "He Remembers Forgotten Beauty" has some memorable lines and images, but decorative, trite imagery like "jewelled crowns," "shadowy pools," "dew-cold lilies" and "grey clouds of incense" shows Yeats' inability to transcend the kind of decorative, impersonal verse typical of many of the Rhymers. The same sort of preference for the remote ideal rather than the immediate real is characteristic of "The Secret Rose," a poem in praise of Ideal Beauty, which Yeats symbolized as a "Far-off, most secret, and inviolate Rose." Many of the poems from this volume have a lyrical grace Yeats never surpassed, but their abstractness or "emptiness" makes one suspect Yeats was creating a poetic fantasy world as an escape from anguish and frustration, such as that caused by his unsuccessful love for Maud Gonne, in the real world.

Yeats found himself as an artist some years after the Rhymers' Club dissolved. Largely because of his deep involvement in the Irish theater movement, he went to live in Ireland and dedicated himself to various Irish nationalistic causes. In various ways, Yeats' later verse reflects this commitment. The volume *The*

Green Helmet reveals Yeats' renewal as man and poet. In "The Fascination of What's Difficult," he complained about the labor involved in carrying on "the day's war with every knave and dolt,/ Theatre business, management of men." Yet it was this very sort of work that remade him. Yeats' love for Maud Gonne found new expression in this volume. Earlier he had imaged her as the incarnation of flawless, unattainable beauty in *The Wind Among the Reeds*. But now in "No Second Troy," he accused her of teaching hate and violence to common people to stir them to rebel against the rich. He portrays her as a modern Helen, who lacks only a "Troy for her to burn." Even though, as in "All Things Can Tempt Me," Yeats often repeats his lament that this devotion to Irish causes cost him dearly in time and energy, it was a major step in his poetic development. By 1920, Yeats was ready to produce the splendid personal poems of wide public interest that made him one of the great poets of the twentieth century, a poetic achievement that grew out of his long apprenticeship in London and Dublin, an achievement that far transcends that of any other poet of the transitional era, and one that has to be compared with that of such modern writers as T. S. Eliot or W. H. Auden.

Although the art for art's sake movement was a major impulse among young poets of the 1880's and 1890's, there were a number of other tendencies which can be regarded as counter-aesthetic. Rather than withdraw from life to pursue ideals of art, such diverse poets as Rudyard Kipling, William Ernest Henley, Thomas Hardy, Alfred Edward Housman, Gerard Manley Hopkins and Francis Thompson differed from art for art's sake poets by their dedication to certain artistic or philosophical ideals which brought them into contact with life. This involvement tended to make their poetry more immediate and rooted in experience than typical aesthetic verse.

Rudyard Kipling pioneered in introducing new forms of realism to English poetry in the 1880's and 1890's. *Departmental Ditties*, the first volume of his verse to be published in England, made an impact on readers and critics because of its exotic Indian subject matter and Kipling's skill as a ballad-writer. No other contemporary poet could approach the narrative facility which distinguished this volume and the even more popular *Barrack-Room Ballads*. In poems like "Fuzzy-Wuzzy" and "Gunga Din," Kipling provided insular Englishmen with insights into army life and stirred them with vigorous rhythms and colorful dialect. The finest of his early ballads may be "Danny Deever" in which Files-on-Parade and the Colour Sergeant discuss the hanging of their comrade Danny.

Although Kipling's early popularity was due to immediately accessible, unintellectual ballads, as the 1890's progressed he published verse in a wide variety of forms, including monologues, hymns and secular songs of various kinds. Furthermore, his later poetry often had a meaning, sometimes a direct message, missing from his earlier verse. For about a decade, Kipling functioned as a kind of spokesman for certain segments of England, as he explicitly advocated ideals of duty, work and commitment to the Empire. In "M'Andrew's Hymn," a dramatic monologue, Kipling used the same type of rugged, colloquial verse as in his ballads. M'Andrew, an obvious spokesman for Kipling, is a man of simple faith who sees in a ship's engines a perfection which is missing from his own life. Could man but live by the machine's rules, "'Law, Order, Duty an' Restraint, Obedience, Discipline!'" his life would be better. Though Kipling's earlier poetry had earned him the labels "jingoist" and "imperialist," several of his poems of the 1890's show the superficiality of this judgment. He saw imperialism as "The White Man's Burden," a phrase common at that time which he used as title for one of his familiar poems. His view of the "new-caught, sullen peoples,/Half-devil and half-child" may not be flattering, by twentieth-century standards, but he clearly saw danger, suffering and sacrifice for the imperialists as well as the natives. The hymn "Recessional" is a blunt warning of another danger implicit in imperialism: conquering nations "drunk with sight of power" may lose the humility and the charity Kipling believed colonizing nations should possess.

Kipling occasionally alluded to the topic of art and the artist in his poems. He had little patience with the art for art's sake approach. For him, life was based on commitment to ideals which found expression in action: travel, warfare, writing. "The Conundrum of the Workshops" may be interpreted as an attack on art for art's sake theorists and poets, and as an affirmation that, while creativity springs from God, criticism is the Devil's work. Modern writers sit in the club-rooms "and scratch with their pens in the mould—/They scratch with their pens in the mould of their graves, and the ink and the anguish start,/For the Devil mutters behind the leaves: 'It's pretty, but is it Art?'"

After 1900, Kipling wrote much more poetry, some of it quite original and experimental, but he never again spoke for a substantial portion of England.

William Ernest Henley's poetry also showed counter-decadent tendencies. His confinement in a hospital for twenty months was the basis of *In Hospital*. The hospital itself, "half-workhouse and half-jail" as he calls it in "Enter Patient," becomes a symbol of modern man's psychic sickness and of his preoccupation with science. In "Before," Henley describes his apprehension before an operation: "A little while, and at a leap I storm/The thick, sweet mystery of chloroform,/The drunken dark, the little death-in-life." Like Kipling, Henley saw the need for man to face life's adversities without despair, and in "Invictus" confidently spoke these sentiments in the well-known lines "I am the master of my fate;/I am the captain of my soul." Henley often took imperialism as his subject, too, and was perhaps even more nationalistic and patriotic than Kipling, as his volumes *The Song of the Sword* and *For England's Sake* show.

Certain transitional poets revealed a deep artistic commitment to the depiction of a variety of life unique to some particular region of England, whose legends, customs, social practices and rituals provided subjects for their poems. In this respect, Thomas Hardy and A. E. Housman have interesting similarities and dissimilarities. The phrase "poet of Wessex" is as appropriate a description of Hardy as the better-known "novelist of Wessex." Born and raised in Dorset, Hardy had intimate contact with the folkways of this region from childhood onward. There were few types of poetry, or subjects for poetry which Hardy did not attempt, but in nearly everything he wrote, contact with rural life left its imprints. He wrote many poems based on legends or real stories of Wessex. *Time's Laughingstocks* contains a group of poems called "A Set of Country Songs" of which "At Casterbridge Fair" is the best known. In "A Trampwoman's Tragedy," one of his most effective ballads, Hardy narrates a tale of a woman's flirtatious jest that leads to three deaths. Many of his other poems are brief, ironic sketches of the passion and tragedy of rural English life.

Hardy's best-known poems are those in which he writes as a "public poet," examining some occurrence of public concern. He often asserts that modern events are merely contemporary reaffirmations of man's unchanging nature, as in "Channel Firing," from *Satires of Circumstance.* Instead of drawing attention to the horror of modern warfare, Hardy's God tells the skeletons who have been awakened by the guns, "'It's gunnery practice out at sea/Just as before you went below;/The world is as it used to be.'" In "The Convergence of the Twain," Hardy does not emphasize the horror, but rather the irony implicit in the sinking of the unsinkable *Titanic.* He visualizes the ship lying at the bottom of the Atlantic, "Deep from human vanity,/And the Pride of Life that planned her...."

Hardy sometimes versified his experience and expressed common human concerns about love, death and absence in highly personal lyric poems. In *Poems of the Past and the Present,* "The Darkling Thrush" shows both public—the ending of the nineteenth century—and private concerns. As the thrush "frail, gaunt, and small" breaks into apparently unmotivated song on a bleak winter afternoon, the poet, despite his depression, at least "could think there trembled through/His happy good-night air/Some blessed Hope, whereof he knew/And I was unaware."

Like Hardy, Alfred Edward Housman exploited the atmosphere, place-names and stories of a specific region of England. Like Hardy's Wessex, Housman's Shropshire was a pastoral locale, relatively unspoiled by industrial forces. But Housman's Shropshire is a kind of fantasy land in which lads drink beer, run races, feel contact with death and loss. It is an impersonal realm, in which no one, apparently, feels much passion for any *living* being.

A key to Housman's conception of poetry may be contained in the half-whimsical poem "Terence, This Is Stupid Stuff" in his first and finest volume of poems, *A Shropshire Lad.* Housman says—perhaps somewhat tongue-in-cheek—that he writes gloomy, death- or misery-centered poetry in order to prepare man to meet the greater troubles of real life. In any case, the dominant note of *A Shropshire Lad* is regret at the passing of love, youth or innocence. Housman never sees loss of these things as a step toward maturation, or even as something to be silently endured. In "Is My Team Ploughing," for instance, the loss of a loved one brings only painful suffering. In "To An Athlete Dying Young," the poet does not lament the early death of one who might have achieved much in later life, but says, "Smart lad, to slip betimes away/From fields where glory does not stay." Better to die young than to "swell the rout/Of lads that wore their honours out." Gloomy as their subject matter often is, Housman's poems are intensely lyrical. In the ballad "Bredon Hill," he skillfully echoes the resonance of church tower bells in the lines "The bells they sound on Bredon,/And still the steeples hum." Housman's poetry evolved little in later volumes. His *Last Poems* and *More Poems* contain the same themes, verse forms and concerns as *A Shropshire Lad*. As poet of this Shropshire fantasy-world, Housman reigns supreme, but he seems minor when compared to poets like Hardy or Yeats.

Gerard Manley Hopkins and Francis Thompson found meaning in life and art by sincere dedication to a religious system. No poet sacrificed more, in secular fame, for such dedication than did Hopkins. After a brilliant career at Oxford, where he was influenced by the teachings of Walter Pater, Hopkins became a Jesuit monk and destroyed most of his early poems. His first major poem as a Jesuit was "The Wreck of the Deutschland," a brillant but difficult ode on five nuns who died in a shipwreck. In the autobiographical first portion of the poem, Hopkins indicated that he had passed through a process of inner remaking which made him see a deeper significance in nature than he had glimpsed before. This response is seen in the nature poems he later wrote. In "The Windhover," Hopkins shares the ecstacy engendered by watching the early-morning flight of a falcon. "Pied Beauty" praises the beauty of dappled things, for in them "He fathers-forth whose beauty is past change:/Praise him." For Hopkins, nature revealed God. In "God's Grandeur," though he laments man's spoilation of the earth, he finds hope that "And for all this, nature is never spent;/There lives the dearest freshness deep down things." Man also revealed God, as Hopkins shows in his poignant elegy "Felix Randal."

Hopkins broke with nineteenth-century poetic tradition in a variety of ways, especially in the handling of metrics and diction. His "sprung rhythm" emphasized the counting of major stresses, not syllables, per line. A foot could consist of a single stressed syllable or a stressed syllable with any number of unstressed syllables. The diction of Hopkins' poems was fully as personal as his conception of metrics. He used usual words in unusual or archaic senses, freely coined new words and yoked words together to form new concepts, as in "Spring and Fall: To a Young Child." Here, Hopkins queries if Margaret is grieving "Over Goldengrove unleaving?" When she grows older, Hopkins observes, she will steel herself against such sorrow "Though worlds of wanwood leafmeal lie." Such innovations of metrics and diction would not have been quietly received by the critical reviews of the 1880's and 1890's, but Hopkins was spared this kind of scrutiny. He published virtually none of his mature poems and permitted only a few friends, including Robert Bridges and Richard Watson Dixon, to read his verses. Bridges finally issued a collected edition of Hopkins' poems in 1918. By then the innovations of late Georgians and war poets made Hopkins' experimentation seem less unusual.

Francis Thompson is another poet for whom the Catholic religion was a source of strength, both personal and poetical. No poet of the era came closer to death by starvation and illness than Thompson did after drifting to London in 1885. He suffered the double agony of penury and drug addiction until he was at least partly rescued and rehabilitated by Wilfred and Viola Meynell. The volume *Poems,* containing his best-known, most sustained achievement "The Hound of Heaven," showed what would have been lost had Thompson died young. The poem also suggests the potent force the English metaphysical poets were beginning to exert on transitional poets. Its elaborate, baroque diction recalls Richard Crashaw. It is autobiographical, but the story of Thompson's alienation from God has been transmuted to allegory, in which the Hound of Heaven, "this tremendous Lover" (God), pursues the beloved (the soul). The poem's diction is sometimes so clotted with obscure archaic language as to be quite unpoetical, but it successfully conveys the poet's impassioned acceptance of Him whom he has fled. Thompson went on to write a substantial body of poetry, including *Sister Songs* and *New Poems,* but his elaborate rhythms and exotic vocabulary did not win critical favor.

When the editor Edward Marsh succeeded in turning his poetic ideals into a series of anthologies of new poetry between 1912 and 1922, he was reacting against the decadent ideal. "I liked poetry," Marsh wrote, "to be all three of the following things: intelligible, musical and racy, and . . . written on some formal principle which I could discern . . . ." Of the five volumes of verse called *Georgian Poetry,* the first two, published in 1912 and 1915, give a clear idea what kind of verse his ideals led Marsh to select. In the main, he chose pastoral poems that sang the joys of rural life, like W. H. Davies' "Days Too Short," or John Drinkwater's "The Fires of God" which contains lines of a pastoral dream-vision, such as, "And I beheld the fruitful earth, with store/Of odorous treasure, full and golden,/Ripe orchard bounty, slender stalks that bore/Their flowered beauty with a meek content. . . ." Marsh's chief supporter was Rupert Brooke, who contributed characteristic Georgian verse to the early volume. Diverse as were the dozens of poets Marsh included in his first two anthologies, Georgian poetry was placid in tone, largely unconcerned with such realities as the war, industrialism and poverty, and often dealt with rural subject matter.

But Marsh's tastes were considerably more catholic than the rather bold statement of his poetic criteria suggests. Though he surely selected some poets for inclusion in *Georgian Poetry* I, such as G. K. Chesterton and John Masefield, in order to lend respectability to the undertaking, his inclusion of D. H. Lawrence must have been motivated by other desires. Marsh published four of Lawrence's poems in the first two numbers of *Georgian Poetry*. He even attempted to give Lawrence lessons on metrics. Marsh had objected that some verses Lawrence had sent him were in *vers libre*. Lawrence retorted, "If your ear has got stiff and a bit mechanical *don't* blame my poetry." "Cruelty and Love," later titled "Love on the Farm," shows how far Lawrence was from being a typically Georgian pastoral poet. A dramatic monologue, the poem is spoken by a woman who watches her man snare and kill a rabbit. He then enters the house and advances on her to make love. She suddenly realizes the similarity between her situation in love and the rabbit's in death; she cries, "God, I am caught in a snare!" In "Snake," Lawrence writes autobiographically of an encounter with a feared, admired snake who "seemed to me again like a king,/Like a king in exile, uncrowned in the underworld,/Now due to be crowned again." After his brief Georgian interlude, Lawrence wrote poetry in many forms.

The contrast between Georgian poetry and that written by the young poets who fought in the First World War is unbelievably stark. If, in fact, Georgian poetic ideals reflected widely-held notions about "the good life," it is little wonder that the sensibilities of young poets were profoundly shocked by their contact with the war. Although the Trench Poets did not constitute a formal movement as the aesthetes and decadents, the Rhymers and the Georgians more or less did, they are linked by the nature of their subject matter. Some of them were simply Georgians turned soldier-poets. Rupert Brooke had contributed to *Georgian Poetry* I a most characteristic poem, "The Old Vicarage, Grantchester." With excruciating sentimentality, Brooke remembers the peace and contentment, the simple beauty, of his childhood home in lines like "Ah God! to see the branches stir/Across the moon at Grantchester:/To smell the thrilling-sweet and rotten/Unforgettable, unforgotten/River-smell, and hear the breeze/Sobbing in the little trees." Brooke took these same rather schoolboyish ideals into battle and in "Peace" thanked God for the War, which he saw as a challenge to call his countrymen from "a world grown old and cold and weary. . . ." Those who died in battle, in "The Dead," became "the rich Dead!" In "The Soldier," Brooke reflects on his own death in battle. Should that happen "there's some corner of a foreign field/ That is forever England. There shall be/In that rich earth a richer dust concealed." In his war poetry, Brooke remained a shocked but very English schoolboy.

Among the many poets who wrote of the First World War from personal experience, Wilfred Owen made one of the most significant contributions to English poetry. In a preface, he spoke of his poems as "elegies," but "to this generation [they are] in no sense consolatory." As to his intention in writing poetry of the war, Owen wrote "All a poet can do to-day is warn. That is why true Poets must be truthful." The poet must abandon his concern with "Poetry," and be faithful to his compassionate vision. In many of Owen's poems pity predominates, as in "Anthem for Doomed Youth." By skillfully contrasting the formal ritual of death at home with impersonal battlefield death, Owen achieves a moving poem. In some poems, however, Owen yields to a didactic impulse and admonishes his countrymen about some of their false impressions of war. "Dulce et Decorum Est" is a conspicuous example. After a vivid account of a gas attack and the agony of a soldier unable to defend himself against it, the poem ends with a direct address to "My friend." Owen says that could his readers have watched the man's suffering they would not tell "To children ardent for some desperate glory,/The old Lie: Dulce et decorum est/Pro patria mori." There is no overt lecturing in "Strange Meeting," Owen's most profound poem. In a kind of dream vision, Owen imagines meeting a man in hell. The man may represent, as Owen says, a German. "'I am the enemy you killed, my friend,'" the man says, but the man had some of the same idealism Owen had, "Whatever hope is yours,/ Was my life also. . . ." Had he lived he would have told the truth about war. Owen here transcends patriotism, duty and honor in a vision of the meeting of two enemies after death.

Isaac Rosenberg's achievement as war poet has in recent years been compared favorably with Wilfred Owen's, even though the bulk of Rosenberg's war verse is small. There are but twenty poems in the "Trench Poems" section of his *Collected Works*. Unlike Brooke, Rosenberg was deaf to the appeals of romantic idealism, and in later poems, the patriotic tone is replaced by a more somber lament for wasted youth and lost hopes. In "Returning, We Hear the Larks," the poet masterfully contrasts the falling of "Music showering on our upturned list'ning faces" with that of death, which "could drop from the dark/As easily as song...." Rosenberg sometimes showed sides of war other than the tragic. "Break of Day in the Trenches" is touched with a restrained humor in the poet's address to a rat, "Now you have touched this English hand/You will do the same to a German...." Rosenberg's finest war poem is "Dead Man's Dump." Mother Earth is here fearfully transmuted to "Maniac Earth!" who waits fretfully for men to die. The poem's dream-clear images of death, "Burnt black by strange decay/Their sinister faces lie,/The lid over each eye...," and the horrors of battle make it one of the finest realistic poems of the war.

DRAMA

The English stage of the mid-nineteenth century was ready for reform. London theaters of the 1860's and 1870's had produced what their audiences wanted–simple-minded comedies such as burlesques, pantomimes and farces, sentimental melodramas like the popular *Lady Audley's Secret* (1863) and lumbering historical plays. Playwrights, producers and theater proprietors composed a vast system dedicated to maintaining the *status quo* by creating and performing innocuous plays that had little connection with the problems or even the realities of life. Rarely did playwrights attempt to criticize or present life realistically. In plays like *Society* (1865) and *Caste* (1867), Tom Robertson used natural dialogue, credible action and characters from the middle and lower classes presented without caricature or exaggeration. Still, his morality remained properly Victorian. In comic operas like *Trial by Jury* (1875) and *Pirates of Penzance* (1880), William Schwenck Gilbert entertained his audiences with humorously satiric comments on such hallowed English institutions as the law, the military and the civil service. But there was as little harshness in his criticism as in the tuneful music of his collaborator, Arthur Sullivan.

A revolt in drama came in the 1880's. In that decade and the next, numerous critics, playwrights and producers cooperated to create an audience for "new drama" in all its manifestations: translations of leading modern continental dramatists, native English dramas which raised questions about adultery and other taboo subjects, plays which ended "realistically" (as demanded by developments in the play not as by the audience) and realistic and poetic Irish drama.

In large measure, the movement was the realists' revolt against the social, political and artistic forces which had kept earlier nineteenth-century dramatists from dealing with "life" and treating characters, dialogue and action credibly. William Archer's *English Dramatists of To-Day* clearly shows the general direction of the movement. Archer, one of the formidable drama critics of the era, preferred even faintly realistic drama to Victorian melodrama. For everybody involved in the "new drama," the age was equal parts excitement and frustration. As in any age of transition, old tendencies and new co-existed, but not without generating friction. Such issues as Ibsen's morality or Shaw's social views, for example, sharply polarized popular and critical opinion. Playwrights had considerable freedom in their choice of subject matter or treatment, but exercising it could cause trouble, as Shaw discovered when *Mrs. Warren's Profession* was declared unproduceable by the British censors.

Plays which dealt with widely recognized social problems were often called "problem plays" in the 1880's and 1890's. The term was widely, and sometimes disparagingly, used by critics to describe the many plays based on such controversial subjects as the new morality, fallen women and the economic structure of society. Though a popular tag at the time, the phrase "problem play" is of limited use to the modern critic since it could cover almost all serious dramatic works; it does, however, suggest the development of English drama toward social realism in these years.

Studying the plays of Henry Arthur Jones chronologically reveals the nature of the revolution in English drama after 1880. His first successful play was *The Silver King*, a melodrama produced in 1882 which featured an incredibly faithful heroine. Even though the play was loaded with coincidence, its success was partly due to Jones' realistic treatment of dialogue and setting. Later he learned to avoid melodramatic devices and turned to problems of sex and marriage. *The Dancing Girl* concerned sexual morality in the life of a mistress. Although Jones left no ambiguity about the relationship between hero and heroine, he sentimentalized the conclusion by allowing a pure virgin to rescue the hero. The concern about a double standard also appears in *Mrs. Dane's Defense*, when a woman lies to conceal immorality in her past. Problems of sexual infidelity are central in some of Jones' comedies, as in *The Liars*. Falkner, passionately in love with Lady Jessica, is kept from an affair by the persuasion of Colonel Sir Christopher Deering, who tells Falkner about women: "They're not worth it." Although his plays came to reflect the new subject matter and treatment characteristic of post-1880 English drama, Jones remained reticent and properly Victorian in his views of sex and marriage.

When first produced, some of Arthur Wing Pinero's plays were considered sensationally frank. In *The Profligate,* he was the first English playwright to portray candidly the effect of previous sexual experience on a married couple. An innocent wife discovers the premarital affairs of her husband and leaves him. The man, in remorse, commits suicide. Such an ending may seem Victorian but, ironically, public sentiment dictated that Pinero substitute a happy ending before the play could be performed. The problem in *The Second Mrs. Tanqueray* was a reversal of that in *The Profligate*: here it is the wife whose prior sexual experiences destroy her marriage and ultimately herself. The heroine of *The Notorious Mrs. Ebbsmith,* who has experienced an unhappy marriage, advocates an intellectual-sexual relationship between man and woman outside marriage. However, she proves too frail to maintain such a position in the harsh glare of society. *Mid-Channel* concerns the strained relationship between wife and husband, both of whom have affairs during the period covered by the play. As usual, the wife is depicted as guiltier than the husband, although his insensitivity to her needs is a basic cause of the conflict. Pinero moved toward the candid representation of problems of real life, but his frequent reuse of situations, characters and outworn dramatic conventions makes one suspect a lack of creativity, as well as his fundamental desire not to offend his audiences.

At first glance, the comedies of Oscar Wilde might seem to fit the pattern of the problem play, since they concern indiscretions of love, parentage or finance, discovered in the pasts of various members of the highest circles of society. But because the problems are the basis for wit and humor rather than for exploration of underlying social issues, his major plays must be considered comedies. The problem in *Lady Windermere's Fan* is preventing a daughter from repeating her mother's indiscretion in love. Wilde might have treated this situation seriously, but he used it only for its inherent suspense and for the comedy which arose from misunderstanding and misinterpretation. In *The Importance of Being Earnest,* the question of the hero's birth and legitimacy might also have formed the basis for a serious exploration of one of society's problems, but *Earnest* is basically a farce. The characters are exaggerations, almost caricatures. The "what's-in-a-name" situation on which the play is based is, however, an oblique criticism of society's obsession with rank. *A Woman of No Importance* concerns a mother who has sinned and—conventionally enough—wishes to hide the truth. In all these plays, Wilde's purpose was to display his scintillating wit. As in Restoration Comedy, sexual indiscretion and the laws of marriage were simply conventions from which to derive glittering epithet and paradoxical phrasing. Wilde's most shocking drama—hardly a problem play—was *Salomé*. In its dramatization of Salomé's perverted desire to possess and kill John the Baptist, the play is an extreme expression of the decadent consciousness.

Although translations of Henrik Ibsen's plays began appearing in England in the late 1870's and 1880's, his influence on English drama was minimal until about 1890. The press reception of the first Ibsen productions in England in 1889-1891 gives a vivid picture of the disparity between artistic intentions and public expectations concerning the stage. Affronted by a foreigner's greater freedom of expression and his choice of subject matter, the guardians of Victoria's decorum recoiled horror-struck. Plays like *A Doll's House, Hedda Gabbler* and *Ghosts* were compared to an open drain, a loathsome sore unbandaged, a dirty act done publicly. Critics rapidly chose sides. The most articulate Ibsenites were William Archer and George Bernard Shaw, while the majority of critics sang a shrill chorus of horror. One ardent Ibsenite, J. T. Grein, made possible the staging of plays by Ibsen and other unconventional dramatists by opening the Independent Theatre in London in 1891. By encouraging composition and performance of radical drama, Grein, as Shaw said, "made a hole in the dyke" of blind prejudice against new drama. Ibsen had considerable impact on later English playwrights. Instead of encouraging innovation of subject matter or treatment, as might have happened had his poetic, idealistic plays like *Peer Gynt* been more popular, his influence primarily encouraged the development of social realism, the treatment of a character's problems as representative of society's.

George Bernard Shaw supported Ibsen with *The Quintessence of Ibsenism* and favorable reviews of his plays. In his own plays, however, it is difficult to trace Ibsen's influence because Shaw's debt to his English contemporaries is so great. A favorite Shavian device, especially in his early plays, was to invert accepted stage conventions. *Arms and the Man,* which portrays war as a humbug, and military men as unwilling warriors, may be studied as a Shavian inversion of the Victorian military play, in which war is glorious and military men are ready to give up all for God and/or Queen. Through such inversions, Shaw criticized over-used theatrical conventions, poked fun at audiences who encouraged their use, and questioned some basic assumptions about the nature of man and society.

In his early plays of the problem play variety, Shaw examines man's blindness concerning society's laws. In *Widowers' Houses,* Shaw's first play, Harry Trench, a young doctor, is horrified to discover that the income of the woman he loves comes from slum rentals. He asks her to give up this income, but she refuses. The tables are turned when Trench learns that part of his own income comes from mortgaged slum property. Here, Shaw is attacking hypocrisy, which is also the behind-the-scenes villain in *Mrs. Warren's Profession,* a play written early in the 1890's but considered too shocking to be performed in England until 1902. Vivie Warren rejects her mother and refuses further financial support after learning that her mother gets her income from managing a string of luxurious brothels. But Vivie ultimately learns that it is respectable society, represented by her mother's friend Sir George Crofts, that finances the brothels, supports prostitution and thrives on income from it. The problem of money is again central in *Major Barbara.* Although Barbara feels that the Salvation Army should not accept money donated by her millionaire father, Andrew Undershaft, because it has come from profits on munitions, the Army thankfully accepts both Undershaft's tainted money and an equal amount from a millionaire distiller. Furthermore, Undershaft himself is an exemplary philanthropist who has established and supports a model town for his employees.

The conflict arising from a lack of harmony between one's own and society's religious principles was one of Shaw's frequent subjects. In *The Shewing-up of Blanco Posnet,* a horse thief impulsively saves a woman with a sick child, although he knows that doing so will lead to his capture and trial. Posnet may have acted on some divinely-given impulse, but no reformation of his character ensues. After his release, Posnet condemns the rottenness of other people and implies that he will henceforth play the hypocritical game society demands. *Androcles and the Lion* makes a less ambiguous statement about faith and life. Shaw depicts a dungeon full of Christians who, although being hauled off to face lions or gladiators, maintain an almost fanatical faith in God's goodness. Their faith is incomprehensible to their pagan captors, but the Christian woman Lavinia explains that their faith gives direction to life. Shaw's most impressive religious drama is *Saint Joan,* whose heroine must choose between affirming or denying visions she believes to have been sent by God. Joan, a typical Shavian heroine, remains true to herself by refusing to recant. She is finally burned at the stake by Christians as a heretic, a more intense, mystical believer than those who persecuted her.

Shaw's philosophy was influenced by a form of anti-Darwinian evolution expounded by Samuel Butler. From it Shaw fashioned a theory of Creative Evolution. The human species was evolving toward more perfect states of being, thanks to the gradual accumulation of knowledge through generations of experience and to man's desire for a more perfect existence. Since human love was but a means to this evolutionary end, it must not be sentimentalized; furthermore, Shaw felt that women rather than men were the aggressors in love because they felt more keenly the drive of the Life Force. In *Pygmalion,* although Higgins has "created" Eliza and does not want her to fall in love with him, she is—in Shaw's view—only a woman and cannot help herself. In *Man and Superman,* Ann Whitefield pursues John Tanner under a similar compulsion. In the central portion of the play, when Tanner dreams of Don Juan in hell, Shaw explicitly states his philosophy. Both men and women serve the Life Force, which gradually perfects "life." *Back to Methuselah,* Shaw's ambitious epic cycle of five plays, traces various stages of man's evolution until immortal supermen look forward to a life without the restrictions of the human body. In Shaw's view of society, then, man can solve the problems of civilization through this self-directed form of evolution.

After 1900, Harley Granville-Barker contributed to the tradition of social realism. Like Shaw, he attacked the hypocrisies that mold the actions and relationships of men and women. Though set in the eighteenth century, *The Marrying of Ann Leete* deals with the attempt of a father to manipulate the lives of his children in matters of marriage, a power that many late Victorian parents still wielded. In his desire for political power, Carnaby Leete is driven to use his children as pawns, but his maneuvering is defeated by his daughter's rebellious marriage to a common gardener and by domestic crises in the marriages of his other children. All that was once noble in an aristocratic family has been destroyed by Leete's craving for political position.

In *The Voysey Inheritance,* Granville-Barker shows a family destroyed by the financial manipulations of at least two generations of Voyseys. The son inherits the burden of lying and scheming to maintain the aristocratic facade of his family's business. When he wishes to reveal the embezzlements of his father, he is forced by family pressure, and even by the woman he loves, to continue the charade of respectability. *Waste* develops a similar theme. The protagonist Trebell, a powerful politician, fears that the discovery of the death of his mistress after an abortion will affect his political career. Trebell has as little interest in his dead love as Carnaby Leete had in the emotions of his own children. Granville-Barker's plays explore the conflict between public and private standards and show that forces of politics or business cripple men's moral sensibilities. Like Shaw, he analyzed the hypocrisy men force upon themselves and upon the people closely associated with them, although his arguments are not as powerful or penetrating as Shaw's.

Prominent during the last two decades of the transitional period, John Galsworthy attempted to present both sides of social questions, a technique which made it difficult for audiences to identify themselves with either side. He showed, through the use of ironically parallel situations, that adherence to the strict lines of "proper" action and law which society had laid down led to the destruction of the individual. His first play, *The Silver Box,* revealed the inequalities of the law for rich and poor. Barthwick, as a drunken prank, steals the purse of a prostitute. Jones, poor husband of the Barthwick's charwoman, takes a silver cigarette case from the Barthwick home. The obvious irony is underscored when Barthwick escapes severe punishment because he is a member of the upper classes and Jones is sent to jail. Parallelism is also evident in *The Eldest Son,* where the sexual indiscretions of a gamekeeper and an aristocratic youth are punished by a double standard. Galsworthy continued his condemnation of the law with *Justice* in which a poor clerk, Falder, who absconds with money to help the woman he loves, is sentenced to prison. Crushed by his prison term, which could have been eased or remitted, Falder cannot obtain employment after his release. Just as a job is found for him with his old employers, he commits another crime and eventually kills himself out of despair. Galsworthy condemns the unbending attitude of the law and the lack of understanding by the members of the society who support such an inflexible institution.

Even so light-hearted a figure as J. M. Barrie was indebted to plays that explored social problems. Although he is usually thought of as the author of *Peter Pan,* in some of his other plays there are touches of social comment. In *The Admirable Crichton,* Barrie suggests that a servant, given the chance, would be as snobbish or class-conscious as people of more exalted rank. *What Every Woman Knows* displays Barrie's gift for revealing the mind of a woman and owes a debt to Pinero's sex-conscious plays. *Quality Street* explores the pathos of the middle-aged spinster. The laughter in these plays is made to serve gently the purpose of social criticism.

Somerset Maugham's early philosophy of the drama would seem to have little in common with that of a typical problem play writer. He believed the essential purpose of plays was entertainment—a joining together of an audience in appreciation of brightly written, cleverly constructed, entertaining plays. His dramas before 1912 are humorous entertainments in which he exploited his flair for romantic, flirtatious dialogue, as in *Jack Straw.* In his early plays, Maugham may be compared with Oscar Wilde or George Bernard Shaw as a writer of dialogue full of witty epigrams and clever verbal tricks, but these plays show no trace of serious interest in social problems.

After 1912, however, Maugham broadened his plays to include serious situations. *Smith* attacks the vapidity of London society both explicitly in dialogue and implicitly (if with small probability) when its Kiplingesque protagonist chooses to marry the parlor maid in preference to a "nice" girl. Although Maugham's post World War I productions include both farces and serious plays, the latter predominate. *The Circle* is a problem play with laughter. In retelling the old story of the couple who give up all for love (despite, in Maugham's version, the example of an older couple who—to their sorrow—did the same thing years before), Maugham uses comedy to underscore the sadness time brings to young lovers. In turning from light entertainments to increasingly serious confrontations of problems, Maugham typifies a gradual darkening of tone in the English drama during and after World War I.

The rise of Irish drama between 1895 and 1920 was the result of many influences, several of an extra-literary nature. Without the extreme self-consciousness and determination fostered by the striving for Irish independence, there would probably have been no Irish literary revival and the substantial body of Irish drama would not have been written. In the 1890's, certain literary men dreamed of an Irish theater modeled after J. T. Grein's Independent Theatre in London. William Butler Yeats gave strong impetus to the Irish literary revival by forming Irish literary societies in London and Dublin early in the decade. He was also a major force in establishing Irish drama by writing plays himself and by encouraging other Irish writers to do so. But in the early 1890's, Yeats could do little but talk, and there seemed small hope of reversing the centuries-old emigration of Irish literary talent to London. When in 1898 Yeats met Lady Augusta Gregory, his dreams for establishing an Irish theater took a great step toward realization. She had similar aims and had the practical knowledge and contacts to enlist financial support. By the next year, The Irish Literary Theatre was born. Using plays by Yeats and Edward Martyn, a company of English actors performed in Dublin.

This method of production was successfully repeated in 1900 and 1901, but the movement—being in several ways more English than Irish—might have perished had not suitable Irish actors been found. The problem was solved in 1912 when George Russell introduced Yeats to the Fay brothers. Still lacking, however, was the physical theater itself. Since 1899, the plays had been performed in various Dublin halls. The London visit of the Irish company in 1903 removed this last obstacle. An English spectator, Miss A. E. F. Hornimann, was so moved by the players' simple, sincere performance that she offered to equip and maintain without cost to the Society a suitable Dublin hall. A theater, "The Mechanic's," and an adjoining building, formerly the city morgue, became the Abbey Theatre. Finally, in December, 1904, Dublin audiences saw plays by Yeats, Lady Gregory and John Millington Synge acted by Irish actors in the Society's own theater.

The dramas that came into being because of the Irish theater movement were as diverse as the backgrounds of the men and women who wrote them, but there were two dominant tendencies. One major stream, the idealistic, can be traced to the gradual awakening of interest in Irish folklore after 1880. Plays of this type were set in the past and dealt with people of a more or less legendary nature and were sometimes little more than dramatized legends or folktales. The other main stream was realistic drama—plays set in the present time or the immediate past, dealing with the lower or middle classes, emphasizing real problems of everyday life. In its early years, the Irish theater movement strongly favored the first ideal, especially evident in the work of Yeats and Lady Gregory, but veered sharply toward the second somewhat later, largely because of the plays of Padraic Colum, T. C. Murray and Lennox Robinson.

Edward Martyn published *The Heather Field* and *Maeve* in 1899 but saw no hope of having them performed in London, as he wished, because of their unconventional subject matter. But after they were brought to the stage, Martyn was regarded as a promising dramatist. In *Maeve*, Martyn explores the mind of a woman torn between the common luxurious life and the worship of beauty. There is much poetry in both the early plays. *The Tale of a Town*, however, which concentrates on the bitter political in-fighting in a small Irish sea town, reveals Martyn's realistic side. His study of Ibsen's plays certainly furthered this realistic bent and helped him see that plays could enlighten as well as entertain. With the help of George Moore and others, Martyn made a sizeable contribution to the Irish theater movement but lacked the professional dedication necessary to move from early promise to substantial achievement.

Isabella Augusta Gregory came closer to the ideal of the "folk playwright" than the others. Although a wealthy landowner, she learned Gaelic to converse with peasants and absorb the folklore and legends of Galway. Her plays, in idiom and subject matter, reveal this influence. Basically she wrote two kinds of drama: comedies of the Irish character and serious drama. Of the former, *Spreading the News* is typical. Thanks to a deaf gossip, the head-strong Jack Smith and the oddities of a new magistrate, half a town is drawn into court on a charge for a murder that never happened. Other plays in this vein are *The Jackdaw* and *The Image*, which show Lady Gregory's belief in the Irish "genius for myth-making" or spinning fantasy webs. Her serious side is evident in *The Rising of the Moon* and *The Gaol Gate*. The Irish peasants of these plays are hard, durable, patriotic. She also wrote tragic folk-history plays, of which the most successful are *Dervogilla* and *Grania*, the latter a tale of seven years' wandering, violent death and the reuniting of

Finn and Grania.

Ideologically, William Butler Yeats stood alone in the Irish theater movement. Diverse as the plays of Martyn and Lady Gregory are, they rarely fulfill Yeats' concept of drama—plays that were "remote, spiritual, ideal." The many plays he wrote for the Irish theater movement before 1910 clearly show his ideals in action. Of course, Yeats was more a poet than a playwright. While he absorbed enough knowledge of stagecraft from his work with Lady Gregory and other Abbey dramatists and from contact with the inner workings of the Abbey Theatre to write idiomatically for the stage, his plays deal more with personifications of abstract ideas or passions than with living beings. Perhaps as a result of the fragile beauty of most of his plays, they are more often read as poetry than performed as drama today.

In his first phase as dramatist, Yeats wrote primarily of Irish peasants. In *The Countess Cathleen,* a dramatization of a folk legend, the Countess agrees to sell her soul to devils to save her people from starvation, but—unlike Faust—she is released from the bargain after her death. *The King's Threshold* ended Yeats' peasant phase. From 1903 to 1910, his years of greatest dramatic achievement, Yeats used kings, lovers and poets as central figures of heroic dramas. Like Lady Gregory, Yeats drew inspiration from Irish myth, especially the Cuchulain group of Old Irish heroic sagas. *On Baile's Strand* depicts the confusion attendant on the slaying of Firmol by his father Cuchulain, who does not recognize his son. *Deirdre,* Yeats' most successful tragedy, is based on a story which appealed to many Irish dramatists: King Conchubar's betrayal of the rebellious young lovers Deirdre and Naise. *The Green Helmet* was the last of Yeats' heroic plays. For years, Yeats had lamented the time and energy his involvement with the Abbey Theatre cost him. As he saw less and less interest among the rising new forces in the Abbey in the "remote, spiritual, ideal" drama he wrote, he left off writing plays. When he resumed some fifteen years later, he no longer wrote as a public, but as a closet playwright.

Despite the ascendency of idealistic drama early in the movement, the tendency to produce realistic drama grew stronger as younger dramatists were attracted to the movement. Yeats' plays were still produced and Lady Gregory continued to write dramas until after 1920, but their dramatic ideals were steadily overshadowed by those of such often-staged Abbey dramatists as J. M. Synge, Padraic Colum, Lennox Robinson, St. John Ervine and T. C. Murray.

In 1899, Yeats met John Millington Synge in Paris and convinced him to give up his life as a critic of French literature and return to his native Ireland. Synge agreed and moved to the Aran Islands where he steeped himself in the humble Irish life of this remote region. Synge's first play, *The Shadow of the Glen,* showed he needed no further apprenticeship. He exploited the age-old May and January situation and gave it an Ibsen twist—the young wife (significantly named Nora) runs away with a more suitable mate to become a wanderer. *Riders to the Sea* is another play of humble peasant life. When the sea, both the sustainer and destroyer of the islanders, claims Maurya's last son, the play achieves the dignity and pathos of tragedy.

Synge's masterpiece, *The Playboy of the Western World,* is realistic in presentation yet tells a fantastic story. A son, for years suppressed and tormented by a tyrannical father, suddenly strikes back, thinks he has killed his father and flees. The play's strength derives from its archetypal theme of patricide with the important variation that Christy Mahon only *thinks* he has killed his father. Christy is a lout, but his tale of murdering his father makes him a hero to the simple villagers. The play caused riots at the Abbey and in the United States because of Synge's stinging satire of the credulous, hero-worshiping Irish. Synge's *Deirdre of the Sorrows* is anything but realistic, except in dialogue. It is a full-scale dramatization of the Deirdre legend. The Greek-like austerity of his best work, evident even in the early *Shadow,* finds noble expression in this play. Deirdre, fully aware of the fate that awaits her in going to Conchubor, heroically yields herself to her fate.

Padraic Colum, who had his first stage success with *Broken Soil* in 1903 when he was only 22, was the youngest of the early Abbey Theatre dramatists. Between then and 1910, he wrote two other plays that marked him as promising—*The Land* and *Thomas Muskerry.* Like Yeats, Colum was basically a poet, but his plays show that the influence of Ibsen's social realism was stronger than the impulse to continue in Yeats' path. *Broken Soil* (later revised as *The Fiddler's House*) is another of the stories of Irish wanderers. After trying unsuccessfully to accept small-farmer life, Conn and his daughter Maire go off to share the life of wandering musicians. Similarly, *The Land* shows the vigorous younger generation, represented by Matt Cosgar, succumbing to the lure of far-off lands of opportunity and leaving

Ireland. Ibsen's influence is especially strong in *Thomas Muskerry,* the story of a man brought to ruin by family pressure.

Of the later dramatists, Lennox Robinson played the most prominent part in the movement from 1908, when his first play was performed at the Abbey, until 1920. He showed a deep knowledge of stagecraft but also had too great reliance on other schools of drama and a deficiency in originality. His most significant contribution was in the sphere of Irish political drama. *The Cross-Roads* is so clearly a problem play that it might almost have been written by Pinero. After an educated girl rejects her city lover to marry a brutal Irish farmer—purely for patriotic motives—her life with her husband (who soon becomes a drunkard) is most unhappy. The crops fail, the cattle die, even the hens refuse to lay. The play's thesis is plain: patriotism is not a sound basis for marriage—a message with palpable political overtones.

Robinson rose above the obvious limits of the thesis play in a group of dramas based on political problems. In *Patriots,* the Irish political scene is the background for real pathos, as James Nugent strives to call the Irish to the cause of freedom. *The Dreamers* treats the ill-fated uprising of Robert Emmet in 1803. Since these plays were produced not long before the Easter Uprising of 1916, they now seem to have been effective calls to arms, whatever they may lack as dramatic entertainments. Robinson's best-known play, *The Whiteheaded Boy,* is a genial satire on the Irish character, more particularly on families like the Geoghegans, who sacrifice themselves in a futile attempt to insure worldly success for favorite, but fallible sons like Denis. Robinson was not a great dramatist, but his role in the Abbey was unique and timely.

T. C. Murray's dramatic themes, in contrast with those of Robinson, were not Irish but universal. His favorite was the destruction of a son by the meddling or tyranny of a parent, a theme of his first Abbey play, *Birthright.* Because of Bat Morrissey's lack of reason and understanding, his son Shane is driven to strangle his brother Hugh in a fight precipitated by Bat's sudden and unmotivated decision to send Hugh to America instead of Shane. *Maurice Harte* tells of Maurice's nervous collapse on the eve of ordination for the priesthood. Earlier, his mother had learned of Maurice's unwillingness to finish his training, but she drove him to return, and hence to the verge of insanity. Murray wrote comparatively few plays and was never highly thought of as a dramatist, partly because of his heavy reliance on chance occurrences to bring about major developments, as in *Spring,* when the old man Andreesh conveniently has a stroke and dies—just to end the play.

St. John Ervine's involvement in the Abbey Theatre was only a brief phase in a long and diverse international career. Nevertheless, in at least one play he showed himself a master of Irish subject matter and a fine playwright in the realistic tradition. *John Ferguson* is the tragedy of a father and the death of his son. Unlike the fathers in Murray's plays, however, Ferguson is a man of honesty, religious ideals and love. He is at the mercy of Witherow, who threatens to foreclose the mortgage. Ferguson's children, Hannah and Andrew, are drawn into the matter when Witherow seduces Hannah, and Andrew—unbeknownst to his father—shoots the seducer-forecloser. But the real villain of the piece is fate: the money from America which would have solved all Ferguson's problems was delayed one day. Despite this flaw, the play is an impressive study of John Ferguson, a Hardyean figure suffering from unjust fate. As early as 1913, Ervine's *Jane Clegg* was produced in Manchester, and after World War I all his plays were English in setting and appeal. In *The Ship* he cast a backward glance at his native Belfast, but never returned to the Irish theater movement.

PROSE

The revolt from Victorian literary tradition, of major importance in tracing developments of other genres, is of less consequence in the era's non-fictional prose. The continuity of Victorian and transitional prose is due in part to the absence of clearly defined traditions of Victorian prose. No tendencies in prose, for example, correspond to the hypocritical, sentimental treatment of love and marriage often characteristic of Victorian novels and plays. Therefore, transitional prosaists lacked targets for their discontent. While they quite frequently disagreed sharply with the ideas of their predecessors, they found little to object to concerning the highly flexible, idiosyncratic forms English prose had assumed earlier in the century.

In the 1880-1920 period, non-fictional prose includes a wide variety of writing, ranging in purpose from the almost pure utilitarianism of a guide to Dorset to the self-conscious artistry of a familiar essay; in subject matter from a chatty nature essay to a book about books; in attitude from a serious disquisition on a literary, social or political topic to the gay flippancy of a parody. Writers of prose, like novelists, poets and dramatists, explored the life and culture of their era. Some took actual journeys to little-known parts of the world and wrote of their experiences. Others explored various aspects of nature, whether of a foreign land or the more familiar English countryside. Some studied man's past in history and biography, while others examined the problems of modern man's existence, and his culture, art and science.

Though better known for his fiction, Robert Louis Stevenson wrote numerous, and popular, books on travel, familiar essays and studies of literature. Stevenson gave careful thought to his travel books. Although based on diaries of his journeys, the books resulted from Stevenson's careful polishing of his first impressions. As he grew older and turned more realist and less romanticist, however, his travel writing became more objective. *Travels with a Donkey* reveals that early in his career Stevenson used his travels primarily to display the charm of his personality, but by the time of *Across the Plains* he had become more concerned with the description and analysis of human beings and customs.

In his personal approach to the essay, Stevenson is a descendant of Charles Lamb. Rather than use the form as a medium to communicate fresh insights or build a life-philosophy, Stevenson, as in *Virginibus Puerisque,* emphasized his experience for its own sake. His subject was usually himself, often his memories of boyhood. His essays tend to be reflective or confessional in mood, as is the somber "Aes Triplex," a meditation on death. "Walking Tours" is written in the more informal style Stevenson used for lighter subjects.

When writing of literature, Stevenson wrote not as a critic but as a man profoundly interested in literature. He pointed out the lessons in living it provided, what one could infer from it concerning good and bad art and the distinctions between various literary genres. In "A Gossip on Romance," Stevenson expresses his preference for romance over more domesticated fiction. In *Familiar Studies,* he emphasizes the moral lessons to be found in the life and work of such figures as John Knox, Robert Burns, Walt Whitman and Henry David Thoreau.

While his diversity in writing won him wide popularity, his style is outstanding. His essay "On Some Technical Elements of Style in Literature" indicates how much importance he placed on a writer's cultivation of style. His own chief stylistic concern was finesse–the blending of sound and sense to produce graceful accuracy of expression.

The travel essay and the nature essay continued nearly unchanged from their Victorian predecessors during the transitional period. Both Darwin's *Voyage of the Beagle* (1839) and Thoreau's *Walden* (1854) were widely read in England in the nineteenth century and had considerable influence on later nature writers. And the stimulus for many of the era's travel writers came from the example of bold ventures into unknown, dangerous lands recorded by earlier explorers like Richard Burton and David Livingstone.

Charles M. Doughty continued the tradition of dangerous exploration and its literary re-creation with his only significant prose work, *Travels in Arabia Deserta*. The composition of it cost him twelve years: two years of living in Arabia and ten years of painful recollection and writing. Doughty's motive in going to Arabia was chiefly archaeological, but he was so stirred by ancient customs and traditions of the Arabs that he abandoned the study of monuments for that of living people. A need to create a style at once uniquely his and suited to his subject may account for his long compositional struggle. By its poetic and archaic qualities, the style he evolved suggests his awareness of the great age of traditions and objects around him. The rhythm of his sentences often echoed the King James Bible; he preferred epithets to simple nouns and pronouns, archaic English words to their modern equivalents; he sometimes used poetically abstract phrases or concepts in preference to the prosaically concrete. Through his style Doughty emphasized the epical qualities of landscape, men and vestiges of the past.

Although W. H. Hudson was born of American parents, lived in South America from birth to age twenty-nine and used South American material in his fiction, the sphere of his explorations as a prosaist was his adopted England. His special interests were the people, flora and fauna of a few English counties. In his prose works these interests are tightly interwoven. In *Hampshire Days,* he displays a naturalist's ability for close scientific description in his account of a cuckoo; and in a passage describing an ancient burial place, reminiscent of Thomas Browne's *Urn Burial,* Hudson shows himself gifted in the contemplative mode. His discussions of Hampshire people show his concern with the racial types of England. Hudson's essays and nature books tend toward the discursive and seem at times utterly without structure. Like Stevenson, he preferred gentle, placid modes of exposition. He was a learned writer with profound sympathies for man and his living environment.

The thread common to virtually all Hudson's prose is his sympathy for humble nature and the ensuing dislike for sociological forces, such as urbanization and mechanization, which tended to spoil "England's green and pleasant land." His respect and love for birds—a recurrent motif in his nature books—is suggestive of his attitude. In "Geese: An Appreciation and a Memory," from *Birds and Man,* he shows that man is amply rewarded by patient attention to the life and habits of the commonest bird. Hudson's sympathy extended to humble men as well. *A Shepherd's Life,* a series of essays based on the life of an actual shepherd, records the suffering of country people in the early years of mechanization. Hudson was no soap-box reformer, but this book conveys his belief in an ideal of well-distributed property and small ownership.

Although Robert Cunninghame-Graham was a close personal friend of W. H. Hudson, he lacked Hudson's insular placidity. Instead, in his ceaseless searching for mystery, adventure or new sensations in such unexpected places as Argentina, Africa, Texas and Morocco, he resembles Richard Burton. *Mogreb-el-Acksa,* a narrative of his dangerous visit to Tarudant, a Moroccan city hitherto unknown to Christians, resembles some of Burton's accounts of visits to sacred shrines of infidels. He differed from Burton, however, in being deeply committed to social causes. His support for Irish Home Rule, for instance, involved him in a bloody riot in London in 1887 and resulted in a prison term.

Cunninghame-Graham's journeys to foreign lands led not only to narratives of his travels but also to historical studies about men and issues associated with the regions he visited. His travels through South America resulted in *Hernando de Soto, The Conquest of New Granada* and *The Conquest of the River Plate.* He has been called a modern conquistador because of his sympathetic studies of historical conquistadors and his fascination with exploration and conquest of new-found lands. His works were never popular, but they won the respect of such diverse authors as George Bernard Shaw and Joseph Conrad.

Though he moved permanently to London in 1877, Richard Jefferies explored his previous twenty-nine years as a Wiltshire man in a series of "country books." All written in the last decade of his life, these include *The Gamekeeper at Home, Wild Life in a Southern County, Round About a Great Estate* and *Field and Hedgerow.* All are collections of essays, sometimes with a unifying theme such as gamekeeping or a certain locale, in which Jefferies reminisces about the satisfactions of country life.

His prose is difficult to classify because of the two distinct sides of his creative self: the mystical and the down-to-earth. The mystical streak, present in *The Amateur Poacher,* is most fully expressed in *The Story of My Heart.* In his visionary moments, Jefferies saw Nature as a veil—in his case an annoyingly opaque one—beneath which he sought to catch glimpses of eternal truths. *The Story* was Jefferies' *Prelude,* but he lacked Wordsworth's powers of recollecting and representing experience. In his nature writings, his realistic side is usually dominant. Like Hudson, Jefferies had sympathy for wildlife, and, as his essay "The Future of Farming" shows, he was disturbed at the alterations in country life produced by such examples of nineteenth-century progress as agricultural mechanization and the railway system. Unlike Hudson, however, who detested blood sports, Jefferies wrote several books, such as *The Gamekeeper at Home* and *The Amateur Poacher,* in fond memory of hunting.

Even though the study of science became more specialized in the nineteenth century, as research into such areas as biology, anthropology and psychology developed, the writings of scientists were often of considerable interest to the average educated man. Purely scientific works, such as Darwin's *The Origin of Species* (1859), sometimes became objects of wide public concern. Like their Victorian counterparts, many men who wrote of their scientific discoveries in the 1880-1920 period had wide literary knowledge. This background undoubtedly affected their style and their choice and treatment of subject matter. In any case, the split between science and literature, identified by C. P. Snow as the "two cultures," is rarely to be seen in transitional literature. Instead, it is often difficult to classify a work as anthropology, history or literary criticism—so diverse are the interests of its author.

The publication of *The Origin of Species* was one of the major events in Samuel Butler's young manhood. He read it while raising sheep in New Zealand in the 1860's and responded warmly to the idea of evolution. Although he remained indifferent to Darwin's theory of natural selection, he published Darwinian sketches in a New Zealand newspaper and wrote Darwin a friendly letter. But Butler's mind was too restless to permit him to play the dutiful disciple to Darwin the master scientist. He wrote a series of works in which he developed his own theory of evolution. Even in the first, *Life and Habit,* Butler had moved toward a new theory, based in part on the findings of Lamarck: evolution proceeds because offspring are a continuation of the personality of their parents; memory of ancestral experiences lies latent until rekindled by a recurrence of associated ideas; organisms change or progress because of a sense of need to be better than or at least different from their parents. Therefore evolution proceeds largely from memory.

Butler reacted to the scholarly silence which greeted *Life and Habit* by writing *Evolution, Old and New,* an attempt to give some of Darwin's predecessors (Erasmus Darwin, Buffon and Lamarck) some of the credit they deserved for anticipating Darwin's theories. Perhaps the most important idea is that there is design to evolution; it proceeds not in random fashion, but as determined by memory and new experience. The splenetic style in which the book is written, however, suggests Butler's real motive for writing: to revenge himself on the Darwinians. His last evolutionary work *Luck, or Cunning?* stresses an organism's adaptation through experience and the passing on of new skills through memory. No scientist, Butler was nonetheless a formidable opponent of men more learned than he because of his skill as an argumentative writer. A master satirist and ironist, Butler made his most impressive contributions to literature in *Erewhon* and *The Way of All Flesh,* two works of fiction which also show his deep concern with evolution.

The comparative method was fundamental to James George Frazer's approach to mythology and anthropology. *The Golden Bough,* the composition, publication and revision of which occupied him for more than five decades, develops the thesis that an "essential similarity" exists among the many systems of myth in which "the human mind has elaborated its first crude philosophy of life." Frazer was engrossed by the motif of the sacrifice of the Divine King, as in the legend of the sacred kingship of Nemi of which Virgil wrote in the sixth book of the *Aeneid.* Frazer wondered why the king-to-be must slay the present king and why he must pluck a branch of a sacred tree. His attempt to find explanations for these queries led to prodigious research into Greek, Scandinavian, Indian and other cultures and to a series of studies which comprise *The Golden Bough*: "The Magic Art and the Evolution of Kings," "Taboo and the Perils of the Soul," "The Dying God," "Attis, Adonis, Osiris," "Spirits of the Corn and of the Wild," "The Scapegoat" and "Balder the Beautiful." Despite the similarities he traced among various systems of mythology, Frazer resisted the temptation to conclude that earlier systems influenced later.

The wide erudition and careful judgment characteristic of his *magnum opus* also distinguish Frazer's shorter scholarly works. In *Folk-Lore in the Old Testament,* Frazer studied the parallels between cataclysmic Old Testament events such as the creation of man and the Great Flood, and similar events described in repositories of folklore. Frazer enhanced the popular appeal of this work by a series of credible, dramatic character studies of Jacob, Samson, Saul and other leading figures of the Old Testament. In *Totemism and Exogamy*, his major anthropological study, Frazer examined the "superstitious respect" with which savages regard certain material objects and their concern with marriage outside the tribe. In the evolution of religion, Frazer attached less importance to totemism than to the worship of the dead, the subject of *The Belief in Immortality and the Worship of the Dead.* In furthering the study of several branches of science, such as mythology, anthropology and comparative religion, Frazer's work was of the first importance. His impact on creative writers was incalculable. By revealing the layers of accumulated significance—symbolism or a sort—that had grown about repeated rituals, holy objects and men who held certain positions in society, Frazer's studies lent impetus to the symbolist movement in literature. And the echoes of Frazer's ideas and words are scattered everywhere in modern literature, as in the works of Joyce, Yeats and Eliot.

In comparison with Frazer, Andrew Lang was a dilettante. He published in many literary genres, and as prosaist he wrote literary criticism and studies of mythology and history without achieving a single great work. "The Divine Amateur," W. E. Henley's description of Lang, suggests the breadth of his literary interests and his lack of specialization. Anthropology appealed to a romantic streak in Lang's personality. In the study of primitive people, Lang felt, "we have a foreboding of a purpose which we know not, a sense as of will, working . . . to a hidden end." His approach to anthropology was not purely scientific. He related it to many other branches of study that interested him. *Myth, Ritual and Religion* is a comparative study of primitive cultures. In his examination of the "civilized" mythology of Egypt, Scandinavia, Greece and Mexico, Lang traced the complex relationship between magic and religion. In *The Making of Religion,* Lang expounded a theory of the origin of religion. From careful study of Australian creeds, he observed that the earliest form of religion was monotheistic—God as loving father and judge of men—and that polytheistic religions were degraded forms. He met the storm of protest this study caused with *Magic and Religion.* Like Frazer, Lang was attracted to the study of totemism, but *The Secret of the Totem* fell short of Frazer's a-achievement.

Lang harmonized his varied literary, historical and anthropological interests in a series of Homeric studies, including

Homer and His Age and *The World of Homer*. In defiance of separatist critics who saw the *Iliad* and the *Odyssey* as the products of several creators and eras, Lang fervently believed in Homer and the unity of the poet's two surviving epics.

Scores of books, letters and essays on socialism, liberalism, Marxism, trade-unionism and feminism appeared between 1880 and 1920. In choosing to explore such socio-economic subject matter, transitional writers continued centuries-old traditions of English prose, especially those developed by major Victorian essayists like Arnold, Ruskin, Carlyle and Mill, all of whom devoted substantial portions of their work to the dissection of society's problems. Transitional social writers were often lit with a reformer's intense desire not simply to diagnose the ill but prescribe the remedy—and sometimes guarantee a cure. The number of utopias they created in plays, novels and prose demonstrates their faith in the power of their various nostrums to heal the body politic.

No author of these years better exemplifies the creative writer as social critic than George Bernard Shaw. In his prose, he expressed his views on modern society with a bluntness missing from the more creative treatment of slum housing, prostitution and the abuses of money or power in his plays. While playgoers must infer from complex, contradictory living examples like Major Barbara and Andrew Undershaft what Shaw is "really saying" about the money-foundation of modern life, play-readers have the benefit of a preface which usually makes Shaw's point clearer. In general, his prefaces are playful and witty, a mixture a literary criticism, autobiography, social commentary—almost anything the discursive but logical Shaw saw fit to include.

The impulse to sport with adversaries or ideas is not absent from his social prose but is subordinated to more serious demands. One side of Shaw was deeply committed to the Fabian [1] view that England's best hope for the future lay in a gradual evolution toward socialism. Although his early optimism underwent considerable change, he held to the end of his life his faith in the

[1] The Fabian Society was formed in 1884 by a group of British socialists who hoped to improve the condition of England by gradual reforms rather than by violent protest. The Society derived its name from the Roman general Quintus Fabius Maximus who defeated Hannibal, in the third century B. C., by avoiding open warfare.

transformational power of socialism. This faith glows in "The Economic Basis of Socialism" and "The Transitional to Social Democracy," which Shaw contributed to *Fabian Essays*.

But Shaw became disillusioned about the efficacy of Fabianism in the 1890's. The movement had little immediate effect on English government, and Shaw gradually saw that to work for change in government before somehow effecting change in human nature was pure folly. In this time of questioning his beliefs, Shaw was sustained by adherence to a quixotic creed demanding abstinence from stimulants and meat, but encouraging spiritual indulgence in the viewing of symbolically rich religious edifices, which he expounded in "On Going to Church." Shaw's faith eventually took the form of Creative Evolution, best represented by *Man and Superman* and its preface. Following Samuel Butler's lead, Shaw saw a Life Force working through all living things towards ever more perfect realization.

Like Shaw, H. G. Wells often looked beyond the muddle of the present to a more hopeful future. *Anticipations* and *A Modern Utopia* reveal many of the fundamental beliefs and passions that permeate Wells' popular scientific romances. *Anticipations*, which he called the main arch of his work, praises managerial, technical men—modern scientific and cultural virtuosos like himself—who would form the ruling class of an elite New Republicanism of the future. *A Modern Utopia* presages the belief, more fully worked out in his later works, that the State of the future could not be confined to a nation or continent but must occupy a planet.

Wells' experience with the London Fabian Society was brief and, personally at least, disastrous. After joining in 1903, Wells became embroiled in angry conflict with older, more established Fabians. Despite these disagreements, however, he made substantial contributions to Fabian literature. Fabians regarded *New Worlds for Old* a sound book on English socialism. In *First and Last Things*, Wells returned to his belief in "the essential fact in man's history . . . the slow unfolding of a sense of community . . . of a synthesis of the species." While his experience with the Fabians may have been more painful, it did not differ in kind from his involvement in other movements. As if seeking an embodiment of his ideal world, Wells enthusiastically embraced and subsequently rejected the Labour Party, the League of Nations and the Soviet Union.

Wells' experience with the Fabians significantly influenced

his artistic vision: almost all his writing after 1908 shows his profound distrust of all social planners other than himself and his increasing desire to sell his visionary schemes of government and education to England and the world. His most massive attempt was *The Outline of History,* an impressionistic précis of man's past, present and future. Although unsystematic and unscholarly, the work shows Wells' genuine concern with problems that beset the England he knew and his desire to help by propagandizing his concept of a World State.

Some of the era's prose writers, for all their interest in the tumultuous present, shared with novelists, dramatists and poets a concern with the people and issues of the past. The era is therefore rich in biographies and studies of historical epochs and the cultures of earlier civilizations. Most of the writers of these works, however, followed well-established paths of historical and biographical writing.

While Hilaire Belloc wrote prose of almost every conceivable type, he did his best work as a historian. Indeed, his approach to most issues may be called historical. Like many Victorians, Belloc wished to apply the lessons of the past to contemporary problems. In this sense, his way of looking at life contrasted sharply with that of Wells and Shaw, who looked to the innovative future rather than to the past. While Belloc wrote large-scale historical studies like *The French Revolution* and *A History of England,* he preferred to see history as the result of the clash of human personalities, as in his two studies of the English Civil War, *Charles the First* and *Cromwell.*

In addition to his English historical studies, Belloc wrote widely about French and European history. Like his studies of the English Civil War, those of the French Revolution centered around analyses of the principal figures, Marie Antoinette, Robespierre and Danton. In these studies, Belloc was moved by the Revolution's insistence on the rights of man. His conviction, most fully stated in *Europe and the Faith,* that "Europe is the faith [i.e. Catholicism], and the faith is Europe" has led to the charge that his studies of European history are biased.

Lytton Strachey provoked controversy because of his innovations in biographical writing and because of his attitude toward leading citizens of Victorian England. As a document of revolt from the ideals of that era, Strachey's *Eminent Victorians* parallels Samuel Butler's *The Way of All Flesh* or George Moore's early novels. Although by the time of its publication (1918), the literary revolution against Victorianism was largely over, the public reputation of such Victorian idols as Florence Nightingale, General Gordan, Cardinal Manning and Dr. Thomas Arnold had never before been so boldly challenged. Strachey's method was to expose the hypocrisy, ambition and short-sightedness of people who seemed above such human fallibilities. One of the founders of the "debunking school" of biography, Strachey often adopted a highly irreverent attitude toward his subjects. In his study of the revered Florence Nightingale, Strachey concluded that her fundamental dissatisfaction with a leisurely, genteel life led to the formation of "a singular craving...to be *doing* something." She triumphed in Scutari, Strachey argued, not as a ministering angel but as a practical-minded, highly efficient nurse with a taste for combat with her superiors.

Rather than maintaining perfect objectivity while examining evidence, Strachey tried to show the person or event "in motion," as in a drama or novel, by the use of interior monologue, dialogue and setting. When his biography rested on solid scholarship and detailed knowledge of his subject, these creative additions provided vividness without disturbing the credibility of his work. In this respect, his study of the most eminent Victorian of all, *Queen Victoria,* is his finest work. He succeeded, through careful scholarship and searching analysis, in creating an unexpectedly sympathetic, convincing portrait of the Queen. Strachey did not see her famous promise "I will be good" as pious ingenuousness, but as a commitment as queen to be herself, to follow her ideals.

As a group, transitional authors were more conscious of art and aesthetic theory than their Victorian counterparts. They sought correspondences between different artistic forms such as music and poetry, or painting and the novel. They examined the correspondence between the spirit of an era like the Renaissance and its art.

The leading critical movement of the late nineteenth century was aestheticism. Walter Pater, its unintentional founder, defined an aesthetic critic as one who need not "possess a correct abstract definition of beauty for the intellect, but a certain kind of temperament, the power of being deeply moved by the presence of beautiful objects." Pater demonstrated his theory in *Studies in the History of the Renaissance.* Pater said in the "Preface" that the aesthetic critic must ask himself, "What is this song or picture, this engaging personality presented in life or in a book, to *me*?" And his sensitive, highly personal rendering of the "Mona Lisa" is typical of his impressionistic critical technique. *The Renaissance* made a deep impression on young men of the era not so much because of the studies themselves as because of Pater's philosophical "Conclusion." Since life is but a series of impressions, Pater mused, we must make the most of our most satisfying or exciting moments. We must avoid all philosophical systems that would force us to sacrifice some of life's experiences.

In a second edition of *The Renaissance*, Pater suppressed the "Conclusion" partly because of violent condemnation by the conservative element at Oxford, but partly too because Pater feared the effect of his artistic hedonism on the young. His concern with the widespread misinterpretation of the "Conclusion" led him to explain his views on art and life in his novel, *Marius the Epicurean*. Although Marius passes through a hedonist phase, he approaches the acceptance of Christianity shortly before his death. Ambiguous as the message of *Marius* is, Pater suggests that life must have philosophical foundations. But *Marius* failed to attain the currency, or even to echo the shock waves which *The Renaissance* generated among the new generations of poets and aesthetes.

For Pater, the scholarly treatise on literature "with its ambitious array of premises and conclusions is the natural art-form of scholastic all-sufficiency." His own essays of literary criticism, as in *Appreciations*, are informal in style, innocent of footnotes or references to weighty authority and chatty. Yet "Style" resembles a treatise in its carefully worked-out distinction between the "masculine" and the "feminine" principles in art: the former is the "controlling, rational, forming power" of the artist which is exercised on the feminine, the unsorted mass of an artist's experience.

Pater's most famous disciple was Oscar Wilde, whose dictum "All art is quite useless" is a natural extension of Pater's theorizing about art for the sake of art. Wilde developed the implications of his theory in *Intentions*, a group of essays on such topics as "The Decay of Lying," "The Critic as Artist" and "The Truth of Masks." Serious as some of his subject matter is, his approach is frequently so paradoxical and whimsical that Wilde's real position is ambiguous. "The Critic as Artist," cast in the form of a dialogue, develops the idea that "In the best days of art there were no art critics," but it is difficult to believe that Wilde is sincere about so sweeping a generalization.

J. A. Symonds resembles Pater in several ways. Both were literary hedonists and both were deeply influenced by ancient Greek and Italian Renaissance cultures. Symonds' major prose work was *The Renaissance in Italy,* which, as a survey of a foreign literature, surpassed Pater's. Symonds' learning was encyclopedic and his sympathy for foreign cultures wide, but his discursiveness tended to dilute his discoveries.

Like Wilde, Arthur Symons was a close friend of many of the aesthetes and decadents of the 1880's and 1890's. His chief contribution to criticism was *The Symbolist Movement in Literature,* a study of eight French writers, whom Symons loosely grouped as symbolists, and their works which he described as "literature in which the visible world is no longer a reality, and the unseen world no longer a dream." Symons' view, perhaps the outgrowth of his association with Yeats, was that symbolism was closely linked with mysticism, "a theory of life which makes us familiar with mystery, and which seems to harmonise those instincts which make for religion, passion, and art. . . ." Although the work is not of first importance either as history or criticism, it had considerable impact on Edwardian and Georgian poets and critics.

For Vernon Lee, an aesthetic experience was a collaboration between the beholder and the object observed. Her critical theories seem a natural development of her experience as a travel writer. As her early travel essays like *Limbo* and *Genius Loci* show, she responded to locale with her total being–mind, heart and spirit. She also overlaid her inner response to scenery with her cumulative knowledge of art, literature and history. In viewing a work of art, she believed, a sensitive person experienced "Empathy," which was compounded of physical sensation and response to beauty. In addition, Empathy combined the totality of a specific remembered experience and the thought of a similar future experience, which united ". . . in our mind, constituting a sort of composite photograph whence all differences are eliminated and wherein all similarities are fused and intensified. . . ." She elaborated this idea in *The Beautiful: An Introduction to Psychological Aesthetics.*

Her interest in words, as evidenced in her definition of

Empathy in *The Beautiful,* led her to a consideration of style in *The Handling of Words.* In this study, she became preoccupied with "the minutest elements to which literary style can be reduced, namely, single words and their simplest combinations." She felt that with her "...gradual recognition of the pattern in which an individual author sets his words, connecting and co-ordinating them in a way peculiar to himself, there also became evident that every such pattern of words exerts its own special power over the Reader, because it has elicited in that Reader's mind conditions, or rather activities, similar to those which have produced that pattern in the mind of the Writer." In *The Handling of Words,* she analyzed the verbs, adverbs and participles of De Quincey, examined the use of the present tense by Carlyle, discussed the verbs, nouns, adjectives of Meredith, Kipling, Stevenson, Hardy and James. In addition, she had a chapter on "The Aesthetics of the Novel" and considered point of view in "On Literary Construction," both important essays on the novel.

Vernon Lee also wrote essays on Italian literature, music and drama for collections like *Studies of the Eighteenth Century in Italy* and *Euphorion.* In "The Italy of the Elizabethan Dramatists," she examined the English writers' concept of Italy. In "Mediaeval Love," she attempted to trace the development of courtly love and the change toward love evinced by Dante. In all her essays, she was leisurely, discursive, erudite, and never hesitated to explore peripheral material.

Both a typical aesthetic writer and a clear-sighted critic, Max Beerbohm used parody and caricature in his criticism. Parodies of his eminent contemporaries like Henry James, Rudyard Kipling and Thomas Hardy in *A Christmas Garland* are effective, if rather underhanded criticisms, and his humorous drawings in *The Poet's Corner* mirror his impatience with pomposity, affectation and hypocrisy–characteristics rampant among writers of the 1880's and 1890's. As a satiric critic of the transitional literary scene, in his drawings and essays he has no peer.

Because Havelock Ellis' research into the psychology of sex aroused such violent controversy in the transitional period, his reputation as a pioneer in sexual study has tended to overshadow his achievement as editor and literary critic. Many of his contemporaries mistook his scientific study of sexual attraction, auto-erotism and homosexuality as prurience, and they were as horrified by the publication of some of these medico-psychological books as they were by *Jude the Obscure* or English translations of Zola's novels. The publication of *Sexual Inversion* in England indirectly involved Ellis in an obscenity trial and made him resolve to publish further volumes of his *magnum opus, Studies in the Psychology of Sex,* in the United States.

In his critical writings, Ellis' sexual research sometimes influenced his choice of subject matter or approach. In *Affirmations,* studies of such "decadents" as Zola, Nietzsche, Huysmans and Casanova, Ellis discussed morality as revealed by literature. Most men, he knew, found the writings of these authors morally questionable, but he believed "our best energies should be spent in attacking and settling of questionable things that so we may enlarge the sphere of the unquestionable...." Ellis exerted literary influence, however, not as author of studies of literary men or eras but rather as a leading editor-critic. As editor for the Mermaid Series of Elizabethan and Restoration plays, he wrote cogent introductions to the works of Ford, Marlowe and others. He wrote many articles on literature for periodicals and included essays on literary topics in the hard-to-classify volumes he called *Impressions and Comments.*

George Saintsbury spent about twenty years (1875-1895) as a London literary journalist but reached his greatest critical fame after becoming Regius Professor of English Literature at the University of Edinburgh (1895-1915). As scholar-editor, Saintsbury prepared editions of little known or undervalued authors for the average reader. Sometimes he angered scholars who expected scrupulous textual accuracy, as in his edition of Dryden which was based largely on Scott's edition rather than on original scholarship. Using modern spelling and keeping editorial minutiae to a minimum, he edited a popular edition of *Caroline Poets* but drew scholarly criticism for his inaccurate manuscript transcription.

His major critical works are four literary histories published after he went to Edinburgh: *A History of Criticism and Literary Taste in Europe, A History of English Prosody, A History of English Prose Rhythm* and *A History of the French Novel.* His approach to literature was, like Pater's, not so much that of a critic or historian as that of a sensitive viewer. Saintsbury defined the aim of his study *Criticism and Literary Taste* as "a reasoned exercise of Literary Taste—the attempt, by examination of literature, to find out what it is that makes literature pleasant, and therefore good ...." Reliance on this "pleasure principle" aligned him with Pater and other impressionistic critics. In *English Prosody,* he pursued the rather elementary notion that "feet or 'spaces' are the integers, the grounds, the secret of English prosody." The work is chiefly valuable for the examples it gives of lines and images Saintsbury found beautiful. A prolific writer for a general as well as a specialized literary audience, Saintsbury, in both literary journalism and more scholarly work, had considerable influence on the era's literary taste.

Perhaps the most imposing figure among the many journalist-critics of the era was that of Gilbert Keith Chesterton. An ally of Hilaire Belloc in the ideological war against social reformers like Shaw and Wells, he enjoyed participating in the "paper battles" that waged in the periodicals of the day. His literary writing was highly journalistic. He once wrote, "I cannot understand the people who take literature seriously; but I can love them, and I do." He was at his best when examining flamboyant authors like Browning and Dickens, with whom he readily identified. In his studies of Stevenson and Shaw, Chesterton exploited an epigrammatic, paradoxical style, sometimes as an end in itself. He wrote about literature more as an enthusiastic appreciator than as one who took it seriously.

Although far less prolific than either Saintsbury or Chesterton, Edmund Gosse made significant contributions to literary criticism: *Northern Studies* was influential in attracting attention to the works of Henrik Ibsen and other Scandinavian authors, and he initiated the revival of interest in Donne with *The Life and Letters of John Donne*. In studies of contemporaries like Swinburne, Gosse painted witty, slightly malicious word-portraits by blending reticence and innuendo. Although his scholarship was attacked early in his career, he went on to gain a considerable reputation as an arbiter of English literary taste in the early decades of the twentieth century.

PART II: INDIVIDUAL AUTHORS AND TERMS

Selective Bibliographies of British Authors 1880-1920 and Definitions of Some Literary Terms

The bibliographies that follow are arranged in alphabetical order by author's last name. Since neither the British Museum nor the Library of Congress is consistent in listing original names and pseudonyms, we have listed all names by which an author is generally known and have used cross references to lead readers to main entries.

These bibliographies are selective, not definitive. They are intended to be a concise guide for further reading and research on individual authors and issues. The listing of primary works includes the author's most important or representative publications, grouped by genre and arranged chronologically. The phrase "and other titles" indicates works not listed here. Wherever possible we have listed standard editions and collected works, as well as letters, journals and other autobiographical materials. The listing of secondary works consists of two parts: bibliographical works on each author, and significant biographical and critical sources. Each part is arranged alphabetically. The list of bibliographical works will assist the student who undertakes an investigation of transitional literature beyond the scope of this book. The list of biographical and critical references, of course, varies considerably in length and type of works listed, according to the kinds of popular and critical interest the author has aroused over the years. Works were selected for inclusion on the basis of usefulness. The assessments at the end of individual bibliographies supplement the introductory essays by giving an evaluation of the author's place in the diverse and, at times, bewildering transitional literary scene.

Dates of books are those of the first editions for wide public distribution. In a few instances, dates are for American editions which have prior claim as first editions. Dates of plays given in italics are for the first year of performance; all publication dates are set in roman.

A few literary definitions, pertinent to the 1880-1920 period, are also included with the alphabetical author listings.

Abbreviations

bio.	biographical; biography
ed.	edition; editor; edited by
intro.	introduction
pub.	published
rvd.	revised
rptd.	reprinted
ser.	series
trans.	translation; translator; translated by
vol.	volume
wks.	works

ABERCROMBIE, LASCELLES (1881-1938)

Poems:

Interludes and Poems, 1908.
The Sale of St. Thomas, 1911. [Completed version, 1931.]
Emblems of Love, 1912.
Deborah, 1913.
Phoenix, 1923.
Twelve Idyls, 1928.
The Poems of Lascelles Abercrombie, 1930.
And other titles.

Prose:

Thomas Hardy: A Critical Study, 1912.
Speculative Dialogues, 1913.
The Theory of Poetry, 1924.
The Idea of Great Poetry, 1925.
Romanticism, 1926.
And other titles.

Bibliographical:

Cooper, Jeffrey. *A Bibliography and Notes on the Works of Lascelles Abercrombie*, 1969.

Biographical and Critical:

Withers, Percy. "Lascelles Abercrombie As I Knew Him," *English*, IV (Autumn, 1943), 174-182.

The overflow of an ardent, sensitive mind, Abercrombie's poems are distinctly un-Georgian. *St. Thomas*, his most substantial achievement, reveals faith in a pantheistic divine spirit and in ideal beauty. His critical works are based on solid scholarship.

AE. see RUSSELL, GEORGE W.

AESTHETICISM [ESTHETICISM]

Aestheticism is the study of the nature of beauty and the standards by which it can be appreciated. Along with decadence, aestheticism was a major concern of many writers of the 1890's. In England, both John Keats and, later, D. G. Rossetti had earlier evinced interest in the aesthetic ideal. And in his "Conclusion" to the *Renaissance*, Pater had attempted to define aesthetic experience, insisting that such experience should be intensified moment by moment for a full appreciation of the beautiful. A somewhat similar movement had also developed in French literature, though with much more freedom about psychological and sexual experience. The French expression "l'art pour l'art" (art for art's sake), a phrase indicating that aesthetic experience should have no moral connection or connotations, was adopted by Oscar Wilde and his followers as a philosophical statement of their own aims in literature and life. Presumably aestheticism differed from decadence, but the distinction became blurred and the two terms were often combined. Since aestheticism made no moral judgments about art or beauty, for the average late-Victorian the dividing line between aestheticism and decadence was hard to distinguish.

ALLEN, GRANT (1848-1899)

Fiction:

The Woman Who Did, 1895.
The British Barbarians: A Hill-Top Novel, 1895.
And other titles.

Biographical and Critical:

Clodd, Edward. *Grant Allen: A Memoir,* 1900. [Bib. pp. 213-222.]

Many readers were shocked by *The Woman Who Did* because the heroine insisted she would live out of wedlock, with the man she truly loved, to initiate a tradition of freedom for all women. Like Hardy's *Tess of the d'Urbervilles*, *The Woman* was considered sensationally frank concerning marriage and sex. But Allen could not match the dramatic power or characterization of Hardy, and *The Woman* is, today, interesting only as evidence of the growing frankness about marriage in the fiction of the 1890's. [1]

ANODOS. *see* COLERIDGE, MARY ELIZABETH.

ANSTEY, F. GUTHRIE. *see* GUTHRIE, THOMAS ANSTEY.

ARCHER, WILLIAM (1856-1924)

Prose:

English Dramatists of To-Day, 1882.
Henry Irving, Actor and Manager: A Critical Study, 1883.
About the Theatre: Essays and Studies, 1886.
Masks or Faces? A Study in the Psychology of Acting, 1888.
William Charles Macready, 1890.
The Theatrical "World" for 1893 (-1897). 5 vols., 1894-1898.
Study and Stage: A Year-Book of Criticism, 1899.
Poets of the Younger Generation, 1902.
The Vedrenne-Barker Season, 1904-1905, 1905.

---

[1]Vivian Cory, a minor novelist, launched her career with an immediate rejoinder to Allen, *The Woman Who Didn't* (1895), which argued that married women should remain faithful, no matter what a husband did, because wedlock was holy. Her title was an obvious attack on Allen, and her pseudonym, "Victoria Cross," implied that Queen Victoria, who set the standard for love within marriage, was "cross" with the woman "who did." Furthermore, she implied that the Victoria Cross, a bronze medal awarded for extraordinary valor, should be presented to women "who didn't."

William Archer

A National Theatre: Scheme and Estimates [with Harley Granville-Barker], 1907.
Play-Making: A Manual of Craftsmanship, 1912.
God and Mr. Wells: A Critical Examination . . ., 1917.
The Old Drama and the New: An Essay in Re-Valuation, 1923.
And other titles.

Plays:

The Green Goddess, 1920.
And other titles.

Biographical and Critical:

Archer, Charles. *William Archer: Life, Work and Friendships*, 1931. [Bib. pp. 419-434.]
Matthews, Brander. "A Critic of the Acted Drama: William Archer," *The Historical Novel and Other Essays*, 1901. Pp. 273-292.
Schmid, Hans. *The Dramatic Criticism of William Archer*, 1964. [Some erratic statements of fact; inconsistent footnotes and quotations.]
Shaw, George Bernard. "How William Archer Impressed Bernard Shaw," *Three Plays*. By William Archer. 1927. Pp. vii-xxxvii.
Woodbridge, Homer E. "William Archer: Prophet of Modern Drama," *Sewanee Review*, XLIV (April-June, 1936), 207-221.

As a critic, Archer insisted that English drama should be tightly constructed, with natural speech and action. He introduced Ibsen to English theaters through his own translations and edited several editions of Ibsen's works. His version of *The Pillars of Society* (1880) was the first Ibsen play produced in London.

ASHFORD, DAISY (1882-1972)

Fiction:

The Young Visiters: or Mr. Salteena's Plan, 1919.
Daisy Ashford: Her Book . . ., 1920. [Reissued, 1965, as *Love and Marriage*. Contains two more pieces of fiction by Daisy, "A Short Story of Love and Marriage" and "The True History of Leslie Woodcock," plus "The Jealous Governess . . . ." by Angela Ashford, Daisy's sister.]

Biographical and Critical:

"Clears Up Origin of 'Young Visiters,'" *New York Times*, November 27, 1923, p. 13.
"Daisy Ashford: Child Author of Best Seller," *The Times* (London), January 17, 1972, p. 12.
Howard, Philip. "The Shy, Giggling Girl Who Wrote a Best Seller at Nine," *The Times* (London), January 17, 1972, p. 1.

Written by a child, *The Young Visiters*, filled with naive situations, stereotyped characters, poor punctuation and misspelling, is a delightful, unconscious parody of popular fiction.

BARKER, HARLEY GRANVILLE. *see* GRANVILLE-BARKER, HARLEY.

BARLAS, JOHN [EVELYN DOUGLAS] (1860-1914)

Poems:

Poems, Lyrical and Dramatic, 1884.
Bird-Notes, 1887.
Holy of Holies: Confessions of an Anarchist, 1887.
Phantasmagoria: "Dream-Fugues," 1887.

John Barlas

Love Sonnets, 1889.
Selections from "Songs of a Bayadere," and "Songs of a Troubadour," 1893.
And other titles.

Biographical and Critical:

Looker, Samuel J. "A Neglected Poet: John Barlas," *Socialist Review,* XIX (January-February, 1922), 28-34; 78-82.
Lowe, David. *John Barlas: Sweet Singer and Socialist,* 1915.
Salt, H. S. "John Barlas's Poetry," *Yellow Book,* XI (October, 1896), 80-90. [Listed in Contents as "The Poetry of John Barlas."]

Barlas is of minor significance for his flirtation with decadence. Poems like "My Lady's Bath," "The Dancing Girl" and "Terrible Love" perfectly catch its nuances. A few of his poems show his interest in humanitarianism and socialism.

BARON CORVO. *see* ROLFE, FREDERICK . . . .

BARRIE, JAMES MATTHEW (1860-1937)

Plays:

The Professor's Love Story, 1894.
Quality Street, 1902.
The Admirable Crichton, 1902.
Peter Pan, 1904.
What Every Woman Knows, 1908.
The Plays of J. M. Barrie. Ed. A. E. Wilson. 1942.
And other titles.

James Matthew Barrie

Fiction:

Auld Licht Idylls, 1888.
A Window in Thrums, 1889.
The Little Minister, 1891.
Sentimental Tommy, 1896.
Tommy and Grizel, 1900.
And other titles.

Letters:

Letters of J. M. Barrie. Ed. Viola Meynell. 1942.

Collected Works:

Works. "Peter Pan Edition." 14 vols., 1929-1931.

Bibliographical:

Garland, Herbert. *A Bibliography of the Writings of Sir James Matthew Barrie*, 1928.
Cutler, Bradley D. *Sir James M. Barrie: A Bibliography*, 1931.

Biographical and Critical:

Asquith, Cynthia. *Portrait of Barrie*, 1954.
Blake, George. *Barrie and the Kailyard School*, 1951.
Dunbar, Janet. *J. M. Barrie: The Man Behind the Image*, 1970. [Bib. pp. 397-398.]
Geduld, Harry M. *Sir James Barrie*, 1971. [Bib. pp. 178-184.]
Green, Roger Lancelyn. *J. M. Barrie*, 1960.
Hammerton, J. A. *Barrie: The Story of a Genius*, 1929. [Too appreciative.]
Mackail, Denis. *The Story of J. M. B.*, 1941.
Moult, Thomas. *Barrie*, 1928.
Roy, James A. *James Matthew Barrie: An Appreciation*, 1937.
Walbrook, Henry. *J. M. Barrie and the Theatre*, 1922.

Barrie is chiefly remembered for the fantasy worlds of his

Peter Pan plays. He had a keen sense of good theater as the durable play *The Admirable Crichton* shows. Though he was the most significant novelist in the Kailyard School, his sentimental, genteel sketches of Scots life *(Sentimental Tommy* and *Tommy and Grizel)* now seem unrealistic and faded.

BEARDSLEY, AUBREY (1872-1898)

Illustrations:

The Works of Aubrey Beardsley. 2 vols., 1899, 1901.
A Second Book of Fifty Drawings, 1899.
The Uncollected Work of Aubrey Beardsley, 1925.
The Best of Beardsley. Ed. R. A. Walker. 1948.
Beardsley: His Best Fifty Drawings. Ed. Kenelm Foss. 1956.
And other titles.

Fiction:

Under the Hill, 1903.
The Story of Venus and Tannhäuser, 1907. [Original, unexpurgated version of *Hill.*]

Letters:

Last Letters of Aubrey Beardsley, 1904.
Letters from Aubrey Beardsley to Leonard Smithers. Ed. R. A. Walker. 1937.
Walker, R. A. (ed.). "Letters of Aubrey Beardsley," *Princeton University Library Chronicle,* XVI (Spring, 1955), 111-144.
The Letters of Aubrey Beardsley. Ed. Henry Maas, J. L. Duncan and W. G. Good. 1970.

Bibliographical:

Gallatin, A. E. *Aubrey Beardsley: Catalogue of Drawings and Bibliography,* 1945.

—, and A. D. Wainwright. *The Gallatin Beardsley Collection in the Princeton University Library,* 1952.

Biographical and Critical:

Brophy, Brigid. *Black and White: A Study of Aubrey Beardsley,* 1968.
Burdett, Osbert H. *The Beardsley Period,* 1925.
Ironside, Robin. "Aubrey Beardsley," *Horizon,* XIV (September, 1946), 190-202.
Jackson, Holbrook. "Aubrey Beardsley," *The Eighteen Nineties,* 1922. Pp. 91-104.
Macfall, Haldane. *Aubrey Beardsley: The Man and His Work,* 1928.
Reade, Brian. *Aubrey Beardsley,* 1967.
Ross, Robert B. *Aubrey Beardsley,* 1909.
Symons, Arthur. *Aubrey Beardsley,* 1905.
Veth, C. *Aubrey Beardsley: 1872-1898,* 1909.
Walker, Rainforth (ed.). *A Beardsley Miscellany,* 1949.
Weintraub, Stanley. *Beardsley: A Biography,* 1967.

Beardsley's forte is most evident in satirical pen-and-ink drawings, which reveal the aberrations and excesses of decadence through the choice of abnormal and sensational subject matter (e.g. his illustrations of Wilde's *Salomé*) and through the blatant sensuality and bestiality of his depiction of men and women. Like Wilde, Beardsley was a center, a major force and a symbol of the 1890's. His most influential teacher was not a school of art but literature, as his illustrations for *Morte d'Arthur* and "Rape of the Lock" suggest. His own prose and poetry are of negligible importance. Beardsley was chief illustrator for *The Yellow Book,* until the Wilde scandal, and later for *The Savoy.* No other artist of the decadent era better captured its essence – a strange obsession with sex, suffering and death.

BEERBOHM, MAX (1872-1956)

Cartoons and Caricatures:

Caricatures of Twenty-five Gentlemen, 1896.
The Poet's Corner, 1904.
A Book of Caricatures, 1907.
Rossetti and His Circle, 1922.
Things New and Old, 1923.
Observations, 1925.
And other titles.

Prose and Parody:

The Works of Max Beerbohm, 1896.
The Happy Hypocrite, 1897.
More, 1899.
Yet Again, 1909.
A Christmas Garland, 1912.
And Even Now, 1920.
Mainly on the Air, 1946.
Around Theatres, 1953.
More Theatres 1898-1903, 1969.
And other titles.

Fiction:

Zuleika Dobson, 1911.
Seven Men, 1919.

Poems:

Max in Verse. Ed. J. G. Riewald. 1964.

Letters:

Max Beerbohm's Letters to Reggie Turner. Ed. Rupert Hart-Davis. 1964.

Bibliographical:

Gallatin, A. E. *Sir Max Beerbohm: Bibliographical Notes*, 1944.

—, and L. M. Oliver. *A Bibliography of the Works of Max Beerbohm*, 1952.

Biographical and Critical:

Behrman, Samuel. *Portrait of Max*, 1960. [Engl. ed. titled *Conversation with Max*].
Boas, Guy. "The Magic of Max," *Blackwood's Magazine*, CCLX (July-December, 1946), 341-350.
Cecil, David. *Max: A Biography*, 1964.
Lynch, J. G. Bohun. *Max Beerbohm in Perspective*, 1921.
Riewald, J. G. *Sir Max Beerbohm*, 1953. [Bib. pp. 213-343.]

A gentle-hearted Swift who could wield the pen to draw as well as write, Beerbohm was at his best when lampooning public failings, whether of leading politicians, literary men, artists or certain classes of society. His caricatures of Browning, Tennyson and Kipling, his prose parodies of Henry James and Thomas Hardy in *A Christmas Garland*, and his gently mocking satire of contemporary manners in *Zuleika Dobson*, all show a mind startled into action by the foolish, extreme, but always laughable qualities of men's mannerisms, prose style or dress. He made a virtue of being a minor writer, but he was master of all he essayed.

BELLOC, JOSEPH, HILAIRE PIERRE RENE (1870-1958)

Prose:

Robespierre, 1901.
The Path to Rome, 1902.
Caliban's Guide to Letters, 1903.
The Old Road, 1904.
The Hills and the Sea, 1906.
Mr. Clutterbuck's Election, 1908.
On Nothing and Kindred Subjects, 1908.
Marie Antoinette, 1909.
The French Revolution, 1911.
Europe and the Faith, 1920.

Hilaire Belloc

A History of England. 4 vols., 1925-1931.
Napoleon, 1932.
Charles the First, King of England, 1933.
Cromwell, 1934.
And other titles.

Poems:

Verses and Sonnets, 1896.
Verses, 1910.
Sonnets and Verse, 1923; rvd. ed., 1938.

Juvenile [nonsense]:

The Bad Child's Book of Beasts, 1896.
More Beasts for Worse Children, 1897.
A Moral Alphabet, 1899.
Cautionary Tales, 1907.

Letters:

Letters from Hilaire Belloc. Ed. Robert Speaight. 1958.

Biographical and Critical:

Braybrooke, Patrick. *Some Thoughts on Hilaire Belloc,* 1923.
Haynes, R. *Hilaire Belloc,* 1953.
Jebb, Eleanor, and Reginald Jebb. *Testimony to Hilaire Belloc,* 1957. [Am. ed. titled *Belloc: The Man.*]
Lowndes, Marie Belloc. *The Young Hilaire Belloc,* 1956.
Mandell, C. C., and E. Shanks. *Hilaire Belloc: the Man and His Work,* 1916.
Morton, J. B. *Hilaire Belloc,* 1955.
Speaight, Robert. *The Life of Hilaire Belloc,* 1957. [Sound, substantial bio.]
Wells, H. G. *Mr. Belloc Objects to "The Outline of History,"* 1926.
Wilhelmsen, Frederick. *Hilaire Belloc: No Alienated Man,* 1953.

Belloc believed that Europe's best hope lay in the return

to the Catholic faith, and this sentiment, which he freely admitted, does appear in his vivid recreation of historical epochs. His descriptions of the Napoleonic era are especially notable. Both children and adults still delight in Belloc's nonsense verse.

BENNETT, ENOCH ARNOLD (1867-1931)

Fiction:

A Man from the North, 1898.
The Grand Babylon Hotel, 1902.
Anna of the Five Towns, 1902.
Tales of the Five Towns, 1905.
Buried Alive, 1908.
The Old Wives' Tale, 1908.
Clayhanger, 1910.
Hilda Lessways, 1911.
These Twain, 1915.
The Pretty Lady, 1918.
Riceyman Steps, 1923.
Elsie and the Child, 1924.
Imperial Palace, 1930.
And other titles.

Plays:

Cupid and Commonsense, 1908.
What the Public Wants, 1909.
The Honeymoon, 1911.
The Great Adventure, 1911.
Body and Soul, 1922.
And other titles.

Prose:

How to Become an Author, 1903.
The Author's Craft, 1914.
And other titles.

Enoch Arnold Bennett

Autobiography, Journals and Letters:

Things That Have Interested Me. 3 ser., 1921, 1923, 1926.
The Journals of Arnold Bennett. Ed. Newman Flower. 1932-1933.
Arnold Bennett's Letters to His Nephew. Ed. Richard Bennett. 1935.
Arnold Bennett and H. G. Wells: A Record of a Personal and a Literary Friendship. Ed. Harris Wilson. 1960.
Letters of Arnold Bennett. Ed. James Hepburn. 3 vols., 1966-1970.

Bibliographical:

Hepburn, James G. "Bibliography," *English Fiction in Transition,* I: 1 (1957), 8-12.
Kennedy, James G. "Arnold Bennett," *English Literature in Transition,* VI: 1 (1963), 19-25.

Biographical and Critical:

Allen, Walter. *Arnold Bennett,* 1948.
Barker, Dudley. *Writer by Trade: A View of Arnold Bennett,* 1966.
Bennett, Dorothy Cheston. *Arnold Bennett: A Portrait Done at Home,* 1935. [Includes 170 letters.]
Hall, James. *Arnold Bennett: Primitivism and Taste,* 1959.
Hepburn, James G. *The Art of Arnold Bennett,* 1963. [Bib. pp. 222-238; important reassessment.]
Lafourcade, Georges. *Arnold Bennett: A Study,* 1939.
Pound, Reginald. *Arnold Bennett,* 1952.
Woolf, Virginia. *Mr. Bennett and Mrs. Brown,* 1924.

Overrated in his own day and seriously underrated for twenty years after Virginia Woolf's scathing criticism, Bennett was one of the novelists who explored the realm of drab urban realism which George Moore, George Gissing and others had begun describing in the 1890's. Bennett's "Five Towns" region, however, was somewhat less grim than the locales of Moore and Gissing. Unfortunately, many of Bennett's novels were mere potboilers. But his fidelity to details of character and setting and his sound sense of structure in novels like *The Old Wives' Tale, The Pretty Lady* and *Riceyman Steps* give him a major place among the realists.

BENSON, ARTHUR CHRISTOPHER (1862-1925)

Prose:

Memoirs of Arthur Hamilton, 1886.
The House of Quiet, 1904. [Spiritual autobio.]
Alfred Tennyson, 1904.
The Isles of Sunset, 1905.
Walter Pater, 1906.
Beside Still Waters, 1907.
Hugh: Memoirs of a Brother, 1915.
And other titles.

Poems:

Le Cahier Jaune, 1892.
Poems, 1893.
The Professor and Other Poems, 1900.
Peace and Other Poems, 1905.
And other titles.

Letters and Journals:

The Diary of Arthur Christopher Benson. Ed. Percy Lubbock. 1926. [Selections.]
Extracts from the Letters of Dr. A. C. Benson to M. E. A. Ed. M. E. Allen. 1926.

Biographical and Critical:

Lubbock, Percy. "Introduction," *The Diary of Arthur Christopher Benson,* 1926. Pp. 11-26.
Ryle, E. H. (ed.). *Arthur Christopher Benson As Seen by Some Friends,* 1925.
Warren, Austen. "The Happy, Vanished World of A. C. Benson," *Sewanee Review,* LXXV (Spring, 1967), 268-281.

Weygandt, Cornelius. "The Poetry of Mr. A. C. Benson," *Sewanee Review*, XIV (October, 1906), 405-421.

Benson simply wrote too much. His poetry is unrelievedly dull; his fiction is still-born; as a biographer he is only competent. He excels in the quasi-religious, quasi-philosophical essays in which his discursive habit of mind and lack of intellectual heat are not serious handicaps. His most lasting work is his diary, which reveals more about himself than he dared or cared to in his creative work.

BENSON, EDWARD FREDERIC (1867-1940)

Fiction:

Dodo, 1893.
The Babe, B. A., 1897.
Mammon and Co., 1899.
The Relentless City, 1903.
Queen Lucia, 1920.
And other titles.

Prose:

The House of Defence, 1906.
Charlotte Brontë, 1932.
Queen Victoria, 1935.
Final Edition, 1940.
And other titles.

Autobiography:

As We Were: A Victorian Peep-Show, 1930.

Benson's many novels, often genial satires on different strata of society, lack bite and conviction. When he turned to biography and history, he produced several significant works, and his *Charlotte Brontë* is a fair, accurate portrayal.

BENSON, ROBERT HUGH (1871-1914)

Fiction:

By What Authority?, 1904.
The History of Richard Raynal, Solitary, 1905.
The Queen's Tragedy, 1906.
The Necromancers, 1909.
A Winnowing, 1910.
Come Rack! Come Rope!, 1912.
Oddsfish!, 1914.
And other titles.

Biographical and Critical:

Benson, Arthur Christopher. *Hugh: Memoirs of a Brother*, 1915.
Braybrooke, Patrick. "Robert Hugh Benson: Novelist and Philosopher," *Some Catholic Novelists*, 1931. Pp. 113-144.
Cornish, Blanche W. *Memorials of Robert Hugh Benson*, 1915.
Martindale, C. C. *The Life of Monsignor Robert Hugh Benson*. 2 vols., 1916.
Reynolds, E. E. "The Historical Novels of Robert Hugh Benson," *Dublin Review*, CXXXIII (Autumn, 1959), 272-278.

Brother of two prolific authors (Arthur Christopher and Edward Frederic Benson), Benson wrote a great deal in his comparatively short life. His novels of modern life, written mainly between 1906 and 1912, are forgotten, but his historical fiction, most of which deals with pre-Reformation England, is vital and compelling. Though his best works, *Richard Raynal* and *By What Authority?*, are poles apart, the former a story of a young hermit, the latter full of slap-dash adventure, both reveal a mind inspired by the glory and mystery of the past.

BENTLEY, EDMUND CLERIHEW [E. CLERIHEW] (1875-1956)

Fiction:

Trent's Last Case, 1913.
Trent's Own Case [with Warner Allen], 1936.
Trent Intervenes, 1938.

Poems [nonsense]:

Biography for Beginners, 1905.
More Biography, 1929.
Baseless Biography, 1939.
Clerihews Complete, 1951.

Autobiography:

Those Days, 1940.

Bentley is remembered for excellent nonsense verse [1] and detective fiction. His Trent stories feature a detective who, especially in *Trent's Last Case*, reveals unexpected human failings in addition to traditional Holmesian shrewdness.

---

[1]Bentley's nonsense verse form, called a Clerihew, contains two couplets of unequal length, with exaggerated rhymes, thumb-nail biography and great use of *non sequitur*. As disciplined nonsense, the Clerihew is rivaled only by the Limerick. Two examples taken from *Clerihews Complete* show Bentley's irreverent approach to literary figures:

Mr. H. G. Wells
Was composed of cells.
He thought the human race
Was a perfect disgrace.

On one occasion when Browning
Saved a débutante from drowning
She inquired faintly what he meant
By that stuff about good news from Ghent.

BERESFORD, JOHN DAVYS (1873-1947)

Fiction:

The Hampdenshire Wonder, 1911.
Jacob Stahl [trilogy], 1911, 1912, 1915.
Goslings, 1913.
The House in Demetrius Road, 1914.
Revolution, 1921.
Unity, 1924.
The Meeting Place, 1929.
The Middle Generation, 1932.
And other titles.

Prose:

H. G. Wells, 1915.
And other titles.

Autobiography:

Writing Aloud, 1928.
What I Believe, 1938.
And other titles.

Bibliographical:

Gerber, Helmut E. "J. D. Beresford: A Bibliography," *Bulletin of Bibliography,* XXI (January-April, 1957), 201-204.

Biographical and Critical:

Gerber, Helmut E. "J. D. Beresford: The Freudian Element," *Literature and Psychology,* VI (August, 1956), 78-86.

Beresford's creative life breaks into three periods: 1911-1923, he wrote autobiographical novels in the tradition of sociological and psychological realism; 1923-1938, he underwent a period of spiritual crisis that brought his work to the verge of mysticism; 1938-1947, under the influence of his collaborator Esmé Wynne-Tyson, he moved into an intensely spiritual phase and based his novels on an idealistic metaphysic with roots in the New Testament and the Eastern mystics. *Jacob Stahl*, his best-remembered work, is a descendant of Butler's *Way of All Flesh*.

BESANT, WALTER (1836-1901)

Fiction:

Ready-Money Mortiboy [with James Rice], 1872.
The Chaplain of the Fleet [with James Rice], 1881.
All Sorts and Conditions of Men, 1882.
Dorothy Forster, 1884.
Children of Gibeon, 1886.
The Rebel Queen, 1893.
No Other Way, 1902.
And other titles.

Autobiography:

Autobiography of Sir Walter Besant. Ed. S. Squire Sprigge. 1902.
As We Are and As We May Be, 1903.

Biographical and Critical:.

Boll, Ernest. "Walter Besant on the Art of the Novel," *English Fiction in Transition*, II: 1 (1959), 28-35.
Boege, Fred. "Sir Walter Besant: Novelist," *Nineteenth-Century Fiction*, X (March, 1956), 249-280; XI (June, 1956), 32-60.

A conscious moral purpose reminiscent of Dickens runs through Besant's work, as in *All Sorts*, in which he calls attention to social evils in East London. He sought lucidity above all, to tell a clear story with simple, instantly recognizable characters. His best work presents a vivid fictional recreation of eighteenth-century life.

BINYON, ROBERT LAURENCE (1869-1943)

Poems:

Lyric Poems, 1894.
Poems, 1895.
First Book of London Visions, 1896.
Porphyrion, 1898.
Second Book of London Visions, 1899.
Odes, 1901.
The Four Years: War Poems, 1919.
The Secret, 1920.
The Sirens: An Ode, 1924.
Collected Poems. 2 vols., 1931.
Dante's *Divina Commedia*. Trans. by Binyon. 1933-1943.
And other titles.

Plays:

Paris and Oenone, 1906.
Attila: A Tragedy, 1907.
Arthur, 1923.
And other titles.

Biographical and Critical:

Clemens, Cyril. "Laurence Binyon on Translating," *Dalhousie Review*, XXXV (Summer, 1955), 168-174.

For many years the keeper of prints and drawings at the British Museum, Binyon was a distinctly minor poet, whose slim verse volumes were the product of his spare time. His verses often seem like captions for photographs: they render some fragment of the London scene with meticulous detail but fail to reveal anything of significance hidden from more ordinary observers. His translation of Dante is his greatest poetic achievement.

BIRRELL, AUGUSTINE (1850-1933)

Prose:

Obiter Dicta. 2 ser., 1884, 1887.
Life of Charlotte Brontë, 1887.
Res Judicatae, 1892.
Essays about Men, Women and Books, 1894.
William Hazlitt, 1902.
Frederick Locker-Lampson, 1920.
Et Cetera, 1930.
And other titles.

Autobiography:

Things Past Redress, 1937.

Both politician and author, Birrell built a slight literary reputation with his essays. Though he survived the shock of forced retirement as chief secretary for Ireland after the 1916 Easter Rebellion, he never equalled the achievement of his early work.

BLACKWOOD, ALGERNON (1869-1951)

Fiction:

The Empty House, 1906.
John Silence, Physician Extraordinary, 1908.
Jimbo, 1909.
The Centaur, 1911.
A Prisoner of Fairyland, 1913.
Julius Le Vallon, 1916.
Promise of Air, 1918.
And other titles.

Autobiography:

Episodes Before Thirty, 1923.

Biographical and Critical:

Hudson, Derek. "A Study of Algernon Blackwood," *Essays and Studies,* XIV (1961), 102-114.

Despite Blackwood's aspiration to be known as a serious novelist, his fame rests on his short tales of the macabre and supernatural. His longer works were often in a similar vein like *Jimbo,* a story of a boy who learns to fly, and *A Prisoner,* a fairy story of children in the Jura. *The Centaur,* which Blackwood thought his best novel, gives a trance-like, mystic vision of man and nature.

BLAND, MRS. HUBERT. *see* NESBIT, E.

BLUNT, WILFRED SCAWEN (1840-1922)

Poems:

Songs and Sonnets. By Proteus, 1875.
The Love Sonnets of Proteus, 1881.
In Vinculis, 1889.
Satan Absolved, 1899.
Esther, Love Lyrics, and Natalia's Resurrection, 1892.
The Seven Golden Odes of Pagan Arabia, 1903.
Poetical Works. 2 vols., 1914.
And other titles.

Prose:

Secret History of the English Occupation of Egypt, 1907.
India under Ripon, 1909.
The Land War in Ireland, 1912.
And other titles.

Autobiography:

My Diaries . . . 1888-1914. 2 vols., 1919-1920.

Biographical and Critical:

Assad, Thomas. "Wilfred Scawen Blunt—Sheikh," *Three Victorian Travelers: Burton, Blunt, Doughty,* 1964. Pp. 53-94.
Finch, Edith. *Wilfred Scawen Blunt, 1840-1922,* 1938. [Bib. pp. 397-402.]
Leslie, Shane. "Wilfred Blunt (1840-1922)," *Men Were Different,* 1937. Pp. 229-287.
Reinehr, Mary Joan. *The Writings of Wilfred Scawen Blunt,* 1940. [Bib. pp. 199-217.]

Blunt's poetry and prose document his vigorous, exotic life. *In Vinculis* tells of the hardships of life in Irish jails, where he was thrown when his activities on behalf of Irish landowners angered the authorities; *Secret History* and *India Under Ripon* were written after several journeys to the East. His prose works foreshadow the interest later writers would have in Eastern lands. As a poet, Blunt failed to attain high rank, despite many fine sonnets (his best form). Usually his poems document important personal experiences, but often he fails to communicate their significance.

BOTTOMLEY, GORDON (1874-1948)

Plays:

King Lear's Wife, 1915.
Britain's Daughter, 1922.
Gruach, 1923.
The Riding to Lithend, 1928.
And other titles.

Poems:

The Mickle Drede, 1896.
Poems at White-Nights, 1899.
The Gate of Smaragdus, 1904.
Chambers of Imagery. 2 ser., 1907, 1912.

Gordon Bottomley

Poems of Thirty Years, 1925.
Poems and Plays. Ed. Claude Colleer Abbott. 1953.

Prose:

A Stage for Poetry: My Purposes with My Plays, 1948.

Letters:

Poet and Painter: Being the Correspondence Between Gordon Bottomley and Paul Nash: 1910-1946. Ed. C. C. Abbott and Anthony Bertram. 1955.

Biographical and Critical:

Abbott, Claude Colleer. "Introduction," *Poems and Plays*, 1953. Pp. 9-19.
Farmer, A. J. "Gordon Bottomley," *Études Anglaises*, IX (October-December, 1956), 323-327.

Bottomley is important chiefly as an exponent of verse drama. Even though his appeal was never wide, he helped prepare a milieu for the later achievements of Eliot and Fry. Some of his plays, like *The Riding to Lithend*, will live, at least as closet drama, because of their subtlety of characterization and poetic conviction. The streak of violence in his later poetry suggests Bottomley's rebellious spirit and his desire to rescue English verse from empty sensuousness and pastoral pleasantries.

BRIDGES, ROBERT SEYMOUR (1844-1930)

Poems:

Poems. 3 ser., 1873, 1879, 1884.
The Growth of Love, 1876 [24 sonnets]; 1890 [79 sonnets].
Poetical Works, 1912.
October, 1920.
New Verse, 1925.
The Testament of Beauty, 1929.
And other titles.

Robert Seymour Bridges

Prose:

Milton's Prosody, 1893.
John Keats, 1895.
The Necessity of Poetry, 1918.
Collected Essays, Papers, Etc. of Robert Bridges. 10 vols., 1927-1936.

Letters:

The Correspondence of Robert Bridges and Henry Bradley 1900-1923, 1940.

Bibliographical:

McKay, George L. *A Bibliography of Robert Bridges*, 1933.

Biographical and Critical:

Beum, Robert. "Profundity Revisited: Bridges and His Critics," *Dalhousie Review*, XLIV (Summer, 1964), 172-179.
Elton, Oliver. *Robert Bridges and The Testament of Beauty*, 1932.
Gordon, G. S. *Robert Bridges*, 1946.
Guerard, Albert J. *Robert Bridges: A Study of Traditionalism*, 1942. [A thorough, sympathetic analysis.]
Ritz, Jean Georges. *Robert Bridges and Gerard Hopkins, 1863-1889*, 1960.
Thompson, Edward. *Robert Bridges, 1844-1930*, 1944.

Despite Bridges' dedication, careful craftsmanship and poet's "ear," his poems are best liked by people who value form more than content, finish more than feeling. His poetry lacks passion and drama, and its concern is with abstractions and generalities, as in *The Growth of Love*, where Bridges writes of Ideal Beauty, not of any specific woman. Like some other poets of the era, Bridges turned away from the excitement and evils of the present, as his reluctance to write patriotic poetry when he was Poet Laureate during World War I suggests, to the time of Milton, Marvell and the classic past for inspiration.

Paradoxically, he achieved popularity with *The Testament of Beauty*, a long philosophical poem ranging over the whole of modern science.

BROOKE, RUPERT (1887-1915)

Poems:

Poems, 1911.
1914, 1915.
Poetical Works. Ed. Geoffrey Keynes. 1946.

Prose:

John Webster and the Elizabethan Drama, 1916.
The Prose of Rupert Brooke. Ed. Christopher Hassall. 1956.

Letters:

Letters from America. Ed. Henry James. 1916.
The Letters of Rupert Brooke. Ed. Geoffrey Keynes. 1968.

Bibliographical:

Keynes, Geoffrey. *A Bibliography of Rupert Brooke*, 1954.

Biographical and Critical:

De la Mare, Walter. *Rupert Brooke and the Intellectual Imagination*, 1919.
Hassall, Christopher. *Rupert Brooke: A Biography*, 1964. [Outstanding bio.]
Marsh, Edward. *Rupert Brooke: A Memoir*, 1918.
Stringer, Arther John. *Red Wine of Youth: A Life of Rupert Brooke*, 1948.

An intelligent, sensitive youth, Brooke matured rapidly through travel and his service in the First World War. But his war experience has been overemphasized as the major factor in his development. He was already a gifted poet by 1914, as his exotic Hawaiian poems show. His poems welcoming the war and "The Soldier" may now seem wrong-headed, but he was a significant commentator on the war. Even his best work lacks finish, but it ably communicates his feelings of love, death and time.

BROOKE, STOPFORD AUGUSTUS (1832-1916)

Prose:

The Life and Letters of Frederick W. Robertson, 1865.
English Literature, 1876; rvd. eds., 1896, 1901, 1924.
Tennyson: His Art and Relation to Modern Life, 1894.
The Poetry of Robert Browning, 1902.
A Study of Clough, Arnold, Rossetti and Morris, 1908. [1913 ed. titled *Four Poets.*]
And other titles.

Biographical and Critical:

Chesterton, G. K. "Stopford Brooke," *Hibbert Journal,* XVI (April, 1918), 377-386.
Drinkwater, John. "Stopford Brooke," *Quarterly Review,* CCXXIX (April, 1918), 526-540.
Jacks, Lawrence P. *Life and Letters of Stopford Brooke,* 1917.

Brooke's *English Literature* influenced a generation of literary study, and his essays on Tennyson and Browning remain valuable. Also, he devoted many volumes to dissecting religious controversies of his day. The Broad Church leanings visible in *Life of Robertson* anticipated his quiet withdrawal from Anglicanism fifteen years later.

BROWN, GEORGE DOUGLAS [GEORGE DOUGLAS, GEORGE HOOD, KENNEDY KING] (1869-1902)

Fiction:

Love and a Sword, 1899.
The House with the Green Shutters, 1901.
And other titles.

Biographical and Critical:

Lennox, Cuthbert. *George Douglas Brown: A Biographical Memoir,* 1903.
Muir, Edwin. "George Douglas," *Latitudes,* 1924. Pp. 31-46.
Scott, J. D. "R. L. Stevenson and G. D. Brown; the Myth of Lord Braxfield," *Horizon,* XIII (May, 1946), 298-310.
Veitch, James. *George Douglas Brown,* 1952.

Brown is chiefly known as the author of *The House,* which has been interpreted as a criticism of the amiable, old-fashioned fiction of the Kailyard School. Brown shows a most unflattering view of Scots life in his depiction of a proud man's failure. Although of smaller stature, the novel belongs with *Clayhanger* and *Father and Son* in the "clash of generations" genre.

BUCHAN, JOHN (1875-1940)

Fiction:

Prester John, 1910.
The Moon Endureth, 1912.
Salute to Adventurers, 1915.
The Thirty-Nine Steps, 1915.
Greenmantle, 1916.
The Power-House, 1916.
Huntingtower, 1922.
The Three Hostages, 1924.
The Dancing Floor, 1926.

Witch Wood, 1927.
The Runagates Club, 1928.
Sick Heart River, 1941. [Am. title *Mountain Meadow*.]
And other titles.

Prose:

The Man and the Book: Sir Walter Scott, 1925.
Montrose, 1928.
And other titles.

Autobiography:

Memory Hold-the-Door, 1940. [Am. title *Pilgrim's Way*.]

Bibliographical:

Cox, J. Randolph. "John Buchan, Lord Tweedsmuir: An Annotated Bibliography of Writings About Him," *English Literature in Transition*, IX: 5-6 (1966), 241-325.
Hanna, Archibald. *John Buchan, 1875-1940: A Bibliography*, 1953.
[Wilmot, B. C.]. *Checklist of Works by and about John Buchan in the John Buchan Collection, Douglas Library, Queens' University, Kingston, Ontario*, 1961.

Biographical and Critical:

Buchan, Anna. *Unforgettable, Unforgotten*, 1945.
Smith, Janet Adam. *John Buchan: A Biography*, 1965. [Bib. pp. 476-479.]
Swiggett, Howard. "Introduction," *Mountain Meadow*, 1941. Pp. v-xlix.
Turner, Arthur C. *Mr. Buchan, Writer*, [1949].
Tweedsmuir, Susan. *John Buchan: By His Wife and Friends*, 1947.
— *The Lilac and the Rose*, 1952.
Usborne, Richard. "John Buchan," *Clubland Heroes*, 1953. Pp. 83-139.

Following the lead of Stevenson and Haggard, Buchan concentrated, in his best known books, on adventure.

His boy's story *Prester John* concerned hidden treasure and native rebellion, but his skill as a writer raised it above the level of Haggard's African entertainments. Buchan saw that high adventure could occur in contemporary England and Europe as well as in exotic countries or in past eras, and he turned his attention to intrigue in the modern world in books like *The Thirty-Nine Steps* and *The Power-House*. His heroes, always "gentlemen" and always believing in old-fashioned fair play, often show ordinary men unwillingly caught in a web-work of espionage or danger.

BUTLER, SAMUEL (1835-1902)

Fiction:

Erewhon, 1872.
Erewhon Revisited, 1901.
The Way of All Flesh. Ed. R. A. Streatfeild. 1903.
Ernest Pontifex or the Way of All Flesh. Ed. Daniel F. Howard. 1964. [Indicates changes and deletions made by Streatfeild.]

Prose:

The Evidence for the Resurrection of Jesus Christ, 1865.
The Fair Haven, 1873.
Life and Habit, 1877.
Evolution, Old and New, 1879.
Unconscious Memory, 1880.
Luck, or Cunning...?, 1887.
Essays on Life, Art and Science. Ed. R. A. Streatfeild. 1904.
God the Known and God the Unknown. Ed. R. A. Streatfeild. 1909.
And other titles.

Letters and Notebooks:

The Note-Books of Samuel Butler. Ed. H. F. Jones. 1912. [Considerable editorial distortion.]

Selections from the Notebooks of Samuel Butler. Ed. A. T. Bartholomew. 1930.
Butleriana. Ed. A. T. Bartholomew. 1932.
Further Extracts from the Note-Books of Samuel Butler. Ed. A. T. Bartholomew. 1934.
Letters Between Samuel Butler and Miss E. M. A. Savage, 1935.
Samuel Butler's Notebooks. Ed. Geoffrey Keynes and Brian Hill. 1951.
The Family Letters of Samuel Butler 1841-1886. Ed. Arnold Silver. 1962.
The Correspondence of Samuel Butler with His Sister May. Ed. Daniel F. Howard. 1962.

Collected Works:

Works. "Shrewsbury Edition." 20 vols., 1923-1926.

Bibliographical:

Harkness, Stanley B. *The Career of Samuel Butler, 1835-1902: A Bibliography,* 1955. [To 1953. The std. bib.]
Hoppé, A. J. *A Bibliography of the Writings of Samuel Butler and of Writings About Him,* 1925. [With some letters from Butler to F. G. Fleay.]

Biographical and Critical:

Cannan, Gilbert. *Samuel Butler: A Critical Study,* 1915.
Fort, J. B. *Samuel Butler 1835-1902,* 1935. [Bib. pp. 487-505.]
Furbank, P. N. *Samuel Butler,* 1948.
Harris, J. F. *Samuel Butler... The Man and His Work,* 1916.
Henderson, Philip. *Samuel Butler: The Incarnate Bachelor,* 1953.
Holt, Lee E. *Samuel Butler,* 1964. [Bib. pp. 167-176.]
Joad, C. E. M. *Samuel Butler,* 1924.
Jones, Henry Festing. *Samuel Butler: A Memoir,* 1917. [Considerable remaking of Butler's character to fit Jones' conception.]
Jones, Joseph Jay. *The Cradle of "Erewhon": Samuel Butler in New Zealand,* 1959.

Muggeridge, Malcolm. *The Earnest Atheist,* 1936. [Controversial.]
Stillman, C. G. *Samuel Butler: A Mid-Victorian Modern,* 1932.
Streatfeild, R. A. *Samuel Butler: A Critical Study,* 1902.

Butler came close to being a Renaissance virtuoso, a man gifted in many areas of art and culture. He exhibited paintings at the Royal Academy, composed music and wrote in a wide variety of forms including art criticism, personal essays and, most notably, though not prolifically, fiction. In all he wrote, he was a brilliant iconoclast who fired scathing volleys at established opinions on art, music, religion, literature and science. In *Erewhon,* the vision is Swiftian: illness is a crime for which man is punished; machines threaten to dominate the functions of man. The work presages *The Way of All Flesh* in suggesting the involuntary transmittal of habit and memory through endless generations. *The Way of All Flesh* attacks entrenched ideals regarding religion, education and marriage. Butler was especially bitter about Victorian methods of child-rearing: the way well-meaning but blind parents molded a child to meet the requirements of their egos or some pre-chosen profession. Butler may justly be called the gadfly of the late Victorian period.

CAINE, HALL. *see* CAINE, THOMAS HENRY HALL.

CAINE, THOMAS HENRY HALL [HALL CAINE] (1853-1931)

Fiction:

The Shadow of a Crime, 1885.
The Deemster, 1887.
The Scapegoat, 1891.
The Christian, 1897.
The Prodigal Son, 1904.
And other titles.

Thomas Henry Hall Caine

Prose:

Recollections of Dante Gabriel Rossetti, 1882; rvd. ed., 1928.
Cobwebs of Criticism, 1883.
Life of Samuel Taylor Coleridge, 1887.
And other titles.

Biographical and Critical:

Kenyon, C. F. *Hall Caine: The Man and The Novelist,* 1901.
Norris, Samuel. *Two Men of Manxland: Hall Caine, Novelist, T. E. Brown, Poet,* 1947.

Almost total oblivion, unrelieved by even scholarly glances, has been the fate of Caine's once-popular blend of sentiment, reform and black-and-white morality. Still worth reading, however, is *Recollections,* which relates the last tortured years of Rossetti's life when Caine acted as secretary for the drug-ridden poet.

CANNAN, GILBERT (1884-1955)

Fiction:

Devious Ways, 1910.
Round the Corner, 1913.
Old Mole, 1914.
Mendel, 1916.
Annette and Bennett, 1922.
And other titles.

Plays:

Miles Dixon, 1910.
The Perfect Widow, 1912.
Mary's Wedding, 1912.
And other titles.

Gilbert Cannan

Prose:

Samuel Butler, 1915.
And other titles.

Biographical and Critical:

Aldington, Richard. *Life for Life's Sake,* 1955. [Passim.]

Cannan's chief love was the theater. He helped found the Manchester Repertory Theatre, acted in plays and composed a number of dramas, some of which reveal a debt to Irish playwrights. They fail, however, to show that Cannan had any particular gift for dramatic composition. As a novelist, he is likely to retain his minor reputation as a clever ironist with no illusions about love or society, as in *Round the Corner.*

CELTIC RENAISSANCE [CELTIC REVIVAL, IRISH LITERARY RENAISSANCE]

The Celtic Renaissance, the sudden surge of interest in Irish history and literature which began about 1880, received impetus from several sources. Chief among non-literary forces was the Irish struggle to gain independence from England, which gave the movement an ideological basis. The increased interest in Irish myth and history stimulated historians, poets and playwrights to use their native land—past or present—as their subject. The movement had deep, immediate effects on some Irish poets, as shown by the marked change in subject matter and mood of W. B. Yeats' poetry after his involvement late in the century. Lesser poets like "AE" (George Russell) and "Fiona Macleod" (William Sharp) also contributed to the movement. The chief genre of the Celtic Renaissance, however, was drama. By 1920, playwrights and managers had established the Abbey Theatre, an Irish national drama group, which produced verse plays of high achievement, largely the work of Yeats, and a variety of more realistic dramas, notably those by Lady Gregory, Edward Martyn and J. M. Synge.

CELTIC REVIVAL. *see* CELTIC RENAISSANCE.

CELTIC TWILIGHT

Yeats' book *The Celtic Twilight,* which illustrated the mysticism of the Irish people through stories about their beliefs in spirits and legends, gave the name to the atmosphere and subject matter typical of many of the poems and tales of the Celtic Renaissance writers – a dreamy, shadowy vision of an unreal world compounded from Irish myth, legend and history. The term is sometimes applied generically (and sarcastically) to the whole Celtic Renaissance.

CHESTERTON, GILBERT KEITH (1874-1936)

Prose:

The Characteristics of Robert Louis Stevenson, 1902.
Robert Browning, 1903.
Charles Dickens, 1906.
All Things Considered, 1908.
Tremendous Trifles, 1909.
George Bernard Shaw, 1910.
A Miscellany of Men, 1912.
The New Jerusalem, 1920.
As I Was Saying, 1936.
And other titles.

Fiction:

The Napoleon of Notting Hill, 1904.
The Wisdom of Father Brown, 1914.
The Man Who Knew Too Much, 1922.
And other titles.

Poems:

The Wild Knight, 1900.

Gilbert Keith Chesterton

The Ballad of the White Horse, 1911.
Poems, 1915.
The Collected Poems . . ., 1927.
And other titles.

Autobiography:

Autobiography, 1936.

Bibliographical:

Sprug, Joseph W. (ed.). *An Index to G. K. Chesterton*, 1966. [Indexed by key words in Chesterton's writing.]
Sullivan, John. *G. K. Chesterton: A Bibliography*, 1958.
— *Chesterton Continued: A Bibliographical Supplement*, 1968. [Includes "A selection of prose and verse by G. K. Chesterton . . . now first collected," pp. 85-113.]

Biographical and Critical:

Braybrooke, Patrick. *Gilbert Keith Chesterton*, 1922.
Bullett, Gerald W. *The Innocence of G. K. Chesterton*, 1923.
Evans, Maurice. *G. K. Chesterton*, 1939.
Furlong, William B. *GBS/GKS: Shaw and Chesterton: The Metaphysical Jesters*, 1970. [Bib. pp. 199-202.]
Hollis, Christopher. *The Mind of Chesterton*, 1970.
Jones, Ada E. *The Chestertons*, 1941.
Lea, Frank A. *The Wild Knight of Battersea: G. K. Chesterton*, 1945.
O'Connor, John. *Father Brown on Chesterton*, 1937.
Reckitt, Maurice B. *G. K. Chesterton*, 1950.
Ward, Maisie. *Gilbert Keith Chesterton*, 1944. [Bib. pp. 671-676.]
— *Return to Chesterton*, 1952.
West, Julius. *G. K. Chesterton: A Critical Study*, 1915. [Bib. pp. 185-191.]
Wills, Garry. *Chesterton: Man and Mask*, 1961. [Bib. pp. 213-215.]

Like Hilaire Belloc, Chesterton had many sides: literary critic, historian, moralist, poet, journalist, fictionist, religious thinker. His studies of Shaw and Dickens display keen insight and a broad sympathy for literature. Similar sympathies for mankind, the past and childhood distinguish his *Autobiography*.

CHILDERS, ERSKINE (1870-1922)

Fiction:

The Riddle of the Sands, 1903.

Bibliographical:

O'Hegarty, Patrick S. *A Bibliography of the Books of Erskine Childers*, 1948.

Biographical and Critical:

Basil, Arthur Frederic. *Erskine Childers, 1870-1922*, 1926.
Scott-James, R. A. "Erskine Childers," *Nineteenth Century and After*, XCIII (January, 1923), 114-121.

Slow in pace compared to modern spy stories, *Riddle of the Sands* was the first good English espionage novel. Depicting the danger of sailing a small ship among the Frisian Islands and the suspense inherent in Germany's plan to invade England, the novel anticipated the work of later high adventure writers like John Buchan.

CLERIHEW, E. *see* BENTLEY, EDMUND CLERIHEW.

COLERIDGE, MARY ELIZABETH [ANODOS] (1861-1907)

Poems:

Fancy's Following, 1896.

Mary Elizabeth Coleridge

Fancy's Guerdon, 1897.
Last Poems, 1905.
Poems. Ed. Henry Newbolt. 1908.
The Collected Poems of Mary Coleridge. Ed. Theresa Whistler. 1954. [Bib. pp. 7-20.]

Prose:

Gathered Leaves from the Prose of Mary E. Coleridge. Ed. Edith Sichel. 1910.

Biographical and Critical:

Bridges, Robert. "The Poems of Mary Coleridge," *Collected Essays, Papers, Etc. of Robert Bridges*, 1931. VI, 205-209.
Sichel, Edith. "Mary Coleridge," *Gathered Leaves...*, 1910. Pp. 1-44.

Coleridge's verse has the epigrammatic precision usually associated with Emily Dickinson. But in contrast to the New England poet, Coleridge lacked the ability to universalize the ordinary and seemed unable to show her real feelings and insights. Her poetic "I" was an abstract dreamer, inspired or troubled by love, beauty and nature.

COLUM, PADRAIC (1881-1972)

Plays:

Broken Soil, 1903. [Rewritten as *The Fiddler's House, 1907*.]
The Land, 1905.
Thomas Muskerry, 1910.
The Desert, 1910. [Later titled *Mogu the Wanderer*.]
And other titles.

Poems:

Wild Earth, 1907.

Dramatic Legends, 1922.
Creatures, 1927.
Poems, 1932.
And other titles.

Biographical and Critical:

Bowen, Zack. *Padraic Colum: A Biographical-Critical Introduction*, 1970. [Bib. pp. 155-157.]
Boyd, E. A. "Poets of the Younger Generation: 'Padraic Colum,'" *Ireland's Literary Renaissance*, 1922. Pp. 261-265.
Denson, Alan. "Padraic Colum: An Appreciation with a Check-list of His Publications," *Dublin Magazine*, VI (Spring-Summer, 1967), 50-67; 83-85.
Levy, William Turner. "Padraic Colum, Poet," *Literary Review*, I (Summer, 1958), 493-504.
Monahan, Michael. "Padraic Colum," *Catholic World*, CXXVII (July, 1928), 449-456.

Colum was, despite his youth, an important dramatist of the Irish theater movement. With *Broken Soil*, he created the Irish peasant play, and *The Land* was one of the Abbey Theatre's early successes. Both plays show his interest in such social problems as Ireland's losing struggle to hold her people. As poet, Colum seems an amalgam of Robert Burns and Robert Browning. With one hand he wrote ballad folk tales, rustic character studies and poems in praise of nature; with the other he mated drama and poetry to write Browningesque lyrics like "The Burial of Saint Brendan."

CONRAD, JOSEPH [JOZEF KONRAD KORZENIOWSKI] (1857-1924)

Fiction:

Almayer's Folly, 1895.
An Outcast of the Islands, 1896.
The Nigger of the "Narcissus," 1897.

Tales of Unrest, 1898.
Lord Jim, 1900.
The Inheritors [with Ford Madox Ford], 1901.
Typhoon, 1902.
Youth: A Narrative, and Two Other Stories [includes *Heart of Darkness*], 1902.
Romance [with Ford Madox Ford], 1903.
Nostromo, 1904.
The Secret Agent, 1907.
A Set of Six, 1908.
Under Western Eyes, 1911.
'Twixt Land and Sea, 1912.
Chance, 1913.
Victory, 1915.
The Shadow-line, 1917.
The Arrow of Gold, 1919.
The Rover, 1923.
Suspense, 1925.
And other titles.

Autobiography:

The Mirror of the Sea, 1906.
Some Reminiscences, 1912. [Rptd. as *A Personal Record,* 1916.]
Notes on Life and Letters, 1921.

Letters:

Conrad to a Friend: 150 Selected Letters from Joseph Conrad to Richard Curle. Ed. Richard Curle. 1928.
Letters From Joseph Conrad, 1895-1924. Ed. Edward Garnett. 1928.
Letters of Joseph Conrad to Marguerite Poradowska. Trans. and ed. John A. Gee and Paul J. Strum. 1940.
Letters to William Blackwood and David S. Meldrum. Ed. William Blackburn. 1958.
Conrad's Polish Background.... Ed. Zdzislaw Najder. 1964.
Joseph Conrad's Letters to R. B. Cunninghame Graham. Ed. C. T. Watts. 1969.

Joseph Conrad

Collected Works:

Works. "Uniform Edition." 22 vols., 1923-1928.
Collected Works. "Memorial Edition." 21 vols., 1925.
Works. "Collected Edition." 24 vols., 1946-1958.

Bibliographical:

Bojarski, Edmund A., and Henry T. Bojarski. "Three Hundred and Thirty-six Unpublished Papers on Joseph Conrad: A Bibliography of Masters Theses and Doctoral Dissertations, 1917-1963," *Bulletin of Bibliography*, XXVI (July-September, 1969), 61-66; 79-83.
Ehrsam, Theodore G. *A Bibliography of Joseph Conrad*, 1969. [The largest primary bib.]
Keating, George. *A Conrad Memorial Library*, 1929.
Lohf, K. A., and E. P. Sheehy. *Joseph Conrad at Mid-Century: Editions and Studies 1895-1955*, 1957.
Teets, Bruce E., and Helmut E. Gerber. *Joseph Conrad: An Annotated Bibliography of Writings About Him*, 1971. [The most thorough secondary bib.]
Wise, Thomas J. *A Bibliography of the Writings of Joseph Conrad, 1895-1920*, 1920.
— *A Conrad Library*, 1928.

Biographical and Critical:

Allen, Jerry. *The Thunder and the Sunshine*, 1958.
— *The Sea Years of Joseph Conrad*, 1965.
Andreach, Robert J. *The Slain and Resurrected God: Conrad, Ford, and the Christian Myth*, 1970.
Aubry, G. J. *Joseph Conrad: Life and Letters*, 1927.
— *The Sea Dreamer....* Trans. H. Sebba. 1957.
Baines, Jocelyn. *Joseph Conrad, a Critical Biography*, 1960. [The best bio.]
Boyle, Ted E. *Symbol and Meaning in the Fiction of Joseph Conrad*, 1965.
Busza, Andrzej. *Conrad's Polish Literary Background...*, 1967.
Conrad, Borys. *My Father: Joseph Conrad*, 1970.
Conrad, Jessie. *Joseph Conrad As I Knew Him*, 1926.
Crankshaw, Edward. *Joseph Conrad: Some Aspects of the*

Art of the Novel, 1936.

Curle, Richard. *The Last Twelve Years of Joseph Conrad*, 1928.

Fleishman, Avrom. *Conrad's Politics: Community and Anarchy in the Fiction of Joseph Conrad*, 1967.

Ford, Ford Madox. *Joseph Conrad, a Personal Remembrance*, 1924.

Gillon, Adam. *The Eternal Solitary: A Study of Joseph Conrad*, 1960.

Graver, Lawrence. *Conrad's Short Fiction*, 1969. [Bib. pp. 215-234.]

Guerard, A. J. *Conrad the Novelist*, 1958.

Gurko, Leo. *Joseph Conrad: Giant in Exile*, 1962.

Hay, Eloise Knapp. *The Political Novels of Joseph Conrad*, 1963.

Hewitt, Douglas. *Conrad: A Reassessment*, 1952.

Hodges, Robert A. *The Dual Heritage of Joseph Conrad*, 1967.

Jablowski, Roza. *Joseph Conrad: 1857-1924*, 1962.

Kirschner, Paul. *Conrad: The Psychologist as Artist*, 1968. [Bib. pp. 288-293.]

Megroz, Rodolphe. *Joseph Conrad's Mind and Method*, 1931.

Meyer, Bernard C. *Joseph Conrad: A Psychoanalytic Biography*, 1967.

Morf, Gustav. *The Polish Heritage of Joseph Conrad*, 1930.

Moser, Thomas. *Joseph Conrad: Achievement and Decline*, 1957.

Newhouse, Neville H. *Joseph Conrad*, 1967.

Palmer, John A. *Joseph Conrad's Fiction: A Study in Literary Growth*, 1968. [Bib. pp. 269-277.]

Rosenfield, Claire. *Paradise of Snakes: An Archetypal Analysis of Conrad's Political Novels*, 1967. [Bib. pp. 177-182.]

Said, Edward W. *Joseph Conrad and the Fiction of Autobiography*, 1966.

Sherry, Norman. *Conrad's Eastern World*, 1966.

Stewart, J. I. M. *Joseph Conrad*, 1968. [Bib. pp. 263-268.]

Yelton, Donald C. *Mimesis and Metaphor: An Inquiry into the Genesis and Scope of Conrad's Symbolic Imagery*, 1967. [Bib. pp. 323-329.]

In his novels and tales, Conrad experimented audaciously with form, abandoning hallowed restrictions of time and point of view to relate his stories of exotic lands and characters in unexpected ways. A Pole who fled to the sea and eventually became an English captain, Conrad found in his early life a rich store of material for his creative imagination. His keen political insight (as seen in *Nostromo*), the rich ambiguity of his symbolism (*Heart of Darkness*) and his grasp of psychology ("The Secret Sharer," *Lord Jim*) mark him as a major novelist and a mirror of his age. In several of his major works, a key situation recurs: a sensitive, isolated man has a comfortable, safe existence disturbed by some unexpected happening, which either destroys (as it does Lord Jim) or completes the man (as in "The Secret Sharer"). Such a situation enabled Conrad to use his favorite character type, the outcast, to probe moral failure and spiritual paralysis. Conrad's work may be studied at many levels, although the more interesting ambiguities of character and symbolism are lacking in his work after 1912. No man of the period made a more significant contribution to the art of the novel than Conrad.

CORELLI, MARIE. *see* MACKAY, MARY.

CORVO, BARON. *see* ROLFE, FREDERICK....

CRACKANTHORPE, HUBERT (1870-1896)

Fiction:

Wreckage, 1893.
Sentimental Studies, and a Set of Village Tales, 1895.
Vignettes, 1896.
Last Studies, 1897.

Hubert Crackanthorpe

Bibliographical:

Danielson, Henry. "Hubert Crackanthorpe (1870-1896)," *Bibliographies of Modern Authors,* 1921. Pp. 19-23.
Harris, Wendell V. "A Bibliography of Writings about Hubert Crackanthorpe," *English Literature in Transition,* VI: 2 (1963), 85-91.

Biographical and Critical:

Frierson, William C. "Hubert Crackanthorpe: Analyst of the Affections," *Sewanee Review,* XXXVI (October, 1928), 462-474.
Harris, Frank. "Lionel Johnson and Hubert Crackanthorpe," *Contemporary Portraits.* 2nd. ser., 1919. Pp. 179-191.
Harris, Wendell V. "Hubert Crackanthorpe as Realist," *English Literature in Transition,* VI: 2 (1963), 76-84.
James, Henry. "Hubert Crackanthorpe," *Last Studies,* 1897. Pp. xi-xxiii.
Peden, William. "Hubert Crackanthorpe: Forgotten Pioneer," *Studies in Short Fiction,* VII (Fall, 1970), 539-548.

Crackanthorpe was a leader among the young writers of the 1890's who brought the English naturalistic short story to a remarkable degree of perfection. He sought to show life (occasionally French life, as in *Village Tales*) as it was, without moral bias and without denying the ugly realities of incompatibility, poverty and psychic distress. He wrote twenty-two stories whose social-geographical range included humble village life and London society (e.g. "The Turn of the Wheel"). Their subject was the play of bitter human passions.

CRAIGIE, PEARL MARY TERESA [JOHN OLIVER HOBBES] (1867-1906)

Fiction:

Some Emotions and a Moral, 1891.
A Bundle of Life, 1894.

Pearl Mary Teresa Cragie

The Herb-Moon: A Fantasia, 1896.
The School for Saints, 1897.
Robert Orange, 1900.
The Serious Wooing, 1901.
The Vineyard, 1903.
And other titles.

Autobiography and Letters:

The Artist's Life, 1904.
Letters from a Silent Study, 1904.
The Life of John Oliver Hobbes Told in Her Correspondence with Numerous Friends, 1911.

Biographical and Critical:

Clarke, I. C. "John Oliver Hobbes," *Six Portraits,* 1935. Pp. 231-246.
Howells, William Dean. "The Fiction of John Oliver Hobbes," *North American Review,* CLXXXIII (December 21, 1906), 1251-1261.

For many readers, Craigie's witty, urbane, slightly cynical society novels have lost their appeal. Readers of her day had their reservations too, as an anonymous rhyme shows:

John Oliver Hobbes, with your spasms and throbs,
How does your novel grow?
With cynical sneers at young love and his tears
And epigrams all in a row.

But in *School for Saints* and *Robert Orange* (virtually halves of one work), she cast cynicism aside to produce a serious, significant study of the painful transition from passionate love and agonized self-scrutiny to certainty and peace. Some readers, like W. D. Howells, have found much to admire in her "shapely, clever and brilliant books."

CROCKETT, SAMUEL RUTHERFORD (1860-1914)

Fiction:

The Stickit Minister, and Some Common Men, 1893.
The Lilac Sunbonnet, 1894.
The Raiders, 1894.
The Men of the Moss-Hags, 1895.
Lochinvar, 1897.
Kit Kennedy, 1899.
And other titles.

Biographical and Critical:

Harper, Malcolm McLachlan. *Crockett and Grey Galloway: The Novelist and His Works,* 1907.
Murray, David Christie. "Mr. S. R. Crockett – Ian Maclaren," *My Contemporaries in Fiction,* 1897. Pp. 99-111.

Although some of his early fiction (*The Lilac Sunbonnet*) was typical of the Kailyard School, Crockett tried a far wider variety than John Watson or even J. M. Barrie. He was a born storyteller, and some of his romantic adventure stories (*Lochinvar*) are still worth reading for their excitement and narrative finesse.

CUNNINGHAME-GRAHAM, R. B. *see* GRAHAM, ROBERT BONTINE CUNNINGHAME.

CUSTANCE, OLIVE. *see* DOUGLAS, MRS. ALFRED.

DARMESTETER, MARY JAMES. *see* DUCLAUX, MARY.

DAVIDSON, JOHN (1857-1909)

Poems:

Diabolus Amans, 1885.
In a Music Hall, 1891.
Fleet Street Eclogues. 2 ser., 1893, 1896.
Ballads and Songs, 1894.
New Ballads, 1897.
The Testament of a Man Forbid, 1901.
The Testament of John Davidson, 1908.
Fleet Street, 1909.
Poems and Ballads. Ed. R. D. Macleod. 1959.
And other titles.

Plays:

Smith, 1888.
Scaramouch in Naxos, 1889.
Self's the Man, 1901.
And other titles.

Fiction:

The North Wall, 1885.
The Great Men and a Practical Novelist, 1891.
A Full and True Account of the Wonderful Mission of Earl Lavender, 1895.
Miss Armstrong's, and Other Circumstances, 1896.
And other titles.

Bibliographical:

Lester, John A. *John Davidson: A Grub Street Bibliography,* 1958.
Stonehill, A., and H. W. Stonehill. "John Davidson," *Bibliographies of Modern Authors.* 2nd ser., 1925. Pp. 3-41.

Biographical and Critical:

Fineman, H. *John Davidson,* 1916.
Lock, D. R. "John Davidson and the Poetry of the 'Nineties,'"

London Quarterly and Holborn Review, CLXI (July, 1936), 338-352.

Macleod, Robert Duncan. *John Davidson: A Study in Personality,* 1957.

Thouless, Priscilla. "John Davidson" and "Davidson's Later Dramas," *Modern Poetic Drama,* 1934. Pp. 76-94; 95-114.

Townsend, J. Benjamin. *John Davidson: Poet of Armageddon,* 1961.

Davidson's turbulent creative life falls into three parts: 1877-1889, he wrote plays (the witty comedy *Scaramouch* is best); 1889-1899, he turned to composing prose and ballads, producing his best work in *Ballads and Songs,* and *New Ballads;* 1899-1909, his lyric impulse yielded to mystical didacticism. Earlier, Davidson's tendency to moralize was tempered by his good humor, but nothing restrained him from impassioned preaching in the *Testaments.* These confused, furious, often powerful outbursts document Davidson's frustration at his lack of worldly achievement and the shock he received from reading Nietzsche.

DAVIES, WILLIAM HENRY (1871-1940)

Poems:

The Soul's Destroyer, 1905.
New Poems, 1907.
Farewell to Poesy, 1910.
Forty New Poems, 1918.
A Poet's Pilgrimage, 1918.
The Song of Love, 1926.
Jewels of Song, 1930.
The Complete Poems. Ed. Osbert Sitwell. 1963.
And other titles.

Fiction:

A Weak Woman, 1911.
The Adventures of Johnny Walker, Tramp, 1926.

William Henry Davies

Autobiography:

The Autobiography of a Super-Tramp, 1908.
The True Traveller, 1912.
Nature, 1914.
Later Days, 1925.

Biographical and Critical:

Kernahan, Coulson. "W. H. Davies, a Nature Poet," *Five More Famous Living Poets,* 1928. Pp. 17-48.
Moult, Thomas. *W. H. Davies,* 1934. [Bib. pp. 147-150.]
Stonesifer, Richard J. *W. H. Davies: A Critical Biography,* 1963. [Bib. pp. 233-234.]

Davies' minor but genuine talent was nurtured by living a tramp's life in England and America. After returning to England, he published *The Soul's Destroyer,* and G. B. Shaw called his earnest primitivism the work of "a genuine innocent." Davies was a kind of Sunday-painter poet whose verses often reflect the people and happenings he saw as a tramp.

DECADENCE

One of a complex of French literary terms current in the 1880's and 90's including *fin de siècle, aestheticisme* and *l'art pour l'art,* decadence suggested a departure from certain moral and ethical standards of bourgeois society, a quest for new sensations and experiences and a preference for artifice over nature. In England, Aubrey Beardsley's drawings, Oscar Wilde's *Salomé*, Ernest Dowson's poems and George Moore's *Confessions of a Young Man* are typical manifestations of decadence.

DE MORGAN, WILLIAM FREND (1839-1917)

Fiction:

Joseph Vance, 1906.
Alice-for-Short, 1907.
Somehow Good, 1908.
It Never Can Happen Again, 1909.
An Affair of Dishonour, 1910.
A Likely Story, 1911.
When Ghost Meets Ghost, 1914.
And other titles.

Biographical and Critical:

Cartwright, Julia. "William De Morgan: A Reminiscence," *Littel's Living Age,* CCXCIII (May 12, 1917), 345-353.
Follett, Helen Thomas. "William De Morgan," *Some Modern Novelists,* 1918. Pp. 151-174.
Hale, Will T. "William De Morgan and the Greater Early Victorians," *Indiana University Studies,* VIII (September, 1921), 3-28.
Phelps, William Lyon. "William De Morgan," *Essays on Modern Novelists,* 1910. Pp. 1-32.
Seymour, Flora Warren. *William De Morgan, A Post-Victorian Realist,* 1920.
Stirling, A. M. D. W. *William De Morgan and His Wife,* 1922.

De Morgan's novels came late in a life devoted primarily to ceramics and other fine arts. In only eight years he wrote several kinds of fiction: ghost stories (*Alice-for-Short* and *A Likely Story*), historical romances (*An Affair of Dishonour*) and realistic novels of a Victorian flavor (*It Never Can Happen Again* and *When Ghost Meets Ghost*). The usual comparison of De Morgan's realistic novels to those of Charles Dickens is not to De Morgan's advantage and makes De Morgan's unassuming tales seem slighter than they are. His fondness for humor, love of detail and genial optimism make his fiction refreshingly old-fashioned. The picaresque *Joseph Vance,* a humorous story of a gutter boy who marries the heroine, is his best work.

DIXON, RICHARD WATSON (1833-1900)

Poems:

Christ's Company, 1861.
Odes and Eclogues, 1884.
Lyrical Poems, 1887.
Songs and Odes. Ed. Robert Bridges. 1896.
The Last Poems of Richard Watson Dixon. Ed. Robert Bridges. 1905.
And other titles.

Prose:

The Life of J. Dixon, D. D., 1874.
History of the Church of England from the Abolition of the Roman Jurisdiction. 6 vols., 1877-1900.

Letters:

The Correspondence of Gerard Manley Hopkins and Richard Watson Dixon. Ed. C. C. Abbott. 1935.

Biographical and Critical:

Coleridge, Mary. "The Last Hermit of Warkworth," *Non Sequitur*, 1900. Pp. 25-41.
Bridges, Robert. "Memoir of Richard Watson Dixon," *Three Friends*, 1932. Pp. 111-147.
Nowell-Smith, Simon. "Some Uncollected Authors XXIX: Richard Watson Dixon, 1833-1900," *Book Collector*, X (Autumn, 1961), 322-328.
Sambrook, James. *A Poet Hidden: The Life of Richard Watson Dixon, 1833-1900*, 1962. [Bib. pp. 124-130.]
— "D. G. Rossetti and R. W. Dixon," *Études Anglaises*, XIV (October-December, 1961), 331-338.

Although Dixon's poetry, like that of Hopkins, was championed by Robert Bridges, it has failed to win lasting admiration. Dixon followed the Pre-Raphaelites in their melancholy tone and religious subject matter. Although his verse after 1883 is superior to his earlier work, he never mastered poetic technique, as his careless, casual approach to metrics shows. And as he found no fresh understanding for age-old problems, his verse is filled with clichés.

DOBSON, HENRY AUSTIN (1840-1921)

Poems:

Vignettes in Rhyme and Vers de Société, 1873.
Proverbs in Porcelain, 1877.
Old-World Idylls, 1883.
At the Sign of the Lyre, 1885.
The Ballad of Beau Brocade and other Poems of the XVIIIth Century, 1892.
The Story of Rosina, 1895.
The Complete Poetical Works . . . . Ed. Alban Dobson. 1923.
And other titles.

Prose:

Hogarth, 1879.
Henry Fielding, 1883.
Richard Steele, 1885.
Life of Oliver Goldsmith, 1888.
Eighteenth Century Vignettes. 3 ser., 1892, 1894, 1896.
At Prior Park, 1912.
Eighteenth Century Studies, 1914.
Later Essays 1917-1920, 1921.
And other titles.

Bibliographical:

Dobson, A. T. A. *A Bibliography of . . . Austin Dobson*, 1925.
— *Catalogue of the Collection of the Works of Austin Dobson (1840-1921)*, 1960.

Henry Austin Dobson

Biographical and Critical:

Dobson, A. T. A. *An Austin Dobson Letter Book,* 1935.
— , et al. *Austin Dobson: Some Notes,* 1928.
Ellis, S. M. "Austin Dobson," *Fortnightly Review,* CX (October, 1921), 640-650. [Rptd. in *Mainly Victorian,* 1925.]
Gosse, Edmund. "Austin Dobson," *Quarterly Review,* CCXXXVII (January, 1922), 53-67.
Lipscomb, Herbert C. "Horace and the Poetry of Austin Dobson," *American Journal of Philology,* L: 197 (1929), 1-20.
Noyes, A. "The Poems of Austin Dobson," *Bookman* (London), LXVI (April, 1924), 13-18.
Robinson, James Keith. "Austin Dobson and the Rondeliers," *Modern Language Quarterly,* XIV (March, 1953), 31-42.

An interest in French literary types and themes common to many English poets of the 1880's and 1890's manifested itself in Dobson's fascination with *vers de société* rather than the usual decadent emphasis on *fleurs du mal.* Dobson wrote poetry about eighteenth-century people ("A Dialogue to the Memory of Mr. Alexander Pope") and objects (ballade on the Marquise de Pompadour's fan) in typically French forms like the ballade and triolet. But the vigor and sentiment of the earlier century were quite beyond the capabilities of his playful, witty verse. At best, he produced only echoes of the past.

DOUGHTY, CHARLES MONTAGU (1843-1926)

Prose:

On the Jöstedal-Brae Glaciers in Norway, 1866.
Travels in Arabia Deserta, 1888.

Poems:

Under Arms, 1900.
The Dawn in Britain, 1906.

The Titans, 1916.
Mansoul, or The Riddle of the World, 1920.

Biographical and Critical:

Armstrong, Martin. "The Works of Charles Doughty," *Fortnightly Review,* CXIX (January, 1926), 21-33.
Bishop, Jonathan. "The Heroic Ideal in Doughty's *Arabia Deserta,*" *Modern Language Quarterly,* XXI (March, 1960), 59-68.
Fairley, Barker. *Charles M. Doughty: A Critical Study,* 1927.
Hogarth, David George. *The Life of Charles M. Doughty,* 1928.
Holloway, John. "Poetry and Plain Language: The Verse of C. M. Doughty," *Essays in Criticism,* IV (January, 1954), 58-70.
Treneer, Anne. *Charles M. Doughty: A Study of His Prose and Verse,* 1935.

Doughty is best remembered for his explorations of *terra incognita,* and his account of them, *Travels in Arabia Deserta.* His sonorous Elizabethan style suited his subject perfectly, even if the language is obscure in spots. Doughty thought *The Dawn,* a 30,000 line blank-verse epic about the coming of civilization to Britain, his masterpiece. It has moments of grandeur, but seems almost a versified travel book, entirely lacking central dramatic action.

DOUGLAS, ALFRED BRUCE (1870-1945)

Poems:

Poems, 1896.
The City of the Soul, 1899.
Sonnets, 1909.
Collected Poems, 1919.
In Excelsis, 1924.
Complete Poems, 1928.
And other titles.

Alfred Bruce Douglas

Autobiography:

Oscar Wilde and Myself [with Thomas Crosland], 1914.
[A virulent attack.]
The Autobiography of Lord Alfred Douglas, 1929.
Without Apology, 1938.
Oscar Wilde: A Summing-up, 1940. [Repudiates much of *Myself.*]

Biographical and Critical:

Brown, W. Sorley. *Lord Alfred Douglas: The Man and the Poet*, 1918.
Braybrooke, Patrick. *Lord Alfred Douglas: His Life and Work*, 1931.
Freeman, William. *Lord Alfred Douglas: The Spoilt Child of Genius*, 1948.
Stopes, Marie. *Lord Alfred Douglas*, 1949.
Croft-Cooke, Rupert. *Bosie: The Story of Lord Alfred Douglas, His Friends and Enemies*, 1963.

Douglas gained more notoriety as intimate friend of Oscar Wilde, virtually the only one who stood beside the fallen idol during his trial, than he did as a poet. His poetic manner had little to distinguish it from that of the usual aesthete-decadent pose. His autobiographical volumes commenting on the 1890's are important, if biased, historical documents.

DOUGLAS, MRS. ALFRED [OLIVE CUSTANCE; OLIVE CUSTANCE DOUGLAS] (1874-1944)

Poems:

Opals, 1897.
Rainbows, 1902.
The Blue Bird, 1905.
The Inn of Dreams, 1911.

Mrs. Alfred Douglas

Bibliographical:

Hawkey, Nancy J. "Olive Custance Douglas: An Annotated Bibliography of Writings About Her," *English Literature in Transition,* XV: 1 (1971), 52-56.

Biographical and Critical:

Douglas, Alfred Bruce. *The Autobiography of Lord Alfred Douglas,* 1929. Pp. 193-209, passim.

Douglas, one of *The Yellow Book* contributors, cultivated a gift for fluid, tuneful verse. Perhaps the strain of marriage to Lord Douglas dried up what had been only a fitful rill of inspiration.

DOUGLAS, EVELYN. *see* BARLAS, JOHN.

DOUGLAS, GEORGE. *see* BROWN, GEORGE DOUGLAS.

DOUGLAS, OLIVE CUSTANCE. *see* DOUGLAS, MRS. ALFRED.

DOWSON, ERNEST CHRISTOPHER (1867-1900)

Poems:

Verses, 1896.
Decorations in Verse and Prose, 1899.
The Poems of Ernest Dowson, 1905.
The Poetical Works of Ernest Christopher Dowson. Ed. Desmond Flower. 1934.
The Poems of Ernest Dowson. Ed. Mark Longaker. 1963.
And other titles.

Ernest Christopher Dowson

Plays:

The Pierrot of the Minute, 1897.

Fiction:

A Comedy of Masks [with Arthur Moore], 1893.
Dilemmas: Stories and Studies in Sentiment, 1895.
Adrian Rome [with Arthur Moore], 1899.
The Stories of Ernest Dowson. Ed. Mark Longaker. 1949.

Letters:

The Letters of Ernest Dowson. Ed. Desmond Flower and Henry Maas. 1967. [Bib. pp. 444-445.]

Bibliographical:

Ramsey, Jonathan. "Ernest Dowson: An Annotated Bibliography of Writings About Him," *English Literature in Transition,* XIV: 1 (1971), 17-42.
Stonehill, C. A., and H. W. Stonehill. *Bibliographies of Modern Authors.* 2nd ser., 1925. Pp. 41-63.

Biographical and Critical:

Gawsworth, John. *The Dowson Legend,* 1939.
Goldfarb, Russell M. *Ernest Dowson: A Study of the Romantic Elements in his Poetry and Prose,* 1961.
— "The Dowson Legend Today," *Studies in English Literature,* IV (Autumn, 1964), 653-662.
Longaker, John Mark. *Ernest Dowson,* 1944. [Bib. pp. 273-277.]
Swann, Thomas B. *Ernest Dowson,* 1964. [Bib. pp. 113-117.]

Dowson, despite the brevity and irregularity of his life, produced a considerable quantity of memorable work. His poetry was influenced by the French decadents Verlaine and Rimbaud, and he achieved some of the finest decadent lyrics. "Non sum qualis eram bonae sub regno Cynarae" with its refrain "I have been faithful to thee, Cynara!

in my fashion'' is the aesthetic-decadent poem *par excellence.* ''Nuns of the Perpetual Adoration'' is a more austere, haunting treatment of Dowson's central poetic concern: how ''the roses of the world . . . . fade, and be trod under by the hurrying feet.'' Only in renunciation of a world wild with desire and pursuit, the theme of ''Benedictio Domini,'' could Dowson see any cause for hope. Otherwise life offered only misery for ''Life-Sick hearts.''

DOYLE, ARTHUR CONAN (1859-1930)

Fiction:

A Study in Scarlet, 1887.
The Sign of Four, 1890.
The White Company, 1891.
The Adventures of Sherlock Holmes, 1892.
The Memoirs of Sherlock Holmes, 1894.
The Exploits of Brigadier Gerard, 1896.
The Hound of the Baskervilles, 1902.
The Return of Sherlock Holmes, 1905.
The Lost World, 1912.
The Valley of Fear, 1915.
His Last Bow, 1917.
The Case-Book of Sherlock Holmes, 1927.
The Annotated Sherlock Holmes. Ed. William S. Baring-Gould. 2 vols., 1968.
And other titles.

Collected Works:

The Principal Works of Fiction of Conan Doyle. 20 vols., 1913.
The Poems of Arthur Conan Doyle, 1922.

Autobiography:

Memoires and Adventures: The Autobiography of Sir Arthur Conan Doyle, 1924.

Arthur Conan Doyle

Bibliographical:

Christ, Jay Finley. *An Irregular Guide to Sherlock Holmes of Baker Street,* 1947.
Locke, H. *A Bibliographical Catalogue of the Writings of Sir Arthur Conan Doyle, 1879-1928,* 1928. [Incomplete.]
Park, Orlando. *Sherlock Holmes, Esq. and John H. Watson, M. D.: An Encyclopedia of Their Affairs,* 1962. [Concordance to Holmes stories; not absolutely complete.]
Smith, Edgar W. *Baker Street Inventory,* 1945.
Waal, Ronald Burt de. "A Bibliography of Sherlockian Bibliographies and Periodicals," *Papers of the Bibliographical Society of America,* LXIV (Third Quarter, 1970), 339-354.

Biographical and Critical:

Baring-Gould, William S. *Sherlock Holmes of Baker Street,* 1962. [Annotated bib. of works about Holmes, pp. 328-336.]
Bell, H. W. *Sherlock Holmes and Dr. Watson,* 1932.
Brend, Gavin. *My Dear Holmes: A Study in Sherlock,* 1951.
Carr, John Dickson. *The Life of Sir Arthur Conan Doyle,* 1948. [Standard life of Doyle; list of "Biographical Archives," pp. 285-295.]
Doyle, Adrian Conan. *The True Conan Doyle,* 1945.
Hall, Trevor H. *Sherlock Holmes: Ten Literary Studies,* 1969.
Hardwick, Michael, and Mollie Hardwick. *The Sherlock Holmes Companion,* 1962.
Holroyd, James Edward. *Baker Street Byways,* 1959.
Klinefelter, Walter. *Sherlock Holmes in Portrait and Profile,* 1963.
Nordon, Pierre. *Sir Arthur Conan Doyle,* 1965.
Pearson, Hesketh. *Conan Doyle: His Life and Art,* 1943.
Smith, Edgar W. (ed.). *Profile by Gaslight: An Irregular Reader About the Private Life of Sherlock Holmes,* 1944.
Starrett, Vincent. *The Private Life of Sherlock Holmes,* 1933.

Doyle's immortal creation, Sherlock Holmes, is an eccentric sleuth who relies heavily on intellection. No fictional character has received so much attention, some of it extremely erudite, much of it facetious, perhaps because no other character more vividly symbolizes man's analytic mind unravelling mysteries and enigmas. By using Holmes' faithful but rather obtuse friend Dr. Watson as a foil and narrator, Doyle set the pattern for countless detective teams which followed in Holmes and Watson's footsteps. Doyle also wrote historical fiction, like *The White Company* in which he tried to epitomize fourteenth-century knighthood, and Napoleonic tales about a light-hearted soldier named Brigadier Gerard. He contributed to the development of science fiction with his stories about Professor Challenger.

DRINKWATER, JOHN (1882-1937)

Poems:

Lyrical and Other Poems, 1908.
Poems of Love and Earth, 1912.
Cromwell, and Other Poems, 1913.
Swords and Ploughshares, 1915.
Poems, 1908-1914, 1917.
Collected Poems, 1923.
New Poems, 1925.
And other titles.

Plays:

The Storm, 1915.
The God of Quiet, 1916.
Abraham Lincoln, 1918.
Oliver Cromwell, 1923.
Collected Plays, 1925.
And other titles.

Prose:

The Pilgrim of Eternity: Byron—A Conflict, 1925.
Victorian Poetry, 1923.

English Poetry: An Unfinished History, 1938.

Autobiography:

Inheritance, 1931.
Discovery, 1932.

Biographical and Critical:

Adcock, Arthur St. John. "John Drinkwater," *Gods of Modern Grub Street,* 1923. Pp. 93-100.
Squire, John Collings. "A Better Play Than Usual," *Books in General: Third Series,* 1921. Pp. 199-205.
Sturgeon, Mary C. "John Drinkwater," *Studies of Contemporary Poets,* 1919. Pp. 327-346.

Drinkwater's early poetry was abstract, cold and rhetorical, but he experienced a conversion after 1912 (described in "The Fires of God") which led him to attempt a different type of poetic expression. The results, poems like "Cromwell" and plays like *Abraham Lincoln,* show Drinkwater's admiration for heroic leaders. Much of his work is colored by humanitarianism blended with Puritanism.

DUCLAUX, MARY [MARY JAMES DARMESTETER, AGNES MARY FRANCES ROBINSON] (1856-1944)

Poems:

A Handful of Honeysuckle, 1878.
The New Arcadia, 1884.
An Italian Garden, 1886.
Retrospect, 1893.
Collected Poems, Lyrical and Narrative, 1902.
L'Oeuvre Poétique de Mary Robinson 1857-1944. Ed. Sylvaine Marandon. 1967.
And other titles.

Mary Duclaux

Fiction:

Arden, 1883.
Marguerites du Temps Passé, 1892. [English ed. titled *A Medieval Garland,* 1898.]

Prose:

The Life of Emily Brontë, 1883.
The End of the Middle Ages, 1889.
La Vie de Ernest Renan, 1898.
La Vie de Émile Duclaux, 1906.
And other titles.

Letters:

Mary Duclaux et Maurice Barrès: Lettres Échangées. Précédé de Les Trois Mary by Daniel Halevy, 1959.

Bibliographical:

Holmes, Ruth Van Zuyle. "Mary Duclaux (1856-1944): Primary and Secondary Checklists," *English Literature in Transition,* X: 1 (1967), 27-46.

Biographical and Critical:

Gunn, Peter. *Vernon Lee, Violet Paget, 1856-1935,* 1964. [Details relationship between Duclaux and Violet Paget, 1880-1887.]
Lynch, Hannah. "A. Mary F. Robinson," *Fortnightly Review,* LXXVII (February 1, 1902), 260-276.

Duclaux has greater interest as a member of two important literary groups (that of London in the 1880's, including George Moore and John Addington Symonds, and that of Paris after 1900) than as a creative writer. Although her only novel was a disaster, her lyric poems have a slight feminine charm derived from *fin de siècle* romantic melancholy. After her marriage to the French orientalist James Darmesteter in 1888, Duclaux moved increasingly in French literary circles.

DU MAURIER, GEORGE LOUIS PALMELLA BUSSON (1834-1896)

Fiction:

Peter Ibbetson, 1892.
Trilby, 1894.
The Martian, 1897.

Prose and Drawing:

English Society at Home, 1880.
Society Pictures, 1891.
English Society, 1897.
Social Pictorial Satire, 1898.
A Legend of Camelot, 1898.

Letters:

The Young George du Maurier. Ed. Daphne du Maurier. 1951. [A selection of letters 1860-1867; bio. appendix by Derek Pepys Whiteley and drawings by du Maurier.]

Biographical and Critical:

Armstrong, T. *Reminiscences of du Maurier*, 1912.
Du Maurier, Daphne. *The du Mauriers*, 1937.
Gilder, J. L., and J. B. Gilder. *Trilbyana: The Rise and Progress of a Popular Novel*, 1895.
Millar, C. C. H. *George du Maurier and Others*, 1937.
Moscheles, Felix. *In Bohemia with du Maurier*, 1896.
Ormond, Leonée. *George Du Maurier*, 1969. [Bib. pp. 499-501.]
Stevenson, Lionel. ''George du Maurier and the Romantic Novel,'' *Essays by Divers Hands*, XXX (1960), 36-54.
Whiteley, Derek P. *George du Maurier: His Life and Work*, 1948.
Wood, T. Martin. *George du Maurier, the Satirist of the Victorians*, 1913.

Du Maurier was more renowned as an artist than as a writer of fiction, although *Trilby* was a best seller. An intelligent, cultivated student of life in France and England, he devoted most of his life to producing satiric drawings and illustrations for *Punch* and *Once a Week*. *Peter Ibbetson* is an interesting blend of romance (supernatural elements) and realism (Du Maurier's memories of his childhood in the Paris suburb Passay). In *Trilby*, candid memories of Paris dominate the supernatural element.

DUNSANY, LORD. *see* PLUNKETT, EDWARD J. M. D., LORD DUNSANY.

EAGLE, SOLOMON. *see* SQUIRE, JOHN COLLINGS.

EASTAWAY, EDWARD. *see* THOMAS, EDWARD.

ELLIS, HENRY HAVELOCK (1859-1939)

Prose:

Man and Woman, 1894.
Sexual Inversion, 1897.
Affirmations, 1898.
The Evolution of Modesty, 1899.
The Soul of Spain, 1908.
Studies in the Psychology of Sex. 6 vols., 1896-1910.
Impressions and Comments. 3 ser., 1914, 1921, 1924.
Kanga Creek: An Australian Idyll, 1922.
Little Essays of Love and Virtue, 1922.
The Dance of Life, 1923.
From Marlowe to Shaw: The Studies, 1876-1936, in English Literature of Havelock Ellis. Ed. John Gawsworth. 1950.
And other titles.

Henry Havelock Ellis

Autobiography:

My Life: Autobiography of Havelock Ellis, 1939.

Bibliographical:

Burne, Glenn S. "Havelock Ellis: An Annotated Selected Bibliography of Primary and Secondary Works," *English Literature in Transition,* IX: 2 (1966), 55-107.

Biographical and Critical:

Calder-Marshall, Arthur. *The Sage of Sex: A Life of Havelock Ellis,* 1959. [Bib. pp. 283-286.]
Collis, John Stewart. *An Artist of Life: A Study of the Life and Work of Havelock Ellis,* 1959.
Freeman-Ishill, Rose. *Havelock Ellis, 1859-1959, Centennial,* 1959.
Goldberg, Isaac. *Havelock Ellis: A Biographical and Critical Survey,* 1926.
Peterson, Houston. *Havelock Ellis: Philosopher of Love,* 1928. [Bib. pp. 394-413.]

With his pioneer studies of sexual psychology, Ellis helped dispel nineteenth-century ignorance, prudery and guilt associated with love and marriage. He interpreted sex not only for doctors (as in *Studies in the Psychology of Sex*) but also for average men (as in *Little Essays*). Too often overshadowed by his work on sexual matters are his incisive essays on literary art.

ERVINE, ST. JOHN GREER (1883-1971)

Plays:

Mixed Marriage, 1911.
The Magnanimous Lover, 1912.
Jane Clegg, 1913.
The Orangeman, 1913.
John Ferguson, 1915.

St. John Greer Ervine

The Wonderful Visit [with H. G. Wells], *1921.*
The Ship, 1922.
The Lady of Belmont, 1923.
And other titles.

Fiction:

Mrs. Martin's Man, 1914.
Alice and a Family, 1915.
Changing Winds, 1917.
The Foolish Lovers, 1920.
The Wayward Man, 1927.
And other titles.

Prose:

Some Impressions of My Elders, 1922.
Parnell, 1925.
How to Write a Play, 1928.
The Theatre in My Time, 1933.
Oscar Wilde: A Present Time Appraisal, 1951.
Bernard Shaw: His Life, Work and Friends, 1956.
And other titles.

Biographical and Critical:

Swinnerton, Frank. "The Critical Theatre," *The Georgian Scene,* 1934. Pp. 211-229.
Woodbridge, Homer E. "Realism and St. John Ervine," *Sewanee Review,* XXXIII (April, 1925), 199-209.

Ervine ranged over the literary scenes of Ireland, England and the U.S., working as playwright, drama critic and novelist. He began as one of the Abbey Theatre writers and was appointed manager of the Theatre in 1915. His work is often grimly realistic. *John Ferguson,* his best play, tells of a mortgage that leads to rape and murder. Ervine is not well known as a novelist, but *Mrs. Martin's Man* and *The Wayward Man* are honest studies of protracted suffering.

ESTHETICISM. *see* AESTHETICISM.

FALKNER, JOHN MEADE (1858-1932)

Fiction:

The Lost Stradivarius, 1895.
Moonfleet, 1898.
The Nebuly Coat, 1903.

Biographical and Critical:

Haley, William. "John Meade Falkner," *Essays by Divers Hands,* XXX (1960), 55-67.
Pollard, Graham. "Some Uncollected Authors XXV: John Meade Falkner, 1858-1932," *Book Collector,* IX (Autumn, 1960), 318-325. [Bib. pp. 323-325.]
Pritchett, V. S. "An Amateur," *The Living Novel,* 1946. Pp. 159-165.

Though Falkner compiled guides and histories of English counties and edited Latin texts of cathedral statutes, he is noted chiefly for his three minor novels. *Moonfleet,* concerning smugglers and hidden treasure, is often bracketed with *Treasure Island* and *Kidnapped* but lacks the subtle characterization of Stevenson. *The Lost Stradivarius,* an excellent supernatural novel, is more restrained in its horror than the ghost stories of Arthur Machen and M. R. James. And *The Nebuly Coat* is a quiet Victorian mystery set in an English cathedral town.

FIN DE SIÈCLE

In the 1890's, this phrase, which means simply "end of the century," was often equated with "decadence." Applied to literature, it suggested the presence of startling, perverse or unnatural subjects or actions; applied to artists, the meaning shifted to include *maladie de fin de siècle,* end of the century sickness, a world-weariness accompanied by a tortured mind and body.

FLECKER, JAMES ELROY (1884-1915)

Poetry:

The Bridge of Fire, 1907.
The Last Generation, 1908.
Thirty-Six Poems, 1910.
Forty-Two Poems, 1911.
The Golden Journey to Samarkand, 1913.
The Burial in England, 1915.
The Collected Poems of James Elroy Flecker. Ed. J. C. Squire, 1916.
And other titles.

Letters:

The Letters of J. E. Flecker to Frank Savery. Ed. Hellé Flecker. 1926.
Some Letters from Abroad . . . , 1930.

Biographical and Critical:

Goldring, Douglas. *James Elroy Flecker,* 1922.
Hodgeson, Geraldine. *The Life of James Elroy Flecker,* 1925.
MacDonald, Alec. "James Elroy Flecker," *Fortnightly Review,* CXV (February, 1924), 274-284.
Mercer, Thomas S. *James Elroy Flecker,* 1952.

Flecker sought to capture the color of the Orient in his verse, but the violence and vivacity of the East are utterly absent. Like the French Parnassian poets, who may have influenced him, Flecker was fascinated by the hypnotic effect that word-sounds and imagery could produce, as in "Yasmin," and he weaves words into beautiful, but meaningless fabrics.

FORD, FORD MADOX. *see* HUEFFER, JOSEPH . . . MADOX.

FORSTER, EDWARD MORGAN (1879-1970)

Fiction:

Where Angels Fear to Tread, 1905.
The Longest Journey, 1907.
A Room with a View, 1908.
Howards End, 1910.
The Celestial Omnibus, 1911.
A Passage to India, 1924.
The Eternal Moment, 1928.
Collected Short Stories, 1948.
Maurice, 1971. [Written 1913-1914.]

Prose:

Aspects of the Novel, 1927.
Goldsworthy Lowes Dickenson, 1934.
Abinger Harvest, 1936.
What I Believe, 1939.
And other titles.

Bibliographical:

Beebe, Maurice, and Joseph Brogunier. "Criticism of E. M. Forster: A Selected Checklist," *Modern Fiction Studies,* VII (Autumn, 1961), 284-292.
Gerber, H. E., et al. "E. M. Forster: An Annotated Checklist of Writings about Him," *English Literature in Transition,* II: 1 (1959), 4-27.
Kirkpatrick, B. J. *A Bibliography of E. M. Forster,* 1965.
McDowell, Frederick P. W. "E. M. Forster: An Annotated Secondary Bibliography," *English Literature in Transition,* XIII: 2 (1970), 93-173.

Biographical and Critical:

Beer, John Bernard. *The Achievement of E. M. Forster,* 1962.

Brander, Laurence. *E. M. Forster: A Critical Study,* 1968.
Crews, Frederick. *E. M. Forster: The Perils of Humanism,* 1962.
Godfrey, Denis. *E. M. Forster's Other Kingdom,* 1968.
Kelvin, Norman. *E. M. Forster,* 1967.
Macaulay, Rose. *The Writings of E. M. Forster,* 1938. [Bib. pp. 301-302.]
McConkey, James. *The Novels of E. M. Forster,* 1957. [Bib. pp. 161-163.]
McDowell, Frederick P. W. *E. M. Forster,* 1969. [Bib. pp. 149-162.]
Oliver, Harold. *The Art of E. M. Forster,* 1960.
Shahane, V. A. *E. M. Forster: A Reassessment,* 1962.
Shusterman, David. *The Quest for Certitude in E. M. Forster's Fiction,* 1965.
Stone, Wilfred. *The Cave and the Mountain: A Study of E. M. Forster,* 1966.
Thomson, George H. *The Fiction of E. M. Forster,* 1967.
Trilling, Lionel. *E. M. Forster,* 1943. [Bib. pp. 185-187.]
Wilde, Alan. *Art and Order: A Study of E. M. Forster,* 1964.

It is only because Forster published much of his fiction before 1920 that he is included in the 1880-1920 period. Even in his early work, Forster is modern in technique and sentiment, and he is closer to writers like Lawrence, Joyce and Eliot than to the transitional figures who dominate the literary scene between 1880 and 1920. Few novelists of the period have received the scrutiny expended on Forster's symbolic fictional art. A novelist of ideas, Forster uses characters to embody concepts and places (like Howards End) to shadow forth tradition and custom; in his fiction, conflict is often the verbal sparring of opposing ideologies. Forster's fundamental concern is man's need for meaningful *contact*—spiritual, intellectual, perhaps physical. In *Howards End,* completeness would be accomplished by a true marriage of the idealistic German Schlegels and the pragmatic English Wilcoxes, but here, as elsewhere, attempts at "connecting" fail. Forster suggests that such contact or connection—impossible for the average man—is beyond the reach of even exceptional humans. Forster's novels show Englishmen who, thanks largely to their upbringing and formal education, have overdeveloped minds and underdeveloped hearts. Together, these flaws may lead to disastrous errors of judgment, as in *A Room with a View* where the freer approach to life in Italy subjects characters to unexpected moments of decision. Forster's work is tragicomic, often wedding an ironic, detached approach to deeply serious matter.

FRAZER, JAMES GEORGE (1854-1941)

Prose:

Totemism, 1887.
The Golden Bough, 1890; rvd. eds., 1900, 1915.
Totemism and Exogamy . . . , 1910.
The Belief in Immortality . . . . 3 vols., 1913-1924.
Folk-Lore in the Old Testament . . . , 1918.
Anthologia Anthropologica . . . A Copious Selection of Passages . . . from the Manuscript Notebooks of Sir James George Frazer . . . . Ed. R. Angus Downie. 4 vols., 1938-1939.
And other titles.

Bibliographical:

Besterman, Theodore. *A Bibliography of Sir James George Frazer,* 1934.

Biographical and Critical:

Downie, R. Angus. *James George Frazer: The Portrait of a Scholar,* 1940.
Hyman, Stanley E. *The Tangled Bank: Darwin, Marx, Frazer and Freud as Imaginative Writers,* 1962. Pp. 187-293.
Malinowski, Bronislaw. "Sir James George Frazer," *A Scientific Theory of Culture . . . ,* 1944. Pp. 179-221.
Vickery, John B. "'The Golden Bough': Impact and Archetype," *Virginia Quarterly Review,* XXXIX (Winter, 1963), 37-57.

James George Frazer

In *The Golden Bough,* Frazer examined in systematic detail the development of human society in terms of magic, religion and science. He led the way in the study of comparative folklore and myth, identifying recurring motifs like the sacrificed man-god, nature gods and the scapegoat as elements of primitive belief. Though some of his theories have been superseded, he influenced an entire generation of researchers in anthropology and mythography.

FREEMAN, JOHN (1880-1929)

Poems:

Twenty Poems, 1909.
Fifty Poems, 1911.
Presage of Victory, 1916.
Stone Trees, 1916.
Memories of Childhood, 1918.
Poems New and Old, 1920.
Collected Poems, 1928.
Last Poems. Ed. J. C. Squire. 1930.
And other titles.

Prose:

The Moderns, 1916.
A Portrait of George Moore in a Study of His Work, 1922.
Punch and Holy Water, 1923.
Herman Melville, 1926.

Letters:

John Freeman's Letters. Ed. Gertrude Freeman and John Squire. 1936.

Biographical and Critical:

Bliss, William. "The Poetry of John Freeman," *London Mercury,* XXI (February, 1930), 325-337.

John Freeman

Freeman, a member of the Georgian poetry group, was a sincere, conscientious poet who lacked originality and power. He reached his apogee with *Poems New and Old,* which showed his love of melodious, slow-flowing verse and mirrored his deep love for the English countryside. A lesser-known facet of Freeman is his sensual love poetry. He explored the nature of the body's relationship to love in the remarkable poems "Judgment Day" and "The Body."

GALSWORTHY, JOHN (1867-1933)

Fiction:

A Man of Devon, 1901.
The Island Pharisees, 1904.
The Man of Property, 1906.
The Country House, 1907.
Fraternity, 1909.
The Patrician, 1911.
The Dark Flower, 1913.
Saint's Progress, 1919.
In Chancery, 1920.
To Let, 1921.
The White Monkey, 1924.
The Silver Spoon, 1926.
Swan Song, 1928.
On Forsyte 'Change, 1930.
Maid in Waiting, 1931.
Flowering Wilderness, 1932.
Over the River, 1933.
And other titles.

Plays:

The Silver Box, 1906.
Strife, 1909.
Justice, 1910.
The Pigeon, 1912.
The Eldest Son, 1912.

John Galsworthy

The Fugitive, 1913.
The Mob, 1914.
A Bit O' Love, 1915.
The Skin Game, 1920.
Loyalties, 1922.
Old English, 1924.
Escape, 1925.
And other titles.

Collected Works:

Caravan: The Assembled Tales of John Galsworthy, 1925.
Works. "Manston Edition." 30 vols., 1923-1936.

Letters:

Letters from John Galsworthy, 1900-1932. Ed. Edward Garnett. 1934.

Bibliographical:

Fabes, Gilbert H. *John Galsworthy: His First Editions: Points and Values,* 1932.
Gerber, Helmut E. "John Galsworthy: An Annotated Checklist of Writings About Him," *English Fiction in Transition,* I: 3 (1958), 7-29.
Humphreys, K. W. *John Galsworthy: Catalogue of the Collection,* 1967. [At the Library, University of Birmingham.]
Marrot, H. V. *A Bibliography of the Works of John Galsworthy,* 1928.
Mikhail, E. H. *John Galsworthy the Dramatist: A Bibliography of Criticism,* 1971.

Biographical and Critical:

Barker, Dudley. *The Man of Principle: A View of John Galsworthy,* 1963.
Coates, R. H. *John Galsworthy As a Dramatic Artist,* 1926.
Croman, Natalie. *John Galsworthy: A Study in Continuity and Contrast,* 1933.
Dupont, V. *John Galsworthy: The Dramatic Artist,* 1943.

Galsworthy, Ada. *Over the Hills and Far Away,* 1937.
Guyot, Edouard. *John Galsworthy: I: Le Romancier,* 1933.
Kaye-Smith, Sheila. *John Galsworthy,* 1916.
Marrot, H. V. *The Life and Letters of John Galsworthy,* 1935.
Mottram, R. H. *For Some We Loved, An Intimate Portrait of Ada and John Galsworthy,* 1956.
— *John Galsworthy,* 1953.
Ould, Hermon. *John Galsworthy,* 1934.
Reynolds, M. E. *Memories of John Galsworthy: By His Sister,* 1936.
Schalit, L. M. *John Galsworthy: A Survey,* 1929.
Smit, J. H. *The Short Stories of John Galsworthy,* [1948].

Though Galsworthy is remembered chiefly for his portrait of the Forsyte family, he also depicted other social levels such as the professional class in *Fraternity,* the landed gentry in *Country House,* and the aristocracy in *The Patrician.* His greatest achievement is the *Forsyte Saga,* which includes nine novels and several short transitional pieces. The Forsytes are representatives of the long-established upper middle classes, comfortably protected by money and "property." Galsworthy was harshly critical of this class, which he knew at first hand as indicated in *The Island Pharisees.* In *The Man of Property,* first volume of the *Forsyte Saga,* Beauty and Love in the person of Irene, who stands outside the Forsyte circle, defeat the Forsyte concept of possession. As successive volumes of the Forsyte chronicle developed, Galsworthy continued to show that "property" could adversely affect later generations, but as he drew farther away from Victorian society, he became less caustic and more nostalgic for a passing way of life. His plays, concerned with the injustices of one class to another *(The Silver Box; Justice),* were, when first produced, vivid condemnations calculated to stir the conscience of the upper classes. However, his plays lack depth of characterization and fail to resolve the problems he depicts.

GBS, G.B.S. *see* SHAW, GEORGE BERNARD.

GEORGE, WALTER LIONEL (1882-1926)

Fiction:

A Bed of Roses, 1913.
Israel Kalisch, 1913.
The Making of an Englishman, 1914. [Am. ed. titled *The Little Beloved.*]
The Second Blooming, 1914.
The Strangers' Wedding, 1916.
Blind Alley, 1920.
Caliban, 1920.
The Confession of Ursula Trent, 1921.
The Triumph of Gallio, 1924.
The Selected Short Stories of W. L. George, 1927.
And other titles.

Biographical and Critical:

Jerrold, Douglas. *Georgian Adventure*, 1937. Passim.
Harris, Frank. "W. L. George," *Contemporary Portraits*. 3rd ser., 1920. Pp. 143-147.

George's work testifies to the importance novelists attached to psychological portrayal after 1900. He is noted for studies of women like the prostitute-heroine of *Bed of Roses*, a novel that gained him considerable notoriety. As novelist, he was handicapped by treating personal matters (e.g. sexual attraction) as social phenomena, with consequent depersonalization of his characters. He was a dedicated writer, deficient in imagination.

GEORGIAN POETRY

The accession of George V in 1910 gave editor Edward Marsh the title for a series of anthologies of modern poetry, which appeared in 1912, 1915, 1917, 1919 and 1922. His "select" poets included Edmund Blunden, Walter de la Mare, D. H. Lawrence and John Drinkwater. Although the work of many poets and poems of different subject matter and form appeared in Marsh's volumes, "Georgian Poetry" came to mean verse of a temperate disposition, possessing a quiet tone, with little tension, conflict or development – verse in reaction against the aesthetic-decadent tendencies of the preceding decades.

GISSING, GEORGE ROBERT (1857-1903)

Fiction:

Workers in the Dawn, 1880.
The Unclassed, 1884.
Demos, 1886.
Isabel Clarendon, 1886.
Thyrza, 1887.
The Nether World, 1889.
New Grub Street, 1891.
Born in Exile, 1892.
The Odd Women, 1893.
Eve's Ransom, 1895.
The Crown of Life, 1899.
Veranilda, 1904.
The House of Cobwebs, 1906.
Sins of the Fathers, 1924.
Stories and Sketches, 1938.
And other titles.

Prose:

Charles Dickens: A Critical Study, 1898.
By the Ionian Sea, 1901.
The Private Papers of Henry Ryecroft, 1903.
Selections, Autobiographical and Imaginative, 1929.
George Gissing: Essays and Fiction. Ed. Pierre Coustillas. 1970.
And other titles.

George Robert Gissing

Letters:

George Gissing and H. G. Wells: Their Friendship and Correspondence. Ed. Royal Gettmann. 1961.
The Letters of George Gissing to Eduard Bertz, 1887-1903. Ed. Arthur C. Young. 1961.
The Letters of George Gissing to Gabrielle Fleury. Ed. Pierre Coustillas. 1964.
Letters of George Gissing to Members of His Family. Ed. Algernon and Ellen Gissing. 1927.
Letters to an Editor. Ed. C. K. Shorter. 1915.
Letters to Edward Clodd from George Gissing, 1914.

Bibliographical:

Coustillas, Pierre, and Paul Goetsch. "George Gissing: An Annotated Bibliography of Writings About Him: Foreign Journals: Supplement II," *English Literature in Transition,* VII: 1 (1964), 14-26.
Coustillas, Pierre. "Gissing's Short Stories: A Bibliography," *English Literature in Transition,* VII: 2 (1964), 59-72.
Wolff, Joseph J. "George Gissing: An Annotated Bibliography of Writings About Him: Supplement," *English Literature in Transition,* III: 2 (1960), 3-33.

Biographical and Critical:

Coustillas, Pierre (ed.). *Collected Articles on George Gissing,* 1968.
Davis, Oswald H. *George Gissing: A Study in Literary Leanings,* 1966.
Donnelly, Mabel Collins. *George Gissing: Grave Comedian,* 1954. [Solid bio.]
Gapp, Samuel Vogt. *George Gissing, Classicist,* 1936.
Korg, Jacob. *George Gissing: A Critical Biography,* 1963.
Roberts, Morley. *The Private Life of Henry Maitland,* 1912. [Novel based on Gissing's life.]
Swinnerton, Frank. *George Gissing: A Critical Study,* 1912.
Ward, A. C. *Gissing,* 1959.
Yates, Annie M. *George Gissing, an Appreciation,* 1922.

Gissing, as H. G. Wells noticed, lacked the reasonable,

affable mask society likes the artist to wear. Instead, in both his life and fiction, Gissing seemed to flaunt his poverty, lack of fame and disdain for society's codes. Self-pity mars much of his work, but he was able to sublimate his feeling of having been wronged when, as in *New Grub Street,* his imagination found a subject that enabled him to project various sides of his complex personality. Its hero, Edmund Reardon, approximates a composite of many of Gissing's protagonists. After an auspicious rise through publication, Reardon marries unwisely and, finding that he can no longer write, separates from his wife to suffer lonely agony until his death. A similar figure is Gilbert Grail *(Thyrza)*, who also represents thwarted ambition and psychic agony. Gissing's essay-fantasia *Henry Ryecroft* expresses concern for society's lack of appreciation of low-born, ill-educated but genuine genius. By using a fictional vantage point of tranquil retirement in *Ryecroft,* Gissing achieved detachment missing from his novels. Though Gissing was not a great novelist, his depiction of the predicament of sensitive, educated misfits in modern society makes his work important.

GOSSE, EDMUND (1849-1928)

Prose:

Life of William Congreve, 1888.
The Life of Philip Henry Gosse, 1890. [Should be compared with *Father and Son.*]
Northern Studies, 1890.
Critical Kit-Kats, 1896.
The Life and Letters of John Donne . . . , 1899.
Ibsen, 1907.
Father and Son: A Study of Two Temperaments, 1907. [Fictionalized autobiography.]
The Life of Algernon Charles Swinburne, 1917.
Books on the Table, 1921.
Aspects and Impressions, 1922.
And other titles.

Edmund Gosse

Poems:

Madrigals, Songs and Sonnets, 1870.
On Viol and Flute, 1873.
New Poems, 1879.
Firdausi in Exile, 1885.
In Russet and Silver, 1894.
The Autumn Garden, 1909.
And other titles.

Collected Works:

Collected Poems, 1911.
Collected Essays. 12 vols., 1912-1927.

Letters:

The Correspondence of André Gide and Edmund Gosse, 1904-1928. Ed. Linnette F. Brugmans. 1959.
Sir Edmund Gosse's Correspondence with Scandinavian Writers. Ed. Elias Bredsdorff. 1961.
Transatlantic Dialogue: Selected American Correspondence of Edmund Gosse. Ed. Paul F. Mattheison and Michael Millgate. 1965.

Bibliographical:

A Catalogue of the Gosse Correspondence in the Brotherton Collection, Consisting Mainly of Letters Written to... Gosse...from 1867-1928, 1950. [University of Leeds, Library Publications No. 3.]
Woolf, James D. "Sir Edmund Gosse: An Annotated Bibliography of Writings About Him," *English Literature in Transition,* XI: 3 (1968), 126-172.

Biographical and Critical:

Braybrooke, Patrick. *Considerations on Edmund Gosse,* 1925.
Charteris, Evan. *The Life and Letters of Sir Edmund Gosse,* 1931.

Edmund Gosse

Gosse's many essays on literary topics are "appreciations" rather than criticism. He was one of the first to introduce Ibsen to England through translations and essays. *Father and Son,* Gosse's most famous work, describes some of the religious problems of both Victorian and anti-Victorian generations. Though not so caustic as *The Way of All Flesh, Father and Son* also shows why so many young men resented their Victorian upbringing after 1880.

GRAHAM, ROBERT BONTINE CUNNINGHAME [R. B. CUNNINGHAME-GRAHAM] (1852-1936)

Essays, "Sketches," "Tales," Fiction, Travel: [It is difficult to categorize Graham's work into precise genres. His "tales" and "sketches" may be mixed together in one volume, partly fiction and partly non-fiction, one blending into the other.]

Mogreb-el-Acksa, 1898.
The Ipané, 1899.
Thirteen Stories, 1900.
Success, 1902.
Hernando de Soto . . . , 1903.
Progress, 1905.
Faith, 1909.
Hope, 1910.
A Hatchment, 1913.
The Conquest of New Granada . . . , 1922.
The Conquest of the River Plate, 1924.
And other titles.

Bibliographical:

Chaundy, Leslie. *A Bibliography of the First Editions of Robert Bontine Cunninghame Graham,* 1924.
West, Herbert Faulkner. *The Herbert Faulkner West Collection of Cunninghame Graham, Presented . . . to Dartmouth College Library . . . ,* 1938.

Robert Bontine Cunninghame Graham

Biographical and Critical:

Macdiarmid, Hugh [Christopher Murray Grieve]. *Cunninghame Graham: A Centenary Study,* 1952.
Tschiffely, A. F. *Don Roberto: Being the Account of the Life and Works of R. B. Cunninghame Graham, 1852-1936,* 1937.
Watts, T. C. "Conrad and Cunninghame Graham," *Joseph Conrad's Letters to R. B. Cunninghame Graham.* Ed. T. C. Watts, 1969. Pp. 3-36.
West, Herbert Faulkner. *A Modern Conquistador. Robert Bontine Cunninghame Graham: His Life and Works,* 1932.

Graham's sketches, tales and historical narratives show his enthusiasm for South America—especially the Argentine Pampas—in their vivid description of folkways, landscape and the country's past. Although Graham resembles William Henry Hudson as an ardent admirer of the South American continent, his style is rougher and less poetic than Hudson's.

GRAHAME, KENNETH (1859-1932)

Fiction:

The Golden Age, 1895.
Dream Days, 1898.
The Wind in the Willows, 1908.

Prose:

Pagan Papers, 1893.

Biographical and Critical:

Chalmers, P. R. *Kenneth Grahame, Life, Letters, Unpublished Work,* 1933.
Graham, Eleanor. *Kenneth Grahame,* 1963.
Green, Peter. *Kenneth Grahame, 1859-1932: A Biography,* 1959.

Kenneth Grahame

In *The Golden Age* and *Dream Days,* Grahame recreates the essence of childhood in nostalgic essays and displays delightful whimsy in the story of "The Reluctant Dragon." His masterpiece, *Wind in the Willows,* is told from the viewpoint of animals and reveals a great love for the earth, its creatures and their responses to the seasons. He avoids sentimentality in *Willows* with a wry sense of humor and reveals deep insight into human nature and human types.

GRANVILLE-BARKER, HARLEY (1877-1946)

Plays:

The Marrying of Ann Leete, 1902.
The Voysey Inheritance, 1905.
Waste, 1907.
The Madras House, 1910.
And other titles.

Prose:

A National Theatre: Scheme and Estimates [with William Archer], 1907.
The Exemplary Theatre, 1922.
Prefaces to Shakespeare. 5 ser., 1927-1948.
On Dramatic Method, 1931.
And other titles.

Biographical and Critical:

Downer, Allan S. "Harley Granville-Barker," *Sewanee Review,* LV (October-December, 1947), 627-645.
Morgan, Margery M. *A Drama of Political Man: A Study in the Plays of Harley Granville Barker,* 1961.
Pearson, Hesketh. "Harley Granville-Barker (1877-1946)," *The Last Actor-Managers,* 1950. Pp. 71-79.
Purdom, C. B. *Harley Granville Barker: Man of the Theatre, Dramatist and Scholar,* 1955. [Appendices include plays produced by Granville-Barker, pp. 290-292, and a detailed bib., pp. 293-309.]

Harley Granville-Barker

Granville-Barker was important as producer and playwright. By successfully staging the early plays of Shaw and those of Ibsen, Galsworthy and Masefield, he gave impetus to the rise of modern drama. In his own major plays, Granville-Barker depicted the corruption of society by presenting individuals in responsible positions whose private morality is completely different from their public image. Political manipulation, with no consideration of individual emotions, and cynical sexuality are displayed in *The Marrying of Ann Leete* and *Waste*. In *The Voysey Inheritance*, he indicts the hypocrisy of a business family whose "inheritance" is really the result of continuous embezzlement.

GREGORY, ISABELLA AUGUSTA [LADY GREGORY] (1852-1932)

Plays:

Spreading the News, 1904.
Kincora, 1905.
The Gaol Gate, 1906.
Dervorgilla, 1907.
The Jackdaw, 1907.
The Rising of the Moon, 1907.
The Unicorn from the Stars [with W. B. Yeats], *1907.*
The Image, 1909.
The Full Moon, 1910.
Grania, 1912.
Hanrahan's Oath, 1918.
The Story Brought by Brigit, 1924.
And other titles.

Prose:

Our Irish Theatre, 1914.
Hugh Lane's Life and Achievement, 1921.
Coole, 1931.
Lady Gregory's Journal, 1916-1930. Ed. Lennox Robinson. 1946.

Isabella Augusta Gregory

Biographical and Critical:

Ayling, Ronald. "'Charwoman of the Abbey,'" *Shaw Review,* IV (September, 1961), 7-15.
Coxhead, Elizabeth. *J. M. Synge and Lady Gregory,* 1962.
— *Lady Gregory: A Literary Portrait,* 1961.
Howarth, Herbert. "Isabella Augusta Gregory," *The Irish Writers 1880-1940,* 1958. Pp. 83-109.
Murphy, Daniel J. "Yeats and Lady Gregory: A Unique Dramatic Collaboration," *Modern Drama,* VII (December, 1964), 322-328.
Saddlemyer, Ann. *In Defence of Lady Gregory, Playwright,* 1966.

A woman of many levels of importance in the Celtic Renaissance, Gregory was a major force in the Abbey Theatre. She collaborated with W. B. Yeats on several plays and wrote a number by herself. Her work may now be overshadowed by the poetic power of Yeats and the greater depth and subtlety of Synge, yet she ably exploited a blend of fantasy and humor and used folk materials (with great success in *The Rising of the Moon*) to produce significant plays.

GROSSMITH, GEORGE (1847-1912) and WALTER WEEDON GROSSMITH (1854-1919)

Fiction:

The Diary of a Nobody, 1892.

The Diary records humorously the every-day tribulations of the lower-middle class life led by Charles Pooter and his family. Though in many ways the characters and situations are similar to those found in the social comedies of H. G. Wells, the Grossmiths lack the subtlety of Wells' fiction.

GUTHRIE, THOMAS ANSTEY [F. GUTHRIE ANSTEY] (1856-1934)

Fiction and Parody:

Vice Versa, 1882.
The Giant's Robe, 1884.
The Tinted Venus, 1885.
Voces Populi. 2 ser., 1890, 1892.
Mr. Punch's Pocket Ibsen, 1893.
Baboo Hurry Bungsho Jabberjee, B. A., 1897.
The Brass Bottle, 1900.
And other titles.

Autobiography:

A Long Retrospect, 1936.

Bibliographical:

Turner, Martin John. *A Bibliography of the Works of F. Anstey,* 1931.

For many years associated with *Punch,* Guthrie perfected an urbane, lightly ironical style for his humorous sketches and novels. His most successful books are fantasies *(Vice Versa, The Giant's Robe, The Tinted Venus*); his serious three-deckers fail lamentably. His work lives both for its fantastic humor and for its satire, as in *Baboo Jabberjee* and the splendid parody of Ibsen.

HAGGARD, HENRY RIDER (1856-1925)

Fiction:

King Solomon's Mines, 1885.
Allan Quatermain, 1887.
She, 1887.
Cleopatra, 1889.
The World's Desire [with Andrew Lang], 1890.

Eric Brighteyes, 1891.
Nada the Lily, 1892.
Montezuma's Daughter, 1893.
Ayesha: The Return of She, 1905.
Red Eve, 1911.
Marie, 1912.
The Holy Flower, 1915.
The Ivory Child, 1916.
She and Allan, 1921.
And other titles.

Autobiography and Letters:

The Days of My Life: An Autobiography. Ed. C. J. Longman. 2 vols., 1926.
Rudyard Kipling to Rider Haggard: The Record of a Friendship. Ed. Morton Cohen. 1965. [2 letters and 27 diary entries by Haggard.]

Bibliographical:

MacKay, George Leslie. *A Bibliography of the Writings of Sir Rider Haggard*, 1930.
—, and J. E. Scott. *Additions and Corrections to the Haggard Bibliography*, 1939.
Scott, J. E. *A Bibliography of the Works of Sir Henry Rider Haggard, 1856-1925*, 1947. [Supersedes all previous bibs.]

Biographical and Critical:

Cohen, Morton. *Rider Haggard: His Life and Work*, 1960; rvd. ed., 1968. [Bib. pp. 307-323.]
Haggard, Lilias Rider. *The Cloak That I Left: A Biography of . . . Rider Haggard . . . by His Daughter*, 1951.
Wheeler, Paul Mowbray. "H. Rider Haggard," *Georgia Review*, XX (Summer, 1966), 213-219.

Haggard specialized in African adventure and made the fantastic events in his stories seem believable. He emphasized lost races hidden in remote parts of the world, who guarded treasures of great value. In *Allan Quatermain*, he created the archetype of all great white hunters, and in

She, he presented the eternally beautiful female who is alluringly sinister because of her immortality. At his best, as in *Cleopatra* and *Eric Brighteyes*, Haggard recaptured a feeling of ancient life and society and combined it with exciting high adventure.

HANKIN, ST. JOHN (1869-1909)

Plays:

The Two Mr. Weatherbys, 1903.
The Return of the Prodigal, 1905.
The Cassilis Engagement, 1907.
The Last of the De Mullins, 1908.
The Plays of St. John Hankin. 2 vols., 1923.
And other titles.

Humor:

Mr. Punch's Dramatic Sequels, 1901.
Lost Masterpieces, 1904.

Biographical and Critical:

Morgan, A. E. "Hankin," *Tendencies of Modern English Drama*, 1924. Pp. 111-120.
Storer, Edward. "St. John Hankin," *Living Age*, CCLXXX (March 28, 1914), 781-784.

Hankin was one of the playwrights who, following GBS, used drama to explore real if overused social problems—women's rights, the control of society and marriage difficulties. In *The Last of the De Mullins*, he attacks complacent middle class morality by siding with the revolt of the younger generation against laws imposed on it by the older. But Hankin's sincerity of purpose fails to make up for his lack of real imagination and vitality. His wooden characters and faded dialogue suggest a man who wrote from conviction rather than inspiration.

HARDY, THOMAS (1840-1928)

Fiction:

Desperate Remedies, 1871.
Under the Greenwood Tree, 1872.
A Pair of Blue Eyes, 1873.
Far From the Madding Crowd, 1874.
The Hand of Ethelberta, 1876.
The Return of the Native, 1878.
The Trumpet Major, 1880.
A Laodicean, 1881.
Two on a Tower, 1882.
The Mayor of Casterbridge, 1886.
The Woodlanders, 1887.
Wessex Tales, 1888.
Tess of the d'Urbervilles, 1891.
A Group of Noble Dames, 1891.
Life's Little Ironies, 1894.
Jude the Obscure, 1895.
A Changed Man, 1913.
And other titles.

Poems:

Wessex Poems, 1898.
Poems of the Past and the Present, 1902.
The Dynasts, 1903-1908. [An "epic drama."]
Time's Laughingstocks, 1909.
Satires of Circumstance, 1914.
Moments of Vision, 1917.
Late Lyrics, 1922.
Human Shows, 1925.
Winter Words, 1928.

Letters and Autobiography:

The Letters of Thomas Hardy. Ed. Carl J. Weber. 1954.
"Dearest Emmie": Thomas Hardy's Letters to His First Wife. Ed. Carl J. Weber. 1963.
Thomas Hardy's Personal Writing: Prefaces, Literary Opinions, Reminiscences. Ed. Harold Orel. 1966.

Thomas Hardy

Collected Works:

Works. "Wessex Edition." 24 vols., 1912-1931.
Collected Poems, 1932.

Bibliographical:

Danielson, Henry. *The First Editions of the Writings of Thomas Hardy and Their Values,* 1916.

Gerber, Helmut E., and W. Eugene Davis. *Thomas Hardy: An Annotated Bibliography of Writings About Him,* 1973. [The most complete secondary bib.]

Purdy, R. L. *Thomas Hardy: A Bibliographical Study,* 1954. [Supersedes earlier bib. studies.]

Webb, A. P. *A Bibliography of the Works of Thomas Hardy 1865-1915,* 1916.

Weber, Carl J. *The First Hundred Years of Thomas Hardy 1840-1940,* 1942.

Biographical and Critical:

Bailey, J. O. *The Poetry of Thomas Hardy: A Handbook and a Commentary,* 1970. [Bib. pp. 675-692.]

— *Thomas Hardy and the Cosmic Mind: A New Reading of the Dynasts,* 1956.

Beach, Joseph Warren. *The Technique of Thomas Hardy,* 1922.

Blunden, E. C. *Thomas Hardy,* 1941.

Brennecke, E. *Thomas Hardy's Universe,* 1924.

Carpenter, Richard C. *Thomas Hardy,* 1964. [Good short intro. to Hardy.]

Chase, Mary Ellen. *Thomas Hardy from Serial to Novel,* 1927.

Chew, Samuel C. *Thomas Hardy, Poet and Novelist,* 1928.

Cox, Reginald G. (ed.). *Thomas Hardy: The Critical Heritage,* 1970.

Deacon, Lois, and Terry Coleman. *Providence and Mr. Hardy,* 1966.

Elliott, A. P. *Fatalism in the Works of Thomas Hardy,* 1935.

Firor, Ruth. *Folkways in Thomas Hardy,* 1931.

Guerard, A. J. *Thomas Hardy: the Novels and Stories,* 1949.

Hardy, Florence Emily. *The Early Life of Thomas Hardy, 1840-1891*, 1928.
— *The Later Years of Thomas Hardy, 1892-1928*, 1930. [Both vols. are virtually autobios. Hardy dictated to his wife.]
Hornback, Bert G. *The Metaphor of Chance: Vision and Technique in the Works of Thomas Hardy*, 1971. [Bib. pp. 171-174.]
Howe, Irving. *Thomas Hardy*, 1967.
Hynes, Samuel. *The Pattern of Hardy's Poetry*, 1961.
Marsden, Kenneth. *The Poems of Thomas Hardy: A Critical Introduction*, 1969.
Miller, J. Hillis. *Thomas Hardy: Distance and Desire*, 1970.
Millgate, Michael. *Thomas Hardy: His Career as a Novelist*, 1971.
Morrell, Roy. *Thomas Hardy: The Will and the Way*, 1965.
Orel, Harold. *Thomas Hardy's Epic-Drama*, 1965.
Pinion, F. B. *A Hardy Companion: A Guide to the Works of Thomas Hardy and Their Background*, 1968. [Bib. pp. 533-550.]
Rutland, W. R. *Thomas Hardy: A Study of His Writings and Their Background*, 1938.
Sankey, Benjamin. *The Major Novels of Thomas Hardy*, 1965.
Southerington, F. R. *Hardy's Vision of Man*, 1971. [Bib. pp. 273-278.]
Southworth, J. G. *The Poetry of Thomas Hardy*, 1947.
Stewart, J. I. M. *Thomas Hardy: A Critical Biography*, 1971. [Bib. pp. 237-239.]
Weber, Carl J. *Hardy of Wessex: His Life and Literary Career*, 1940; rvd. ed., 1966.
Webster, H. C. *On a Darkling Plain: The Art and Thought of Thomas Hardy*, 1947.
Wright, Walter F. *The Shaping of "The Dynasts": A Study in Thomas Hardy*, 1967. [Bib. pp. 320-324.]

As man and artist, Hardy remains a paradox. Despite his sensitive nature, he often bowed to demands of Victorian editors by bowdlerizing his novels for serialization; despite the placid, stoic mask he wore, his works show an inordinate interest in grotesque, violent aspects of life; despite his realistic use of south-western English settings (the Wessex of virtually all his novels and stories), he was fascinated with forces, motives and deeds beyond the borders of the normal or natural. After failing to establish himself as a poet in the 1860's, Hardy turned to writing lucrative magazine fiction in such conventional Victorian modes as the bucolic love story *(Under the Greenwood Tree)* and the suspense story *(Desperate Remedies)*. He became popular with the publication of *Far From the Madding Crowd* and *The Return of the Native*. In later novels, he turned to increasingly frank studies of such delicate aspects of Victorian life as religion and extramarital love (notably in *Tess of the d'Urbervilles* and *Jude the Obscure*), which shocked late-Victorian readers. From 1895 until his death, he published almost nothing but poetry. Hardy's achievement in verse is very uneven, and he seems never to have thrown a poem away. Occasionally, his finest poems are responses to happenings of public significance, such as the approach of World War I ("Channel Firing") or the sinking of the *Titanic* ("The Convergence of the Twain"). More often, they result from his being reminded of the great losses of life—youth, love faith—as in "The Oxen" and his love poems on his first wife. *The Dynasts*, an epic drama of the Napoleonic era, brilliantly displays Hardy's narrative and poetic genius: it is a fitting capstone to his creative life.

HARLAND, HENRY [SIDNEY LUSKA] (1861-1905)

Fiction:

The Yoke of the Thorah, 1887.
Grey Roses, 1895.
Comedies and Errors, 1898.
The Cardinal's Snuff-Box, 1900.
The Lady Paramount, 1902.
And other titles.

Born in America, Harland gained some reputation for his Sidney Luska stories of Jewish-American life in 1885-1890 before going to England. Despite his later novels, which reveal a playful and shallow mind, he is mainly remembered as literary editor of *The Yellow Book*.

HARRIS, FRANK (1856-1931)

Prose:

Contemporary Portraits. 4 ser., 1915, 1919, 1920, 1923.
Oscar Wilde: His Life and Confessions, 1916.
Frank Harris on Bernard Shaw, 1931.
And other titles.

Fiction:

Elder Conklin, 1894.
The Bomb, 1908.
And other titles.

Autobiography:

My Life and Loves. 4 vols., 1922-1927. [One vol. ed. by John F. Gallagher, 1963, is the first complete, unexpurgated Eng. or Am. ed.]

Letters:

Moore vs. Harris: An Intimate Correspondence Between George Moore and Frank Harris, 1925.
Frank Harris to Arnold Bennett, 1936.

Biographical and Critical:

Brome, Vincent. *Frank Harris*, 1959. [Bib. pp. 234-240.]
Lunn, Hugh Kingsmill. *Frank Harris*, 1932.
Root, E. Merrill. *Frank Harris*, 1947.
Tobin, A. I., and Elmer Gertz. *Frank Harris. A Study in Black and White*, 1931. [Bib. pp. 359-379.]

The unexpurgated publication of *My Life* has given Harris greater renown than he achieved in his own lifetime. To his peers, he was many things: a great editor of *Fortnightly Review, Saturday Review* and *Vanity Fair,* a blackmailing blackguard and, occasionally, a creative writer of substantial power. *The Bomb* is a moving account of an incident in the Chicago Haymarket riots. His most engrossing aspect is still his erratic, dynamic life, which touched many aspects of the literary and social scenes of the period.

HAWKINS, ANTHONY HOPE [ANTHONY HOPE] (1863-1933)

Fiction:

The Prisoner of Zenda, 1894.
The Dolly Dialogues, 1894.
The God in the Car, 1894.
Rupert of Hentzau, 1898.
The King's Mirror, 1899.
Double Harness, 1903.
Lucinda, 1920.
And other titles.

Autobiography:

Memories and Notes, 1927.

Biographical and Critical:

Mallet, Charles. *Anthony Hope and His Books,* 1935.

Like H. Rider Haggard, Hawkins will be remembered as a successful practitioner of adventurous romance, even though his fiction lacks the variety and verisimilitude of Haggard's. Despite his productivity, he owed his popularity largely to *Zenda* with its pleasant blend of humor and romance.

HENLEY, WILLIAM ERNEST (1849-1903)

Poems:

A Book of Verses, 1888.
London Voluntaries, 1893.
London Types, 1898.
Poems, 1898.
Hawthorn and Lavender: Songs and Madrigals, 1899.
In Hospital, 1901.
Lyrics, 1903.
And other titles.

Prose and Letters:

Pictures at Play . . . by Two Art-Critics [with Andrew Lang], 1888.
Views and Reviews: Essays in Appreciation, 1890.
Some Letters of William Ernest Henley, 1933.
And other titles.

Biographical and Critical:

Buckley, Jerome Hamilton. *William Ernest Henley*, 1945.
Connell, John. *W. E. Henley*, 1949.
Flora, Joseph M. *William Ernest Henley*, 1970. [Bib. pp. 157-162.]
Looker, Samuel J. *Shelley, Trelawny and Henley: A Study of Three Titans*, 1950.

Henley's work was a reaction against the aesthetic-decadent mode. In his "hospital verse," he experimented with surprisingly modern free verse—unrhymed, irregular in meter and quite unpoetic in subject matter. Unlike the decadents, he was deeply immersed in the affairs of his country. He championed Imperialism, as in "England, My England," while editing the *National Observer*.

HEWLETT, MAURICE HENRY (1861-1923)

Fiction:

The Forest Lovers, 1898.
Little Novels of Italy, 1899.
The Life and Death of Richard Yea-and-Nay, 1900.
The Queen's Quair, 1904.
Halfway House, 1908.
Open Country, 1909.
Rest Harrow, 1910.
And other titles.

Poetry:

Artemision, 1909.
The Agonists: A Trilogy of God and Man, 1911.
The Song of the Plough, 1916.
And other titles.

Prose and Letters:

In a Green Shade, 1920.
Wiltshire Essays, 1921.
Extemporary Essays, 1922.
Last Essays, 1924.
The Letters of Maurice Hewlett . . . [*and*] *A Diary in Greece*. Ed. Lawrence Binyon. 1926.

Bibliographical:

Muir, Percy. *A Bibliography of the First Editions of Works by Maurice Henry Hewlett*, 1927.

Biographical and Critical:

Bronner, Milton. *Maurice Hewlett*, 1910.
Church, Richard. "Maurice Hewlett Reconsidered," *Fortnightly Review*, CXXXV (January, 1934), 96-102.
Freeman, John. "The 'English' Poems of Maurice Hewlett," *Quarterly Review*, CCXXXVI (July, 1921), 112-128.
Gwynn, Stephen. "Maurice Hewlett," *Edinburgh Review*,

CCXXXIX (January, 1924), 61-72.

Sutherland, Arthur Bruce. *Maurice Hewlett: Historical Romancer,* 1938. [Bib. pp. 189-199.]

Despite a determined effort to be known as serious novelist, essayist and poet, in the public eye Hewlett was a romancer, whose early works *The Forest Lovers* and *Richard Yea-and-Nay* established his reputation. He failed to outgrow this stereotype largely because of want of ideas and originality. Whether writing romances or, from 1904-1914, "modern" novels, he was a follower of other men's paths. Hewlett thought himself a poet, but produced little of value except *The Song of the Plow,* an "epic" of the life of Hodge, the traditional English peasant. But it too is derivative, pedestrian, colorless.

HICHENS, ROBERT SMYTHE (1864-1950)

Fiction:

The Coastguard's Secret, 1886.
The Green Carnation, 1894.
The Londoners, 1898.
The Garden of Allah, 1904.
Mrs. Marden, 1919.
The Afterglow, 1935.
And other titles.

Autobiography:

Yesterday, 1947.

Hichens will be remembered for his witty satire of Oscar Wilde and the aesthetes in *The Green Carnation.* His romantic adventure stories (e.g. *The Garden of Allah*) have faded into oblivion.

HINKSON, MRS. *see* TYNAN, KATHARINE.

HOBBES, JOHN OLIVER. *see* CRAIGIE, PEARL MARY THERESA.

HOOD, GEORGE. *see* BROWN, GEORGE DOUGLAS.

HOPE, ANTHONY. *see* HAWKINS, ANTHONY HOPE.

HOPKINS, GERARD MANLEY (1844-1889)

Poems:

Poems. Ed. Robert Bridges. 1918; rvd. ed., 1930.
A Vision of the Mermaids, 1929.
Poems and Prose of Gerard Manley Hopkins. Ed. W. H. Gardner. 1953.
The Poems of Gerard Manley Hopkins. Ed. W. H. Gardner and N. H. Mackenzie. 1967.

Prose:

The Sermons and Devotional Writings of Gerard Manley Hopkins. Ed. Christopher Devlin. 1959.

Letters, Journals, and Notebooks:

The Correspondence of Gerard Manley Hopkins and Richard Watson Dixon. Ed. Claude Colleer Abbott. 1935.
The Letters of Gerard Manley Hopkins to Robert Bridges. Ed. Claude Colleer Abbott. 1935.
The Note-Books and Papers of Gerard Manley Hopkins. Ed. Humphry House. 1937; rvd. ed., 1959.
Further Letters of Gerard Manley Hopkins. Ed. Claude Colleer Abbott. 1938; rvd. ed., 1956.

Bibliographical:

Borrello, Alfred (ed.). *A Concordance of the Poetry in*

English of Gerard Manley Hopkins, 1969.
Charney, Mauria. *A Bibliographical Study of Hopkins Criticism, 1918-1949,* 1950.
Cohen, Edward H. *Works and Criticism of Gerard Manley Hopkins: A Comprehensive Bibliography,* 1969.
Dilligan, Robert J., and Todd K. Bender. *A Concordance to the English Poetry of Gerard Manley Hopkins,* 1970.
Patricia, Mary (Sister). "Forty Years of Criticism: A Chronological Check List of Criticism of the Works of Gerard Manley Hopkins from 1909 to 1949," *Bulletin of Bibliography,* XX (May-August, 1950), 38-44; (September-December, 1950), 63-67.
Seelhamer, Ruth. *Hopkins Collected at Gonzaga,* 1970.

Biographical and Critical:

Bender, Todd K. *Gerard Manley Hopkins: The Classical Background and Critical Reception of His Work,* 1966.
Boyle, Robert Richard. *Metaphor in Hopkins,* 1961.
Cohen, Selma J. *The Poetic Theory of Gerard Manley Hopkins,* 1947.
Downes, David A. *Gerard Manley Hopkins: A Study of His Ignatian Spirit,* 1959.
Gardner, W. H. *Gerard Manley Hopkins (1844-1889)...,* 1944.
Grigson, Geoffrey. *Gerard Manley Hopkins,* 1955.
Hart, Mary Adouta (Sister). *The Christocentric Theme in Gerard Manley Hopkins' "The Wreck of the Deutschland,"* 1952.
Heuser, Alan. *The Shaping Vision of Gerard Manley Hopkins,* 1958.
Holloway, Marcella Marie (Sister). *The Prosodic Theory of Gerard Manley Hopkins,* 1947.
Johnson, Wendell Stacy. *Gerard Manley Hopkins: The Poet as Victorian,* 1968.
Keating, John Edward. *The Wreck of the Deutschland: An Essay and a Commentary,* 1963.
Kelly, Bernard. *The Mind and Poetry of G. M. Hopkins,* 1935.
Lahey, G. F. *Gerard Manley Hopkins,* 1930.
Lees, Francis Noel. *Gerard Manley Hopkins,* 1966.
McChesney, Donald. *A Hopkins Commentary: An Explanatory Commentary on the Main Poems, 1876-1889,* 1968.
Mariani, Paul L. *A Commentary on the Complete Poems of*

Gerard Manley Hopkins, 1970. [Bib. pp. 337-352.]
Peters, W. A. M. *Gerard Manley Hopkins: A Critical Essay Towards the Understanding of His Poetry*, 1948.
Pick, John. *Gerard Manley Hopkins: Priest and Poet*, 1942.
Ritz, Jean-Georges. *Robert Bridges and Gerard Hopkins, 1863-1889: A Literary Friendship*, 1960.
Ruggles, Eleanor. *Gerard Manley Hopkins—A Life*, 1944.
Schneider, Elisabeth W. *The Dragon in the Gate: Studies in the Poems of G. M. Hopkins*, 1968.
Thomas, Alfred. *Hopkins the Jesuit: The Years of Training*, 1969. [Bib. pp. 257-263.]
Wain, John. *Gerard Manley Hopkins: An Idiom of Desperation*, 1960.

No one, except Robert Bridges and a few others, heard Hopkins' powerful, eccentric poetic voice during his lifetime. Although Hopkins had links with English poetic tradition, notably with the metaphysicals and, in his own time, with Anglican and Roman Catholic visionary poets, the peculiar qualities of his poetry were largely the result of his experimentation with metrics and diction. His "sprung rhythm," the use of unstressed syllables according to the dictates of inspiration, helped free poetry from too-rigid metrical demands. As a linguistic innovator, Hopkins made words serve his own poetic ends by coining new ones or by yoking old ones together to form new groupings, as in the lines describing clouds in autumn, "... wilder, wilful-wavier/Meal-drift moulded ever and melted across skies?" His poetry seems "modern" because of its frequent ambiguities and verbal experimentation, as in "The Windhover." His most ambitious—and perplexing—work is the narrative-contemplative poem "The Wreck of the Deutschland." Whatever his obscurities or excesses, Hopkins was an important force on later poetry.

HOUGHTON, WILLIAM STANLEY (1881-1913)

Plays:

The Dear Departed, 1908.

William Stanley Houghton

The Younger Generation, 1910.
Hindle Wakes, 1912.
Ginger, 1913.
Five One-Act Plays, 1913.
The Works of Stanley Houghton. Ed. Harold Brighouse. 3 vols., 1914.
And other titles.

Biographical and Critical:

Morgan, A. E. "Houghton," *Tendencies of Modern English Drama,* 1924. Pp. 177-182.
Storer, Edward. "Stanley Houghton," *Living Age,* CCLXXX (February, 1914), 413-417.

A disciple of GBS, Houghton was handicapped by reticence, and his plays lacked humor—that saving grace of didactic Shavian drama. Yet he knew his craft and wrote competently. *Hindle Wakes,* his best play, examines one of his favorite themes: the conflict between generations.

HOUSMAN, ALFRED EDWARD (1859-1936)

Poems:

A Shropshire Lad, 1896.
Last Poems, 1922.
More Poems, 1936.
A Shropshire Lad. Ed. Carl J. Weber. 1946. [Bib. of various eds., pp. 87-105.]
The Manuscript Poems of A. E. Housman: Eight Hundred Lines of Hitherto Uncollected Verse from the Author's Notebooks. Ed. Tom Burns Haber. 1955. [Housman authorities question accuracy of transcription; shows Housman's method of composition.]
Collected Poems. Ed. John Sparrow. 1956.
Complete Poems. Ed. Tom Burns Haber. 1959. [Discusses textual problems.]
Collected Poems. Ed. John Carter. 1965.

Alfred Edward Housman

Prose:

The Name and Nature of Poetry, 1933.
Selected Prose. Ed. John Carter. 1961.
The Confines of Criticism . . . 1911. Ed. John Carter. 1969.

Letters:

The Letters of A. E. Housman. Ed. Henry Maas. 1971.

Bibliographical:

Carter, John, and John Sparrow. *A. E. Housman: An Annotated Hand-List,* 1952. [Most recent and most thorough bib.]
Ehrsam, Theodore G. *A Bibliography of Alfred Edward Housman,* 1941. [Incomplete; often inaccurate.]
Hyder, Clyde Kenneth. *A Concordance to the Poems of A. E. Housman,* 1940. [Does not always use reliable texts.]
Stallman, Robert W. "Annotated Bibliography of A. E. Housman: A Critical Study," *Publications of the Modern Language Association of America,* LX (June, 1945), 463-502. [Adds to Ehrsam.]

Biographical and Critical:

Gow, A. S. F. *A. E. Housman: A Sketch Together with a List of His Writings and Indexes to His Classical Papers,* 1936.
Haber, Tom Burns. *A. E. Housman,* 1967. [Bib. pp. 212-214.]
Housman, Laurence. *A. E. H.: Some Poems, Some Letters and a Personal Memoir,* 1937. [Am. ed. titled *My Brother, A. E. Housman: Personal Recollections together with Thirty Hitherto Unpublished Poems,* 1938; includes description of note-books and list of dated poems.]
— *The Unexpected Years,* 1937.
Leggett, B. J. *Housman's Land of Lost Content: A Critical Study of "A Shropshire Lad,"* 1970. [Bib. pp. 139-150.]
Marlow, Norman. *A. E. Housman: Scholar and Poet,* 1958.
Richards, Grant. *Housman: 1897-1936,* 1941. [Includes Cockerell list of dated poems.]

Ricks, Christopher (ed.). *A. E. Housman: A Collection of Critical Essays,* 1968.
Scott-Kilvert, Ian. *A. E. Housman,* 1955.
Watson, George L. *A. E. Housman: A Divided Life,* 1957.
Withers, Percy. *A Buried Life: Personal Recollections of A. E. Housman,* 1940.

Housman's poetry is a pleasant blend of lyricism and cynicism. He is cynical about young love, friendship and the promise of youth. He often versified the obvious, repeated himself by using similar subject matter, imagery and mood in many poems, and rarely offered man any hope. In his best poems ("Bredon Hill," "Loveliest of Trees"), images of lost hope and evanescent beauty are made memorable by the lyricism of his verse. His subject matter and poetic technique changed little throughout his life; he early discovered his *métier* and never explored beyond its narrow boundaries.

HOUSMAN, CLEMENCE ANNIE (1861-1955)

Fiction:

The Were-Wolf, 1896.
The Unknown Sea, 1898.
The Life of Sir Aglovale de Galis, 1905.

Biographical:

[Minor refs. to Housman appear in books on A. E. Housman and in Laurence Housman's *The Unexpected Years.*]

The sister of A. E. and Laurence Housman, Housman wrote three novels which are heavy with fantasy. *The Were-Wolf* is pseudo-Norse saga; *Sir Aglovale* is drawn from Malory. *The Unknown Sea,* her most original work, is an attempt at Christian allegory and concerns a girl without a soul, but Housman's style is often tedious, her characterization wooden.

HOUSMAN, LAURENCE (1865-1959)

Poems:

Green Arras, 1896.
Spikenard, 1898.
The Little Land, 1899.
Rue, 1899.
The Heart of Peace, 1918.
Collected Poems, 1937.
And other titles.

Plays:

Prunella [with Harley Granville-Barker], *1904.*
Angels & Ministers, 1921.
Little Plays of St. Francis. 3 ser., 1922, 1931, 1935.
Victoria Regina, 1935.
And other titles.

Fiction [Includes fairy stories, short stories, "tales," satires, novels.]:

A Farm in Fairyland, 1894.
The House of Joy, 1895.
The Field of Clover, 1898.
An English Woman's Love-Letters, 1900.
The Blue Moon, 1904.
John of Jingalo, 1912.
And other titles.

Autobiography:

The Unexpected Years, 1937.
[Passing refs. to L. Housman in books about A. E. Housman.]

Housman once wrote: "I have written more books than I should have done had I given more time to second thoughts . . . ." His poetry is mediocre and expresses conventional thoughts in conventional poetic diction. His dramas often deal with religious matters or royalty. His favorite dramatic device was to structure his plays in long series of short scenes rather than in acts. Though several were successfully staged, the lack of definite dramatic acts makes them seem like closet drama (e.g. *Little Plays of St. Francis* and *Victoria Regina*). Housman's fiction ranges through Victorian fairy stories (both sentimental and bitter), almost unclassifiable short tales and political satires like *John of Jingalo*.

HUDSON, WILLIAM HENRY (1841-1922)

Fiction:

The Purple Land That England Lost, 1885.
A Crystal Age, 1887.
Fan, 1892.
El Ombú, 1902. [Retitled *South American Sketches,* 1909.]
Green Mansions, 1904.
A Little Boy Lost, 1905.
Dead Man's Plack and An Old Thorn, 1920.
And other titles.

Prose:

Idle Days in Patagonia, 1893.
Birds and Man, 1901.
Hampshire Days, 1903.
The Land's End, 1908.
A Shepherd's Life, 1910.
And other titles.

Collected Works:

Collected Works. 24 vols., 1922-1923.

Autobiography and Letters:

Far Away and Long Ago: A History of My Early Life, 1918.
A Hundred and Fifty-Three Letters from W. H. Hudson. Ed. E. Garnett. 1923.

W. H. Hudson's Letters to R. B. Cunninghame-Graham. Ed. R. Curle. 1941.

Bibliographical:

Tate, Marie T. "Bibliographies, News and Notes: W. H. Hudson," *English Literature in Transition,* VI: 1 (1963), 36-48.

Wilson, George F. *A Bibliography of the Writings of William Henry Hudson,* 1922.

Biographical and Critical:

Charles, R. H. "The Writings of W. H. Hudson," *Essays and Studies,* XX (1934), 135-151.

Fletcher, J. V. "The Creator of Rima, W. H. Hudson: A Belated Romantic," *Sewanee Review,* XLI (January-March, 1933), 24-40.

Hamilton, Robert. *W. H. Hudson: The Vision of Earth,* 1946.

Haymaker, Richard E. *From Pampas to Hedgerows and Downs: A Study of W. H. Hudson,* 1954.

Several elements are common to almost all of Hudson's works: a deep delight in the variety and beauty of nature, a fine sense of style, a hatred of blood sports and sportsmen and a dislike of the finiteness of time. *Green Mansions* is Hudson's most popular novel. Even if, as he wrote, "the story doesn't move—it simmers placidly away," the descriptions of nature and the bird-girl Rima reveal considerable descriptive and creative power. In *Hampshire Days,* Hudson shows himself one of the gifted nature essayists of the period.

HUEFFER, JOSEPH LEOPOLD FORD HERMANN MADOX [FORD MADOX FORD] (1873-1939)

Fiction:

The Shifting of the Fire, 1892.

The Inheritors [with Joseph Conrad], 1901.

Romance [with Joseph Conrad], 1903.
The Fifth Queen, 1906.
Privy Seal, 1907.
The Fifth Queen Crowned, 1908. [With two preceding vols. forms Katherine Howard trilogy.]
Mr. Apollo, 1908.
The Panel, 1912. [Rvd. Am. ed. *Ring for Nancy,* 1913.]
The Young Lovell, 1913.
The Good Soldier, 1915.
The Marsden Case, 1923.
Some Do Not, 1924.
No More Parades, 1925.
A Man Could Stand Up, 1926.
Last Post, 1928. [With three preceding vols. forms *Parade's End* tetralogy.]
No Enemy, 1929. [Fictional autobio.]
And other titles.

Poetry:

Poems for Pictures, 1900.
From Inland, 1907.
Songs from London, 1910.
High Germany, 1911.
On Heaven, 1918.
New Poems, 1927.
Collected Poems, 1936.
And other titles.

Prose:

Ford Madox Brown, 1896.
Rossetti: A Critical Essay on His Art, 1902.
Hans Holbein the Younger, 1905.
The Pre-Raphaelite Brotherhood, 1907.
The Critical Attitude, 1911.
Henry James: A Critical Study, 1913.
Joseph Conrad: A Personal Remembrance, 1924.
A Mirror to France, 1926.
The English Novel..., 1930.
Critical Writings of Ford Madox Ford. Ed. Frank MacShane. 1964.
And other titles.

Joseph Leopold Ford Hermann Madox Hueffer

Autobiography and Letters:

Ancient Lights and Certain New Reflections, 1911. [Am. ed. *Memories and Impressions.*]
Thus to Revisit, 1921.
Return to Yesterday, 1931.
It Was the Nightingale, 1934.
Letters of Ford Madox Ford. Ed. Richard M. Ludwig. 1965.

Bibliographical:

Harvey, David Dow. *Ford Madox Ford: 1873-1939: A Bibliography of Works and Criticism,* 1962. [Supersedes all earlier bib. works.]

Biographical and Critical:

Andreach, Robert J. *The Slain and Resurrected God: Conrad, Ford and the Christian Myth,* 1970.
Cassell, Richard. *Ford Madox Ford: A Study of the Novels,* 1961.
Goldring, Douglas. *The Last Pre-Raphaelite: A Record of The Life and Writings of Ford Madox Ford,* 1948. [Am. ed. *Trained for Genius,* 1949.]
Gordon, Ambrose. *The Invisible Tent: The War Novels of Ford Madox Ford,* 1964. [Bib. pp. 145-147.]
Hoffman, Charles G. *Ford Madox Ford,* 1967.
Leer, Norman. *The Limited Hero in the Novels of Ford Madox Ford,* 1966.
Lid, R. W. *Ford Madox Ford: The Essence of His Art,* 1964. [Bib. pp. 195-201.]
MacShane, Frank. *The Life and Work of Ford Madox Ford,* 1965. [Bib. pp. 271-274.]
Meixner, John Albert. *Ford Madox Ford's Novels,* 1962. [Bib. pp. 288-293.]
Ohmann, Carol. *Ford Madox Ford: From Apprentice to Craftsman,* 1964.
Soskice, Juliet (Hueffer). *Chapters from Childhood,* 1921. [Reminiscences by Ford's sister.]
Wiley, Paul L. *Novelist of Three Worlds: Ford Madox Ford,* 1962.
Young, Kenneth. *Ford Madox Ford,* 1956.

Joseph Leopold Ford Hermann Madox Hueffer

Hueffer was trained for genius, but recognition of its particular kind and quality came slowly. In his Pre-Raphaelite, highly literate boyhood environment, the writing of stories and verse came naturally. At age 25, he was presented to Joseph Conrad as an eminent English stylist. Their collaboration probably benefited Hueffer more than the older author, as the psychological approach of the Katherine Howard trilogy (which Conrad called "the swan song of Historical Romance") attests. On his 40th birthday, Hueffer began what he envisioned to be his own swan song as a novelist, *The Good Soldier*. For its intensity and technical virtuosity it is his best novel; fortunately, however, it was not his last. The Tietjens tetralogy (called in the U. S. *Parade's End*) is a logical development in narrative manner (modified stream-of-consciousness) and psychology from his earlier work. Its occasional dullness is counterbalanced by cumulative effect and the sense of a changing social order. Although Hueffer is chiefly known as a novelist, he exerted another significant literary force as editor, gifted with the power of attracting work of new writers, of *The English Review* and later *Transatlantic Review*.

IRISH LITERARY RENAISSANCE. *see* CELTIC RENAISSANCE.

IRON, RALPH. *see* SCHREINER, OLIVE . . . .

JACOBS, WILLIAM WYMARK (1863-1943)

Fiction:

Many Cargoes, 1896.
The Skipper's Wooing, 1897.
Over the Side, 1899.
A Master of Craft, 1900.
Dialstone Lane, 1904.

At Sunwich Port, 1906.
Salthaven, 1908.
Deep Waters, 1919.
And other titles.

Biographical and Critical:

Bennett, Arnold. "W. W. Jacobs and Aristophanes," *Books and Persons,* 1917. Pp. 53-56.
Priestley, J. B. "In Praise of Mr. Jacobs," *London Mercury,* IX (November, 1923), 26-36.
Pritchett, V. S. "W. W. Jacobs," *Books in General,* 1953. Pp. 235-241.
Whitford, Robert C. "The Humor of W. W. Jacobs," *South Atlantic Quarterly,* XVIII (July, 1919), 246-251.

Jacobs' macabre tale "The Monkey's Paw" has obscured his greater popular renown as writer of land-based sea humor. *Many Cargoes* presents the humorous difficulties of sailors ashore in small shipping towns. Despite his rapid development in narrative skill during 1885-1910, he never rose above the level of gifted entertainer. Of his novels, perhaps *At Sunwich Port* and *Dialstone Lane* are best.

JAMES, MONTAGUE RHODES (1862-1936)

Fiction:

Ghost Stories of an Antiquary, 1904.
More Ghost Stories of an Antiquary, 1911.
A Thin Ghost, and Others, 1919.
The Five Jars, 1922.
A Warning to the Curious, 1925.
Collected Ghost Stories, 1931.

Letters:

Letters to a Friend. Ed. Gwendolen McBryde. 1956. ["Introduction," pp. 7-26, is a rambling memoir of James.]

Montague Rhodes James

Bibliographical:

Cox, J. Randolph. "Montague Rhodes James: An Annotated Bibliography of Writings About Him," *English Literature in Transition,* XII: 4 (1969), 203-210.

Biographical and Critical:

Cox, J. Randolph. "Ghostly Antiquary: The Stories of Montague Rhodes James," *English Literature in Transition,* XII: 4 (1969), 197-202.
Gaselee, Stephen. "Montague Rhodes James: 1862-1936," *Proceedings of the British Academy,* XXII (1936), 418-433.
Lubbock, S. G. *A Memoir of Montague Rhodes James,* 1939. [Includes A. F. Scholfield, "List of Writings," pp. 47-87, a thorough bib.]
Penzolt, Peter. "Dr. M. R. James (1862-1936)," *The Supernatural in Fiction,* 1952. Pp. 191-202.

James was a noted paleographer, biblical scholar and cataloger of manuscript collections. His ghost stories, at times slow in pace and weak in construction, created superlative horror. Rather than use misty specters, James preferred tangible manifestations like malignant hair growing from wallpaper, revengeful spiders and bestial teeth unexpectedly found under pillows. Despite a weak beginning, *The Five Jars* is a pleasant fairy tale.

JEFFERIES, RICHARD (1848-1887)

Prose:

The Gamekeeper at Home, 1878.
Wild Life in a Southern County, 1879.
The Amateur Poacher, 1879.
Round About a Great Estate, 1880.
Nature Near London, 1883.
The Life of the Fields, 1884.
Red Deer, 1884.
The Open Air, 1885.

Field and Hedgerow . . . , 1889.
The Nature Diaries and Note-Books of Richard Jefferies . . . . Ed. Samuel J. Looker. 1941.
And other titles.

Fiction:

Greene Ferne Farm, 1880.
Wood Magic: A Fable, 1881.
Bevis: The Story of a Boy, 1882.
The Dewy Morn, 1884.
After London: or, Wild England, 1885.
Amaryllis at the Fair, 1887.
And other titles.

Autobiography:

The Story of My Heart: My Autobiography, 1883; also, *The Story of My Heart. Edited With the First Draft of the Author's Manuscript.* Ed. Samuel J. Looker. 1947.

Biographical and Critical:

Arkell, Reginald. *Richard Jefferies,* 1933; rptd. as *Richard Jefferies and His Countryside . . . ,* 1946.
Besant, Walter. *The Eulogy of Richard Jefferies,* 1888.
Drew, Philip. "Richard Jefferies and the English Countryside," *Victorian Studies,* XI (December, 1967), 181-206.
Keith, W. J. *Richard Jefferies: A Critical Study,* 1965. [Bib. pp. 170-194.]
Looker, Samuel J. (ed.). *Concerning Richard Jefferies,* 1944.
—. (ed.). *Richard Jefferies: A Tribute,* 1946.
—, and Crichton Porteous. *Richard Jefferies: Man of the Fields,* 1965. [Bib. pp. 244-258.]
Salt, Henry S. *Richard Jefferies: A Study,* 1894.
Thomas, Edward. *Richard Jefferies: His Life and Work,* 1909. [Bib. pp. 329-335.]

In his essays and best novels, Jefferies displayed an intense love of nature and a gift for detailed observation. As he gradually came to find more delight in cataloging the characteristics of wild life than in destroying it, he changed from sportsman-hunter to naturalist. A hint of mysticism is present in his work since nature aroused in him feelings of religious awe.

JEROME, JEROME KLAPKA (1859-1927)

Fiction:

Three Men in a Boat, 1889.
John Ingerfield, 1894.
Paul Kelver, 1902.
The Angel and the Author — And Others, 1908.
Malvina of Brittany, 1916.
And other titles.

Plays:

Barbara, 1886.
Sunset, 1888.
The Passing of the Third Floor Back, 1907.
Fanny and the Servant Problem, 1908.
The Master of Mrs. Chilvers, 1911.
And other titles.

Prose:

Idle Thoughts of an Idle Fellow, 1886.
Stage-Land, 1889.
The Second Thoughts of an Idle Fellow, 1898.
Three Men on the Bummel, 1900.
And other titles.

Autobiography:

My Life and Times, 1926.

Biographical and Critical:

Leslie, Anita. *The Remarkable Mr. Jerome,* 1954.
Moss, Alfred. *Jerome K. Jerome: His Life and Works,* 1929.

Jerome achieved about equal fame as novelist and dramatist, but revealed rather different sides of his creative self in the two genres. Many of his plays showed commitment to such current social-political issues as woman suffrage in *The Master of Mrs. Chilvers.* His fiction was usually humorous, like the immensely popular *Three Men in a Boat,* although his autobiographical novel *Paul Kelver* was quite as earnest as his plays.

JOHNSON, LIONEL PIGOT (1867-1902)

Poems:

Poems, 1895.
Ireland, 1897.
Poetical Works of Lionel Johnson, 1915.
The Complete Poems of Lionel Johnson. Ed. Iain Fletcher. 1953.

Prose:

The Art of Thomas Hardy, 1894.
Post Liminium, 1911. [Selection of critical essays.]
Reviews and Critical Papers. Ed. R. Shafer. 1921.
And other titles.

Biographical and Critical:

Charlesworth, Barbara. "Lionel Johnson," *Dark Passages . . . ,* 1965. Pp. 81-95.
Evans, B. Ifor. "Ernest Dowson, Lionel Johnson, and the Poetry of the Eighteen-Nineties," *English Poetry in the Later Nineteenth Century,* 1933. Pp. 314-332.
Fletcher, Iain. "Lionel Johnson: 'The Dark Angel,'" *Interpretations: Essays on Twelve English Poems.* Ed. John Wain. 1955. Pp. 153-178.
Weygandt, Cornelius. "Lionel Johnson, English Irishman," *Tuesdays at Ten,* 1928. Pp. 62-73.

Johnson, an alienated young Bohemian who burned himself out after a brief flowering of exceptional promise, closely fit the decadent paradigm. His love of the exotic helps explain his affection for Ireland and his conversion to Catholicism—both important subjects of his poetry. Its most pressing concern, however, is sin. Much of his poetry lacks urgency of communication, but "The Dark Angel" documents real internal strife. His book on Hardy is a valuable and beautifully written study.

JONES, HENRY ARTHUR (1851-1929)

Plays:

The Silver King, 1882.
The Dancing Girl, 1891.
The Masqueraders, 1894.
The Case of Rebellious Susan, 1894.
The Liars, 1897.
Mrs. Dane's Defense, 1900.
Dolly Reforming Herself, 1908.
And other titles.

Essays:

The Renascence of the English Drama, 1895.
The Foundations of a National Drama, 1913.
The Theatre of Ideas, 1915.
And other titles.

Biographical and Critical:

Allen, Percy. "Henry Arthur Jones," *Fornightly Review,* CXXV (May, 1929), 692-699.
Cordell, Richard. *Henry Arthur Jones and the Modern Drama,* 1932.
Jones, Doris Arthur. *Taking the Curtain Call: The Life and Letters of Henry Arthur Jones,* 1930. [List of plays and bib. pp. 363-384.]
Northend, Marjorie. "Henry Arthur Jones and the Develop-

ment of the Modern English Drama,'' *Review of English Studies*, XVIII (October, 1942), 448-463.

In subject matter, Jones broke sharply with the Victorian tradition of drama. The heroine of *The Dancing Girl* is a mistress; a man gambles for a wife in *The Masqueraders;* a woman hides her earlier seduction in *Mrs. Dane's Defense*. Even comedies like *Rebellious Susan* and *The Liars* concern wives who wish to change the double moral standard of society. But Jones also clung to many Victorian conventions and diminished the effectiveness of his realistic subjects with sentimentality, melodrama and, usually, a comparatively happy ending.

KAILYARD SCHOOL

When editor William Robertson Nicoll began encouraging J. M. Barrie, John Watson, S. R. Crockett and lesser writers to describe humble Scots life, the result was amiable, sentimental fiction, which had wide appeal in the 1890's. The name ''Kailyard School'' was derived from the Scots word for the cabbage patch commonly associated with humble dwellings. Compared with more radical and influential movements in English fiction of the 1880's and 90's, Kailyard fiction, with its sentimentality, naive optimism and dialectal charm was an anachronism. The movement waned as new social and political forces rose in the closing years of the 1800's. The probable *coup de grace* was George Douglas Brown's novel *The House with the Green Shutters* which showed pride, greed and hypocrisy flourishing in a typical Kailyard setting.

KAYE-SMITH, SHEILA (1887-1956)

Fiction:

The Tramping Methodist, 1908.
Starbrace, 1909.

Sheila Kaye-Smith

Spell Land, 1910.
Isle of Thorns, 1913.
Three Against the World, 1914.
Willow's Forge, 1914.
Green Apple Harvest, 1920.
Joanna Godden, 1921.
The End of the House of Alard, 1923.
And other titles.

Poems:

Saints in Sussex, 1923.
And other titles.

Autobiography:

Three Ways Home, 1937.
All the Books of My Life, 1956.

Biographical and Critical:

Hopkins, R. Thurston. *Sheila Kaye-Smith and the Weald Country,* 1925.
Kernahan, Coulson. "Sheila Kaye-Smith as a Poet," *Nineteenth Century,* XCVII (June, 1925), 910-924.
Malone, Andrew E. "The Novelist of Sussex: Sheila Kaye-Smith," *Fortnightly Review,* CXX (August, 1926), 199-209.

Kaye-Smith is the novelist of Sussex. Her art is intensely serious, her view of love, tragic. *Joanna Godden* is still impressive for its depiction of vigorous country living. In *House of Alard,* she aimed at tragedy in her depiction of the *Götterdämmerung* of the country gentry's way of life, but the book is shrill and unconvincing. Like some of her other novels, it is more a tract for the times than creative fiction. She had all the great novelist's requisites except genius.

KING, KENNEDY. *see* BROWN, GEORGE DOUGLAS.

KIPLING, RUDYARD (1865-1936)

Poems:

Departmental Ditties, 1886.
Barrack-Room Ballads, 1892.
The Seven Seas, 1896.
The Five Nations, 1903.
Songs from Books, 1912.
The Years Between, 1919.
[Many poems included in collections of stories.]

Fiction:

Plain Tales from the Hills, 1888.
Soldiers Three, 1888.
In Black and White, 1888.
The Phantom 'Rickshaw, 1888.
The Story of the Gadsbys, 1888.
Under the Deodars, 1888.
Wee Willie Winkie, 1888.
The Courting of Dinah Shadd, 1890.
The Light That Failed, 1890; rvd. ed., 1891.
Life's Handicap, 1891.
Many Inventions, 1893.
The Jungle Book, 1894.
The Second Jungle Book, 1895.
Captains Courageous, 1897.
The Day's Work, 1898.
Stalky and Co., 1899.
Kim, 1901.
Just So Stories, 1902.
Traffics and Discoveries, 1904.
Puck of Pook's Hill, 1906.
Actions and Reactions, 1909.
A Diversity of Creatures, 1917.
Debits and Credits, 1926.
And other titles.

Prose:

A Fleet in Being, 1898.

Rudyard Kipling

From Sea to Sea, 1899.
Letters of Travel: 1892-1913, 1920.
A Book of Words, 1928.
Something of Myself for My Friends Known and Unknown, 1937. [Autobio.]
And other titles.

Collected Works:

Works. "Bombay Edition." 31 vols., 1913-1938.
Works. "Sussex Edition." 35 vols., 1937-1939.
Rudyard Kipling's Verse: Definitive Edition, 1940.

Letters:

Rudyard Kipling to Rider Haggard: The Record of a Friendship. Ed. Morton N. Cohen. 1965.

Bibliographical:

Gerber, Helmut E., and Edward S. Lauterbach (eds.). "Rudyard Kipling: An Annotated Bibliography of Writings About Him," *English Fiction in Transition,* III: 3, 4, 5 (1960), 1-235. [Comprehensive.]

Lauterbach, Edward S. (ed.). "An Annotated Bibliography of Writings About Rudyard Kipling: First Supplement," *English Literature in Transition,* VIII: 3, 4 (1965), 136-241. [Continues Gerber and Lauterbach.]

Livingston, Flora V. *Bibliography of the Works of Rudyard Kipling,* 1927. [Often inaccurate.]

— *Supplement to Bibliography of Works of Rudyard Kipling,* 1938. [Corrects errors of previous Livingston bib.]

Martindell, E. W. *A Bibliography of the Works of Rudyard Kipling, 1881-1923,* 1923. [Rvd. ed.]

Stewart, James McG. *Rudyard Kipling: A Bibliographical Catalogue.* Ed. A. W. Yeats. 1959. [Though only "a partial check-list," this is the most comprehensive bib. of Kipling.]

Biographical and Critical:

Beresford, G. C. *Schooldays with Kipling,* 1936.

Bodelsen, C. A. *Aspects of Kipling's Art,* 1964.
Braybrooke, Patrick. *Kipling and His Soldiers,* 1926.
Brown, Hilton. *Rudyard Kipling: A New Appreciation,* 1945.
Carrington, Charles E. *Rudyard Kipling,* 1955. [Authorized bio.; both Eng. and Am. eds. carelessly proofread, resulting in errors in some book titles; bib. unspecific, esp. where newspapers are concerned.]
Cornell, Louis L. *Kipling in India,* 1966.
Croft-Cooke, Richard. *Rudyard Kipling,* 1948.
Dobrée, Bonamy. *Rudyard Kipling,* 1951.
— *Rudyard Kipling: Realist and Fabulist,* 1967.
Durand, Ralph A. *A Handbook to the Poetry of Rudyard Kipling,* 1914.
Falls, Cyril Bentham. *Rudyard Kipling: A Critical Study,* 1915.
Gilbert, Eliot L. *The Good Kipling: Studies in the Short Story,* 1970.
— (ed.). *Kipling and the Critics,* 1965.
Green, Roger Lancelyn (ed.). *Kipling: The Critical Heritage,* 1971.
— , and R. E. Harbord. *The Readers' Guide to Rudyard Kipling's Work,* 1961- [In process of completion; detailed annotation of uncommon words, allusions, refs. in individual Kipling stories and poems.]
Knowles, Frederic Lawrence. *A Kipling Primer,* 1899.
Munson, Arley. *Kipling's India,* 1915.
Shanks, Edward. *Rudyard Kipling: A Study in Literature and Political Ideas,* 1940.
Stewart, J. I. M. *Rudyard Kipling,* 1966.
Tompkins, J. M. S. *The Art of Rudyard Kipling,* 1959.
Weygandt, Anne M. *Kipling's Reading and Its Influence on His Poetry,* 1939.
Worster, W. J. Alexander. *Merlin's Isle: A Study of Rudyard Kipling's England,* 1920.
Young, William Arthur. *A Dictionary of the Characters and Scenes in the Stories and Poems of Rudyard Kipling . . . ,* 1911; rvd. ed. by W. A. Young and John H. McGivering, *A Kipling Dictionary,* 1967.

Kipling burst on the English literary scene as interpreter of India in volumes of short stories such as *Plain Tales from the Hills* and *The Phantom 'Richshaw.* His Indian fiction includes sketches and anecdotes like "The Bisara of Pooree" and "Lispeth," but Kipling also took a satiric view of Anglo-Indian society and the hypocritical maneuverings of both the English and Indians. In "Without Benefit of Clergy," he studies the tragic result of an Englishman's marriage to an Indian woman. As Kipling traveled throughout the world his fictional subjects widened, and he wrote of any place with ease, using vigorous idiom and dialect, capturing a sense of locality. And as his compassion for man deepened, his stories often concerned psychological problems, as seen in "The Gardener" and in "The House Surgeon." His late fiction, like "The Bull That Thought," "The Prophet and the Country" and "Mrs. Bathurst" is often obscure and complex in terms of symbol and myth.

Like his fiction, Kipling's poetry also took its initial inspiration from India, as in *Departmental Ditties* and *Barrack-Room Ballads*. His verse, with its rugged rhythms and stern no-nonsense approach to life, made Kipling the uncrowned laureate, though the sentiment in these poems was criticized as jingoistic. But he saw both triumph and burden, power and danger, in the extension of Empire, as poems like "Recessional" and "The White Man's Burden" show. For Kipling, Empire and other systems of law were vital for men, since men needed action, work and duty to fulfill themselves. As in his fiction, Kipling captured the idiom and color of whatever he described in verse, even, on occasion, the sounds of machinery.

Many of Kipling's delightful stories for children also derived from his Indian experiences. In the two *Jungle Books*, he endows animals with speech and human emotions; in *Just So Stories*, he explains whimsically the peculiarities of various animals. *Kim* is a high adventure panorama of India, filled with the energy and color of many races jostled together in a vast wondrous land.

KORZENIOWSKI, JOZEF KONRAD. *see* CONRAD, JOSEPH.

LADY GREGORY. *see* GREGORY, ISABELLA AUGUSTA.

LANG, ANDREW (1844-1912)

Prose:

Custom and Myth, 1884.
Letters to Dead Authors, 1886.
Books and Bookmen, 1886.
Myth, Ritual and Religion, 1887.
Essays in Little, 1891.
Pickle the Spy, 1897.
The Making of Religion, 1898.
Magic and Religion, 1901.
Adventures Among Books, 1905.
The Puzzle of Dickens's Last Plot, 1905.
The Secret of the Totem, 1905.
The World of Homer, 1910.
And other titles.

Poems:

XXII Ballades in Blue China, 1880.
Helen of Troy, 1882.
Rhymes à la Mode, 1884.
Grass of Parnassus, 1888.
Poetical Works, 1923.
And other titles.

Bibliographical:

Green, Roger Lancelyn. "Descriptions from the Darlington Collection of Andrew Lang," *Indiana University Bookman*, No. 7 (April, 1965), 73-101.

Biographical and Critical:

Green, Roger Lancelyn. *Andrew Lang: A Critical Biography*, 1946. [Bib. pp. 236-259.]
— "Andrew Lang, 'The Greatest Bookman of His Age,'" *Indiana University Bookman*, No. 7 (April, 1965), 10-72.
Maurer, Oscar. "Andrew Lang and *Longman's Magazine*, 1882-1905," *University of Texas Studies in English*, XXIV (1955), 152-178.

Andrew Lang

Murray, Gilbert. *Andrew Lang the Poet,* 1948.
Webster, A. Blyth (ed.). *Concerning Andrew Lang,* 1949.

Bookman, littérateur and prolific essayist, Lang combined a pleasant style with considerable erudition. His range of interests was wide, including Homer, folk-lore, anthropology, history, criticism, forgery, controversy and parody. He was one of the first scholars to note that similar motifs were repeated in the folk-lore of widely different races. He also compiled and edited collections of fairy stories which have delighted millions of children.

LAWRENCE, DAVID HERBERT (1885-1930)

Fiction:

The White Peacock, 1911.
The Trespasser, 1912.
Sons and Lovers, 1913.
The Prussian Officer, 1914.
The Rainbow, 1915.
The Lost Girl, 1920.
Women in Love, 1921.
Aaron's Rod, 1922.
St. Mawr, 1925.
Lady Chatterley's Lover, 1928 [Florence]; 1932 [London].
The Tales of D. H. Lawrence, 1934.
And other titles.

Poems:

Love Poems and Others, 1913.
Amores, 1916.
Look! We Have Come Through!, 1917.
New Poems, 1918.
Tortoises, 1921.
Birds, Beasts and Flowers, 1923.
Pansies, 1929.
Nettles, 1930.
Last Poems. Ed. Richard Aldington and Giuseppi Orioli. 1932.

The Ship of Death, 1933.
The Complete Poems of D. H. Lawrence. Ed. Vivian de Sola Pinto and Warren Roberts. 2 vols., 1964.
And other titles.

Plays: [Many of Lawrence's plays were not performed until years after their publication.]

The Widowing of Mrs. Holroyd, 1914.
Touch and Go, 1920.
David, 1926.
The Plays of D. H. Lawrence, 1933.
A Collier's Friday Night, 1934.
And other titles.

Prose:

Twilight in Italy, 1916.
Sea and Sardinia, 1921.
Psychoanalysis and the Unconscious, 1921.
Fantasia of the Unconscious, 1922.
Studies in Classic American Literature, 1923.
Mornings in Mexico, 1927.
Pornography and Obscenity, 1929.
Phoenix: The Posthumous Papers of D. H. Lawrence. Ed. E. D. McDonald. 1936.
Phoenix II: Uncollected, Unpublished, and Other Prose Works by D. H. Lawrence. Ed. Warren Roberts and Harry T. Moore. 1968.
And other titles.

Letters:

Letters of D. H. Lawrence. Ed. Aldous Huxley. 1932.
D. H. Lawrence: Reminiscences and Correspondence, 1934. [Letters to Earl H. Brewster and Achsah Brewster, with reminiscences by them.]
Letters to Bertrand Russell. Ed. H. Moore. 1948.
Selected Letters. Ed. Diana Trilling. 1958.
The Collected Letters of D. H. Lawrence. Ed. Harry T. Moore. 2 vols., 1962.
Lawrence in Love: Letters to Louie Burrows. Ed. James

T. Boulton. 1968.
The Quest for Rananim: D. H. Lawrence's Letters to S. S. Koteliansky 1914-1930. Ed. George J. Zytaruk. 1970.

Bibliographical:

Fabes, Gilbert H. *D. H. Lawrence, His First Editions: Points and Values*, 1933.
MacDonald, E. D. *A Bibliography of the Writings of D. H. Lawrence*, 1925.
— *The Writings of D. H. Lawrence 1925-1930*, 1931.
Powell, Lawrence Clark. *The Manuscripts of D. H. Lawrence*, 1937.
Roberts, Warren. *A Bibliography of D. H. Lawrence*, 1963.
Tedlock, Ernest W. *The Frieda Lawrence Collection of D. H. Lawrence Manuscripts*, 1948.

Biographical and Critical:

Aldington, R. *D. H. Lawrence: Portrait of a Genius, But...*, 1950.
Alldritt, Keith. *The Visual Imagination of D. H. Lawrence*, 1971.
Beal, Anthony. *D. H. Lawrence*, 1961.
Corke, Helen. *D. H. Lawrence: The Croydon Years*, 1965. [Includes selection from author's unpub. autobio.]
Cowan, James C. *D. H. Lawrence's American Journey: A Study in Literature and Myth*, 1970. [Bib. pp. 146-154.]
Daleski, Herman M. *The Forked Flame: A Study of D. H. Lawrence*, 1965.
Delavenay, Emile. *D. H. Lawrence and Edward Carpenter: A Study in Edwardian Transition*, 1971.
Draper, Ronald P. *D. H. Lawrence*, 1964.
— (ed.). *D. H. Lawrence: The Critical Heritage*, 1970.
Ford, George Henry. *Double Measure: A Study of the Novels and Stories of D. H. Lawrence*, 1965.
Goodheart, Eugene. *The Utopian Vision of D. H. Lawrence*, 1963.
Gordon, David J. *D. H. Lawrence as a Literary Critic*, 1966.
Gregory, Horace. *Pilgrim of the Apocalypse*, 1934.
Hochman, Baruch. *Another Ego: The Changing View of Self*

and Society in the Work of D. H. Lawrence, 1970.
Hough, Graham Goulden. *The Dark Sun: A Study of D. H. Lawrence*, 1956.
Kenmare, Dallas. *Firebird: A Study of D. H. Lawrence*, 1951.
Lawrence, Ada, and Stuart G. Gelder. *Young Lorenzo: Early Life of D. H. Lawrence*, 1931.
Lawrence, Frieda. *"Not I, But the Wind,"* 1934.
Leavis, Frank R. *D. H. Lawrence, Novelist*, 1955.
Moore, Harry T. *The Intelligent Heart: The Story of D. H. Lawrence*, 1955.
Moynahan, Julian. *The Deed of Life: The Novels and Tales of D. H. Lawrence*, 1963.
Sagar, Keith M. *The Art of D. H. Lawrence*, 1966.
Spilka, Mark. *The Love Ethic of D. H. Lawrence*, 1955. [Bib. pp. 237-240.]
Stoll, John E. *The Novels of D. H. Lawrence: A Search for Integration*, 1971. [Bib. pp. 251-263.]
Vivas, Eliseo. *D. H. Lawrence: The Failure and Triumph of Art*, 1960. [Bib. pp. 293-300.]
Weiss, Daniel A. *Oedipus in Nottingham: D. H. Lawrence*, 1962.
Widmer, Kingsley. *The Art of Perversity: D. H. Lawrence's Shorter Fictions*, 1962.
Yudhishtar [sic]. *Conflict in the Novels of D. H. Lawrence*, 1969. [Bib. pp. 302-306.]

Like E. M. Forster, Lawrence belongs in many respects to the modern era, but since much of his early work, including *Sons and Lovers*, appeared before 1920, he is part of the transitional era. As novelist, poet and critic, Lawrence was indeed a force to be reckoned with; as man, he was an odd composite of iconoclast, romantic and social critic. His fiction reveals the struggle early twentieth-century novelists had in finding their way toward new modes of expression. *Sons and Lovers*, with its clearly marked story line and emphasis on a single character, might have been written by Gissing or Hardy. But Lawrence broke with such traditions in *The Rainbow*, which follows the development of human attitudes and tendencies through several generations. Lawrence is an emphatically "modern" novelist in his recurrent emphasis on sex and sensuality, in his depiction of man's struggle with the dark power of industrialism and in his use of symbolism — all of which appear in *Women in Love*, probably his finest novel. These attitudes are also apparent in his short stories. Lawrence's intellectual power and imagistic skill make his poetry effective. He also had the gift of communicating his keen perceptions in memorable images, as in "Piano." He probably furthered the tendency toward experimentation with metrical patterns and authorial disregard of the reader's expectations through his highly individual "private" verse. As essayist, Lawrence wrote with vigor and insight about a host of topics: literature, countries, psychology. His letters are of extraordinary interest as the spontaneous, uninhibited record of a seminal mind.

LEDWIDGE, FRANCIS (1891-1917)

Poems:

Songs of the Fields, 1916.
Songs of Peace, 1917.
Last Songs, 1918.
The Complete Poems of Francis Ledwidge, 1919.

Biographical and Critical:

Drinkwater, John. "Francis Ledwidge," *The Muse in Council . . .*, 1925. Pp. 289-303.
Tynan, Katherine. "Francis Ledwidge," *The Years of the Shadow*, 1919. Pp. 288-298.
Zucker, Louis C. "The Art of a Minor Poet," *South Atlantic Quarterly*, XXI (July, 1922), 259-269.

Ledwidge's poetic being was formed in Meath, the region of Ireland in which he was raised. His pre-war poetry, full of the flora and fauna of the land, drew Lord Dunsany's encouragement. During World War I, no other poet was as full of home-thoughts from abroad. All he experienced in Flanders was thrown against the background of the pastoral, lost world of childhood ("In France"). Occasionally Ledwidge approached the sensuous lyricism of Keats, as in "Before the Tears."

LEE, VERNON. *see* PAGET, VIOLET.

LEE-HAMILTON, EUGENE (1845-1907)

Poems:

Poems & Transcripts, 1878.
Gods, Saints and Men, 1880.
The New Medusa, 1882.
Apollo and Marsyas, 1884.
Imaginary Sonnets, 1888.
The Fountain of Youth, 1891.
Sonnets of the Wingless Hours, 1894.
Dramatic Sonnets, Poems and Ballads, 1903.
Mimma Bella, 1908.

Fiction:

The Lord of the Dark Red Star, 1903.
The Romance of the Fountain, 1905.

Biographical and Critical:

Lyon, Harvey T. "When Paris Was in Flames," *Colby Library Quarterly,* IV (November, 1955), 73-78.
— "A Publishing History of the Writings of Eugene Lee-Hamilton," *Papers of the Bibliographical Society of America,* LI (Second Quarter, 1957), 141-159.
MacBeth, George. "Lee-Hamilton and the Romantic Agony," *Critical Quarterly,* IV (Summer, 1962), 141-150.
Pantazzi, Sybille. "Eugene Lee-Hamilton," *Papers of the Bibliographical Society of America,* LVII (First Quarter, 1963), 92-94.

Eugene Lee-Hamilton

Lee-Hamilton's best poems were composed during a mysterious 20-year illness that kept him bedridden. Unlike Henley's hospital verse, Lee-Hamilton's is neither realistic nor autobiographical. He created fantasies, based on historical or imaginary subjects, tinged with the horror of his life. His thwarted, violent desires and suffering often found expression in poems like "Sister Mary of the Plague." His favorite form was the sonnet, sometimes a vehicle for the confessions of others, sometimes for his own personal experiences, as in the sequence "A Wheeled Bed." His concept of life as an agony to which man must submit was the mainspring of darkly powerful poems.

LE GALLIENNE, RICHARD (1866-1947)

Prose:

George Meredith: Some Characteristics, 1890.
Prose Fancies, 1894.
Retrospective Reviews .... 2 vols., 1896.
Rudyard Kipling: A Criticism, 1900.
Attitudes and Avowals ..., 1910.
The Romantic '90s, 1925.
And other titles.

Poems:

Volumes in Folio, 1889.
English Poems, 1892.
New Poems, 1910.
And other titles.

Fiction:

The Quest of the Golden Girl, 1896.
And other titles.

Richard Le Gallienne

Bibliographical:

Lingel, R. J. C. *A Bibliographical Checklist of the Writings of Richard Le Gallienne,* 1926.

Biographical and Critical:

Whittington-Egan, Richard, and Geoffrey Smerdon. *The Quest of the Golden Boy: The Life and Letters of Richard Le Gallienne,* 1960. [Bib. pp. 553-561.]

Le Gallienne attenuated his creative talent by writing too much. His verse was overrated; its amorphous sweetness, which pleased readers of the 1890's, has lost all appeal. Le Gallienne's *Retrospective Reviews* have some interest as comment on the contemporary literary scene. His greatest achievement is, probably, his work as editorial reader for John Lane, a position which enabled him to place in print the works of many of his literary friends.

LINDESAY, ETHEL FLORENCE. *see* RICHARDSON, HENRY HANDEL.

LORD DUNSANY. *see* PLUNKETT, EDWARD J. M. D., LORD DUNSANY.

LUCAS, EDWARD VERRALL (1868-1938)

Prose and Autobiography:

Highways and Byways in Sussex, 1904.
The Life of Charles Lamb, 1905.
Old Lamps for New, 1911.
What a Life! An Autobiography by E. V. L. and G. M., 1911.

A Wanderer in Florence, 1912.
Cloud and Silver, 1916.
Adventures and Enthusiasms, 1920.
Reading, Writing and Remembering, 1932.
English Leaves, 1933.
And other titles.

Poems:

Sparks from Flint, 1891.
Songs of the Bat, 1892.
All the World Over, 1898.
And other titles.

Fiction:

Listener's Lure, 1906.
Over Bemerton's, 1908.
London Lavender, 1912.

Biographical and Critical:

Lucas, Audrey. *E. V. Lucas: A Portrait,* 1939.

Lucas shared his quiet enthusiasm for art, foreign lands and the English countryside in his essays. Not a man of profound learning in any academic area, he wrote as a journalist, relating his travels and observations to a select circle of readers. Essayist and *bon vivant,* Lucas idolized Charles Lamb, to whom he paid gracious tribute in a biography and by collecting Lamb's works and letters.

LUSKA, SIDNEY. *see* HARLAND, HENRY.

MACAULAY, ROSE (1889-1958)

Fiction:

Abbots Verney, 1906.
The Furnace, 1907.
The Secret River, 1909.
The Valley Captives, 1911.
Views and Vagabonds, 1912.
What Not, 1918.
Potterism, 1920.
Dangerous Ages, 1921.
Told by an Idiot, 1923.
And other titles.

Letters:

Letters to a Friend, 1950-1952. Ed. Constance Babington-Smith. 1961.
Last Letters to a Friend, 1952-1958. Ed. Constance Babington-Smith. 1963.

Biographical and Critical:

Bensen, Alice R. "The Skeptical Balance: A Study of . . . 'Going Abroad,'" *Papers of the Michigan Academy of Science, Arts and Letters,* XLVIII (1963), 675-683.
Irwin, W. R. "Permanence and Change in *The Edwardians* and *Told by an Idiot,*" *Modern Fiction Studies,* II (May, 1956), 63-67.
Lockwood, William J. "Rose Macaulay," *Minor British Novelists.* Ed. Charles A. Hoyt. 1967. Pp. 135-156.
Swinnerton, Frank R. "Rose Macaulay," *Kenyon Review,* XXIX (November, 1967), 591-608.

Macaulay's abiding concern was life in the post World War I era. Her manner, which placed wit before compassion and satire before understanding, makes her seem shallow, if not simply heartless. Her early books are probably her best: *Potterism* is still effective satire and *Views and Vagabonds* is an interesting mingling of her comic and tragic, satiric and compassionate instincts.

MACHEN, ARTHUR (1863-1947)

Fiction:

The Great God Pan, 1894.
The Three Impostors, 1895.
The House of Souls, 1906.
The Hill of Dreams, 1907.
The Angels of Mons: The Bowmen..., 1915. [Created myth of Angels of Mons during World War I.]
And other titles.

Prose:

Hieroglyphics, 1902.
Dog and Duck, 1924.
And other titles.

Collected Works:

Works. "Carleon Edition." 9 vols., 1923.

Autobiography:

Far Off Things, 1922.
Things Near and Far, 1923.
The London Adventure, 1924.

Bibliographical:

Danielson, Henry. *Arthur Machen: A Bibliography,* 1923. [Brief comments by Machen between bib. entries.]
Goldstone, Adrian, and Wesley Sweetser. *A Bibliography of Arthur Machen,* 1965.
Sweetser, Wesley D. "Arthur Machen: A Bibliography of Writings About Him," *English Literature in Transition,* XI: 1 (1968), 1-33.

Biographical and Critical:

Gekle, William Francis. *Arthur Machen: Weaver of Fantasy.* 1949.

Reynolds, Aidan, and William Charlton. *Arthur Machen: A Short Account of His Life and Work,* 1963.
Sewell, Brocard (ed.). *Arthur Machen,* 1960.
Sweetser, Wesley D. *Arthur Machen,* 1964.

Though Machen published work in nearly every genre except drama, he is noted especially for stories of supernatural horror. His characters often experience the literal disintegration of both soul and body after the use of strange drugs or encounters with primordial creatures such as Pan or baleful Little People. His imperfect *Hill of Dreams* is interesting as a tragic maturation novel and as an early attempt at stream-of-consciousness technique.

MACKAY, MARY [MARIE CORELLI] (1855-1924)

Fiction:

A Romance of Two Worlds, 1886.
Barabbas, 1893.
The Sorrows of Satan, 1895.
The Young Diana, 1918.
The Secret Power, 1921.
And other titles.

Poems:

Poems. Ed. B. Vyver. 1925.
And other titles.

Biographical and Critical:

Bell, R. S. W., and T. F. G. Coates. *Marie Corelli: The Writer and the Woman,* 1903.
Bigland, Eileen. *Marie Corelli: The Woman and the Legend,* 1953.
Bullock, G. *Marie Corelli: The Life and Death of a Best-Seller,* 1940.
Carr, Kent. *Miss Marie Corelli,* 1901.

Scott, William Stuart. *Marie Corelli: The Story of a Friendship,* 1955.
Vyver, B. *Memoirs of Marie Corelli,* 1930.

Both as woman and author, Mackay was an earnest eccentric. Her novels are of great length and wide scope but evince little more than mild talent. Today *Sorrows of Satan,* which broke all previous sales records, will be read chiefly as an index of public literary taste. She saw herself as a quasi-divinity, gifted with insight so rare, and compositional ability so consummate, as to place her above her critics, who continued to attack her works as incredible and badly written.

MACKENZIE, EDWARD MONTAGUE COMPTON (1883-19)

Fiction:

The Passionate Elopement, 1911.
Carnival, 1913.
Sinister Street. 2 vols., 1913-1914.
Guy and Pauline, 1915.
Vestal Fire, 1927.
Extraordinary Women, 1928.
Our Street, 1931.
And other titles.

Prose:

Gallipoli Memories, 1929.
First Athenian Memories, 1931.
Greek Memories, 1939.
And other titles.

Autobiographical:

My Life and Times. 9 vols., 1963-197 . [9 vols. to date; 10 vols. projected.]

Edward Montague Compton Mackenzie

Biographical and Critical:

Fytton, Francis. "Compton Mackenzie: Romance versus Realism," *Catholic World,* CLXXXII (February, 1956), 358-363.
Robertson, Leo. *Compton Mackenzie,* 1954.

Mackenzie's early works bore high promise, especially *Sinister Street,* a memorable picture of Oxford life and a conversion to Catholicism. But after his own conversion in 1914, his work failed to progress. His handicaps were his multiplicity of interests, traces of fanaticism toward government and religion and a desire to please a widely diversified reading public too much of the time.

MACLAREN, IAN. *see* WATSON, JOHN.

MACLEOD, FIONA. *see* SHARP, WILLIAM.

MALLOCK, WILLIAM HURRELL (1849-1923)

Fiction:

The New Republic, 1877.
The New Paul and Virginia..., 1878.
The Old Order Changes, 1886.
A Human Document, 1892.
The Individualist, 1899.
An Immortal Soul, 1908.

Prose:

Social Equality, 1882.
Atheism and the Value of Life, 1884.
Aristocracy and Evolution, 1898.
A Critical Evaluation of Socialism, 1907.

William Hurrell Mallock

Autobiography:

Memoirs of Life and Literature, 1920.

Bibliographical:

Nickerson, Charles C. "A Bibliography of the Novels of W. H. Mallock," *English Literature in Transition,* VI: 4 (1963), 190-198.

Biographical and Critical:

Adams, A. B. *The Novels of W. H. Mallock,* 1934.
Nickerson, Charles C. "The Novels of W. H. Mallock: Notes Towards a Bibliography," *English Literature in Transition,* VI: 4 (1963), 182-189.
— "W. H. Mallock's Contribution to 'The Miscellany,'" *Victorian Studies,* VI (December, 1962), 169-177.
Tucker, A. V. "W. H. Mallock and Late Victorian Conservatism," *University of Toronto Quarterly,* XXI (January, 1962), 223-241.

Mallock had a quick mind best suited to light satire and unpretentious fiction. *New Paul* was his most amusing novel, and *The Old Order Changes* was his most popular. *The New Republic,* an attack on certain eminent Victorians, showed Mallock's dissatisfaction with the Victorian point of view. His serious religious, sociological and political work, now totally forgotten, resulted from his commitment to certain theories of property rights and the distribution of wealth.

MANSFIELD, KATHERINE. *see* MURRAY, KATHLEEN BEAUCHAMP.

MARTIN, VIOLET FLORENCE [MARTIN ROSS] (1862-1915)

Fiction [All with Edith Oenone Somerville]:

Naboth's Vineyard, 1891.
The Real Charlotte, 1894.
The Silver Fox, 1897.
Some Experiences of an Irish R. M., 1899.
And other titles.

Prose [All with Edith Oenone Somerville]:

All on the Irish Shore, 1903.
Some Irish Yesterdays, 1906.
Irish Memories, 1918.
Stray-Aways, 1920.

Bibliographical:

Hudson, Elizabeth. *A Bibliography of the First Editions of the Works of E. OE. Somerville and Martin Ross,* 1942.
Vaughan, Robert. *The First Editions of Edith Oenone Somerville and Violet Florence Martin,* 1952.

Biographical and Critical:

Powell, Violet. *The Irish Cousins: The Books and Background of Somerville and Ross,* 1970.
Watson, Cresap S. "Realism, Determinism and Symmetry in *The Real Charlotte,*" *Hermathena,* LXXXIV (November, 1954), 26-44.

The lives and work of Martin and her collaborator-cousin Edith Oenone Somerville seem anachronistic since they lived in and wrote of Ireland without displaying awareness of their country's struggle. Perhaps for that reason, however, their works have importance in revealing a passing way of Irish life, that of "the English garrison." *The Real Charlotte,* their finest novel, is one of the better collaborative novels of the period, and *Some Experiences* is certainly one of the funniest.

MARTYN, EDWARD (1859-1923)

Plays:

The Heather Field, 1899.
Maeve, 1900.
An Enchanted Sea, 1902.
The Tale of a Town, 1905.
Grangecolman, 1912.
The Dream Physician, 1914.
And other titles.

Biographical and Critical:

Boyd, Ernest A. "Edward Martyn," *Contemporary Drama of Ireland,* 1917. Pp. 12-32.
Courtney, Marie-Thérèse (Sister). *Edward Martyn and the Irish Theatre,* 1957. [Bib. pp. 172-187.]
Gwynn, Denis. *Edward Martyn and the Irish Literary Revival,* 1930.
Ryan, Stephan P. "James Joyce and Edward Martyn," *Xavier University Studies,* I (December, 1962), 200-205.
Setterquist, Jan. *Ibsen and the Beginnings of Anglo-Irish Drama: II Edward Martyn,* 1960.

Martyn was one of the first Celtic Renaissance playwrights to show Ibsen's influence, manifested in the use of symbolism (as in *The Heather Field*) and demon-haunted characters (as in *Maeve*). However, though Martyn's first plays were important contributions to the Irish theater movement, his comparative ignorance of stagecraft and a lack of discipline kept him from fulfilling his early promise.

MASON, ALFRED EDWARD WOODLEY (1865-1948)

Fiction:

The Courtship of Morrice Buckler, 1896.
Clementina, 1901.
The Four Feathers, 1902.

Alfred Edward Woodley Mason

At the Villa Rose, 1910.
The Witness for the Defence, 1913.
The Winding Stair, 1923.
The House of the Arrow, 1924.
And other titles.

Mason's creative life falls in two periods: from 1895 to 1901, he wrote romances; after 1901, he turned to novels of contemporary life and detective fiction. The impulse to stimulate his audiences with mystery and adventure was of equal importance in both. A few of his high adventure novels are still read (notably *The Four Feathers*). As writer of detective diversions, Mason will probably be remembered for *The House of the Arrow*, which features the police detective M. Hanaud.

MAUGHAM, WILLIAM SOMERSET (1874-1966)

Fiction:

Liza of Lambeth, 1897.
The Making of a Saint, 1898.
Orientations, 1899.
The Hero, 1901.
The Merry-Go-Round, 1904.
The Explorer, 1907.
Of Human Bondage, 1915.
The Moon and Sixpence, 1919.
The Trembling of a Leaf, 1921.
The Painted Veil, 1925.
Ashenden; or, The British Agent, 1928.
Cakes and Ale: or, The Skeleton in the Cupboard, 1930.
The Mixture as Before, 1940.
And other titles.

Plays:

A Man of Honor, 1903.
Jack Straw, 1908.
Smith, 1909.

The Tenth Man, 1910.
Landed Gentry, 1910.
Home and Beauty, 1919.
Caesar's Wife, 1919.
The Circle, 1921.
The Collected Plays of W. S. Maugham. 3 vols., 1952.
And other titles.

Autobiography:

The Summing Up, 1938.
Strictly Personal, 1941.
A Writer's Notebook, 1949.

Bibliographical:

Bason, F. *A Bibliography of the Writings of William Somerset Maugham,* 1931.
Jonas, Klaus W. *A Bibliography of the Writings of W. Somerset Maugham,* 1950. [Derivative; based, according to Stott, on *Maughamiana* and other bibs.]
Sanders, Charles (ed.). *W. Somerset Maugham: An Annotated Bibliography of Writings About Him,* 1970.
— "W. Somerset Maugham: A Supplementary Bibliography," *English Literature in Transition.* XV: 2 (1972), 168-173.
Stott, Raymond Toole. *Maughamiana: A Handlist of Works by W. S. Maugham,* 1950.
— *The Writings of William Somerset Maugham: A Bibliography,* 1956; supplement, 1961. [The definitive bib.]

Biographical and Critical:

Brander, Laurence. *Somerset Maugham, A Guide,* 1963. [Bib. pp. 215-218.]
Brophy, John. *Somerset Maugham,* 1952.
Cordell, Richard A. *W. Somerset Maugham,* 1937.
— *Somerset Maugham: A Biographical and Critical Study,* 1961.
Jensen, Sven A. *William Somerset Maugham: Some Aspects of the Man and His Work,* 1957.
Jonas, Klaus W. *The Gentleman from Cap Ferrat,* 1956.
Kanin, Garson. *Remembering Mr. Maugham,* 1966.

McCarthy, Desmond. *William Somerset Maugham: 'The English Maupassant,'* 1934.
McIver, Claude S. *William Somerset Maugham: A Study of Technique and Literary Sources,* 1936.
Maugham, Robin. *Somerset and All the Maughams,* 1966.
Nichols, Beverly. *A Case of Human Bondage,* 1966.
Pfeiffer, Karl G. *W. Somerset Maugham: A Candid Portrait,* 1959.
Ward, R. H. *William Somerset Maugham,* 1937.

Probably no other author of the period had such wide appeal to large segments of both the intellectual and popular reading audiences as Maugham. Reasons for this popularity include his versatility as author of fiction, plays and autobiographical essays; his conspicuous internationalism (his fiction is set in England, America, the Far East, the Riviera); and his willingness to feed his heterogeneous audience the kind of creative fare it had accepted so willingly in the past. In his fiction, detachment, which may be traced to his early medical experience, often gives rise to cold, inquisitive, objective dissections of man and society, with little sympathy for the fallen or joy for the triumphant. In his best-known novel, *Of Human Bondage,* Maugham describes Phillip's loss of faith but passes no judgment against religion or the church, as Samuel Butler might have done. Similarly, in "Rain," Maugham uses the tale of a missionary's fall from virtue solely as a case history. Authorial sympathy does, however, lend warmth to some of his work, like *Cakes and Ale*. As playwright, Maugham thought himself a writer of comedies, yet his situations are often simply farcical. He was also a gifted autobiographer, as *The Summing Up* testifies.

MERRICK, LEONARD. *see* MILLER, LEONARD.

MEYNELL, ALICE CHRISTIANA GERTRUDE THOMPSON (1847-1922)

Poems:

Preludes, 1875.
Poems, 1893.
Later Poems, 1902.
Poems on the War, 1915.
The Last Poems of Alice Meynell, 1923.
And other titles.

Prose:

The Life and Work of Holman Hunt, 1893.
London Impressions, 1898.
John Ruskin, 1899.
And other titles.

Bibliographical:

Stonehill, Charles A., and Helen W. Stonehill. *Bibliographies of Modern Authors*, 1925. Pp. 79-125.

Biographical and Critical:

Chesterson, Gilbert K. "Alice Meynell," *Dublin Review*, CCXX (Autumn, 1947), 3-12.
Meynell, Viola. *Alice Meynell: A Memoir*, 1929.
Tuell, Anne K. *Mrs. Meynell and Her Literary Generation*, 1925.

Meynell was at the center of Roman Catholic literary life of the period. Although her poetic output was small—due to her unusual reticence and demand for perfection—some of her religious poems, like "Meditation," may last. She wrote effectively in the sonnet form, as "I Touched the Heart that Loved Me" shows.

MILLER, LEONARD [LEONARD MERRICK] (1864-1939)

Fiction:

Mr. Bazalgette's Agent, 1888.
Violet Moses, 1891.
This Stage of Fools, 1896.
The Actor-Manager, 1898.
The Worldlings, 1900.
To Tell You the Truth, 1922.
The Works of Leonard Merrick. 14 vols., 1918-1922.
[Intros. by M. Hewlett, W. D. Howells, N. Munro, H. G. Wells *et al.*]
And other titles.

Despite the admiration of contemporary writers, Miller was never popular with the public. His fiction lacks either the sincere confrontation of serious matters that would have earned him critical acclaim, or wholehearted abandon to one of the popular modes. Serious concerns exist in his fiction but they are veiled by comedy, and his humor is somewhat mitigated by pathos and tragedy. He was chiefly a minor entertainer for a select group of other writers.

MONKHOUSE, ALLAN NOBLE (1858-1936)

Plays:

Reaping the Whirlwind, 1908.
Mary Broome, 1911.
Resentment, 1912.
The Education of Mr. Surrage, 1912.
The Conquering Hero, 1924.
The Hayling Family, 1924.
Sons and Fathers, 1926.
And other titles.

Allan Noble Monkhouse

Fiction:

Love in a Life, 1903.
Dying Fires, 1912.
Men and Ghosts, 1918.
My Daughter Helen, 1922.
And other titles.

Prose:

Books and Plays, 1894.

Biographical and Critical:

Garnett, Edward. "The Work of Allan Monkhouse," *Adelphi*, I (May, 1924), 1092-1101.
Pratt, Tinsley. "The Manchester Dramatists," *Papers of the Manchester Literary Club*, XL (July, 1914), 213-229.
Sutton, Graham. "The Plays of Allan Monkhouse," *Fortnightly Review*, CXVI (October, 1924), 547-557.

Monkhouse wrote plays for the Gaiety Theatre, Manchester, which sometimes follow Ibsen in making past errors the cause of present revelation, as in *The Hayling Family*. His forte was comedy, as in *The Education of Mr. Surrage*, where the conflict-between-generations theme is handled cleverly. Echoes of such writers as Shaw and Meredith in Monkhouse's novels and plays suggest a bookish, insufficiently original mind.

MONTAGUE, CHARLES EDWARD (1867-1928)

Fiction:

The Morning's War, 1913.
Fiery Particles, 1923.
Rough Justice, 1926.
And other titles.

Charles Edward Montague

Prose:

Dramatic Values, 1911.
Disenchantment, 1922.
The Right Place, 1924.
A Writer's Notes on His Trade, 1930.

Biographical and Critical:

Elton, Oliver. *C. E. Montague: A Memoir,* 1929.
Irwin, W. R. "Experiment in Irony: Montague's 'A Hind Let Loose,'" *Modern Fiction Studies,* III (Summer, 1957), 141-146.
Priestley, J. B. "C. E. Montague," *London Mercury,* XVIII (August, 1928), 381-390.
Sastri, C. L. R. "C. E. Montague," *Calcutta Review,* XLVIII (August, 1933), 193-209.
Ward, A. C. "C. E. Montague: 'Fiery Particles,'" *Aspects of the Modern Short Story,* 1924. Pp. 255-267.

Montague's relatively slight reputation rests about equally on his essays and his fiction. In the former, he revealed a considerable critical faculty (especially in *Dramatic Values*) and a deep involvement in World War I. The war also contributed to his fiction and figures importantly in *Fiery Particles,* his best volume of stories. Apparently, his was a clear, bright intellect best suited to shorter forms, for despite his lean, accurate style and his creative prowess, his novels suffer from serious structural flaws.

MOORE, GEORGE (1852-1933)

Fiction:

A Modern Lover, 1883.
A Mummer's Wife, 1885.
A Drama in Muslin, 1886.
Mike Fletcher, 1889.
Esther Waters, 1894.

Evelyn Innes, 1898.
Sister Teresa, 1901.
The Untilled Field, 1903.
The Lake, 1905.
The Brook Kerith, 1916.
Héloïse and Abélard, 1921.
And other titles.

Poems:

Flowers of Passion, 1878.
Pagan Poems, 1881.

Plays:

The Strike at Arlingford, 1893.
The Bending of the Bough [with Edward Martyn], *1900.*
Elizabeth Cooper, 1913. [Rvd. as *The Coming of Gabrielle, 1923.*]

Prose:

Literature at Nurse, or Circulating Morals, 1885.
Impressions and Opinions, 1891.
Modern Painting, 1893.
Avowals, 1919.
Conversations in Ebury Street, 1924.
And other titles.

Autobiography and Letters:

Confessions of a Young Man, 1888.
Memoirs of My Dead Life, 1906.
Hail and Farewell, I *Ave*, 1911; II *Salve*, 1912; III *Vale*, 1914.
Letters from George Moore to Édouard Dujardin 1886-1922. Trans. John Eglinton. 1929.
Letters of George Moore, 1942. [To John Eglinton.]
Letters to Lady Cunard 1895-1933. Ed. Rupert Hart-Davis. 1957.
George Moore in Transition: Letters to T. Fisher Unwin and Lena Milman, 1894-1910. Ed. Helmut Gerber. 1968.

George Moore

Collected Works:

Works. "Carra Edition." 21 vols., 1922-1924.
Works. "Uniform Edition." 20 vols., 1924-1933.
Works. "Ebury Edition." 20 vols., 1936-1938.

Bibliographical:

Gerber, Helmut. "George Moore: An Annotated Bibliography of Writings About Him," *English Fiction in Transition,* II: 2 (1959), 3-91; "Supplement," *Ibid.,* III: 2 (1960), 34-46; "Supplement II," *Ibid.,* IV: 2 (1961), 30-42.
Gilcher, Edwin. *A Bibliography of George Moore,* 1970.
Williams, I. A. *George Moore,* 1921.

Biographical and Critical:

Brown, Malcolm. *George Moore: A Reconsideration,* 1955.
Collett, Georges Paul. *George Moore et la France,* 1957.
Cunard, Nancy. *GM: Memories of George Moore,* 1956.
Ferguson, Walter D. *The Influence of Flaubert on George Moore,* 1934.
Freeman, John. *A Portrait of George Moore in a Study of His Work,* 1922. [Bib. pp. 235-278.]
Goodwin, Geraint. *Conversations with George Moore,* 1929.
Hone, Joseph. *The Life of George Moore,* 1936.
Hughes, Douglas A. (ed.). *The Man of Wax: Critical Essays on George Moore,* 1971.
Noël, Jean C. *George Moore: l'homme et l'oeuvre,* 1966.
Owens, Graham (ed.). *George Moore's Mind and Art,* 1968.
Wolfe, Humbert. *George Moore,* 1931.

Moore was, as he said himself, as receptive to impressions as a sheet of wax. He lived for extended periods in England, France and his native Ireland and each place shaped what he wrote. *Flowers of Passion* and *Confessions of a Young Man* document the impact such nineteenth-century French writers as Balzac, Zola and Flaubert made on Moore while he was studying art in Paris. From 1880 to 1901, he lived in England and wrote his best fiction, which blends a realist's concern for the life of the lower class with shocking frankness of presentation (as in *A Mummer's Wife* and *Esther Waters,* his masterpiece). During his decade as a major light in the Celtic Renaissance, he wrote fiction (*The Untilled Field*) and plays (*The Bending of the Bough*) which are faithful reflections of Irish life as Moore saw it. These years also provided Moore material for his finest non-fictional work, *Hail and Farewell.* Later, he turned to biblical and other exotic subject matter in *The Brook Kerith* and *Héloïse and Abélard.* His work has been called a series of experiments, but this designation obscures the perfection he demanded regarding form and style. Rather, each work was an end in itself, a culmination of certain tendencies and desires.

MOORE, THOMAS STURGE (1870-1944)

Poems:

The Vinedresser, 1899.
The Centaur's Booty, 1903.
Danaë, 1903.
The Gazelles, 1904.
A Sicillian Idyll, and Judith, 1911.
Judas, 1923.
The Poems of T. Sturge Moore. 4 vols., 1931-1933.
And other titles.

Plays:

Aphrodite Against Artemis, 1901.
Absalom, 1903.
Mariamne, 1911.
Tragic Mothers, 1920.
The Powers of the Air, 1920.
And other titles.

Prose:

Correggio, 1906.
Art and Life, 1910.

Thomas Sturge Moore

Armour for Aphrodite, 1929.
And other titles.

Letters:

Yeats & Moore. W. B. Yeats and T. Sturge Moore: Their Correspondence, 1901-1937. Ed. Ursula Bridge. 1953.

Biographical and Critical:

Bickley, Francis. "The Poetry of T. Sturge Moore," *To-Day,* III (March, 1918), 10-15.
Gwynn, Frederick L. *Sturge Moore and the Life of Art,* 1952. [Bib. pp. 123-135.]
Jones, Llewellyn. "T. Sturge Moore: Poet and Critic," *American Review,* I (September-October, 1923), 540-549.
McDowall, Arthur. "The Poetry of Mr. Sturge Moore," *London Mercury,* V (April, 1922), 607-616.
Winters, Yvor. "The Poetry of T. Sturge Moore," *Southern Review,* II (Winter, 1966), 1-16.

Moore was a poet's poet and a descendant of the art for art's sake movement. A sincere, dedicated craftsman with definite aims, he wished to purify poetic diction. He had a predilection for mythological subjects (as in *Danaë*). But despite the admiration of Yeats and other poets, Moore remained virtually unknown to the public. His work was probably too abstract and dealt with situations and beings too remote from present life to engage wide interest.

MORRISON, ARTHUR (1863-1945)

Fiction:

Martin Hewitt: Investigator, 1894.
Tales of Mean Streets, 1894.
Adventures of Martin Hewitt, 1896.
A Child of the Jago, 1896.
To London Town, 1899.

The Hole in the Wall, 1902.
Green Ginger, 1909.
And other titles.

Biographical and Critical:

Bell, Jocelyn. "A Study of Arthur Morrison," *Essays and Studies,* V (1952), 77-89.
Pritchett, V. S. "An East End Novelist," *The Living Novel,* 1946. Pp. 152-158.

As serious novelist of London slum life (e.g. *Hole in the Wall*), Morrison may be compared with Gissing. He was the first to portray slum life as it really was. When he wrote detective fiction, he created a most ordinary sleuth, thereby breaking with the tradition of the detective-as-eccentric.

MUNRO, HECTOR HUGH [SAKI] (1870-1916)

Fiction:

Reginald, 1904.
Reginald in Russia, 1910.
The Chronicles of Clovis, 1912.
Beasts and Super-Beasts, 1914.
The Toys of Peace, 1919.
The Square Egg, 1924.
And other titles.

Bibliographical:

Drake, Robert. "Saki: Some Problems and a Bibliography," *English Fiction in Transition,* V: 1 (1962), 6-26. [Annotated bib. of wk. about.]

Biographical and Critical:

Drake, Robert. "The Sauce for the Asparagus: A Reappraisal of Saki," *Saturday Book,* XX (1960), 61-73.

Gillen, Charles H. *H. H. Munro (Saki)*, 1969. [Bib. pp. 171-175.]
Lambert, J. W. "Introduction," *The Bodley Head Saki*, 1963. Pp. 7-62.
Munro, Ethel M. "Biography of Saki," *The Square Egg*, 1924. Pp. 3-120. [Chief bio. source.]
Spears, George James. *The Satire of Saki: A Study of the Satiric Art of Hector H. Munro*, 1963. [Bib. pp. 123-127, though adds items not listed in Drake, is careless with names, dates, magazine titles, and ignores most of the wks. listed by Drake; no index; use with caution.]

Munro's short stories and novels, which at first appear to deal only with practical jokes, cruelty or supernatural animals, are crystal-hard sketches of hypocritical Edwardian society. His story tellers are young and cynical, with a mannered arrogance that delights in the discomfiture of human beings; his children, who delight in murder and sadism, often appear less bestial than adults surrounding them; his animals ironically often overcome human law and order. His brilliant, bitter epigrams easily rival Wilde's.

MUNRO, NEIL (1864-1930)

Fiction:

The Lost Pibroch, and Other Sheiling Stories, 1896.
John Splendid..., 1898.
Gilian the Dreamer, 1899.
Children of Tempest: A Tale of the Outer Isles, 1903.
The Vital Spark and Her Queer Crew, 1906.
The Daft Days, 1907.
Ayreshire Idylls, 1912.
Jaunty Jock, 1918.
And other titles.

Prose:

Hungry Ireland, 1898.

Neil Munro

The Clyde River and Firth, 1907.
And other titles.

Collected Works:

The Works of Neil Munro. 9 vols., 1935.

Biographical and Critical:

Keith, C. "Neil Munro, The Savage from Inverary," *Queens Quarterly,* LVI (Summer, 1949), 203-213.

Munro was the leading Scots novelist of his era. He gained wide popularity with his early novels (e.g. *Gilian the Dreamer),* which were unashamedly romantic portrayals of Scottish characters and scenes. When, after 1903, he turned to gentle realism, his audience decreased as the grimmer realism of George Douglas and others put Scottish pastorals out of fashion.

MURRAY, THOMAS C. (1873-1959)

Plays:

Birthright, 1910.
Maurice Harte, 1912.
Spring, 1918.
Aftermath, 1922.
Autumn Fire, 1924.
The Pipe in the Fields, 1927.
And other titles.

Biographical and Critical:

Conlin, Matthew. "T. C. Murray: Ireland on the Stage," *Renascence,* XIII (Spring, 1961), 125-131.
— "The Tragic Effect in *Autumn Fire* and *Desire Under the Elms,*" *Modern Drama,* I (February, 1959), 228-235.
Óh-Aodha, Michéal. "T. C. Murray and Some Critics," *Studies: An Irish Quarterly Review,* XLVII (Summer, 1958), 185-191.

Thomas C. Murray

Murray, a minor Irish dramatist, is credited with furthering the drift toward realism in the Abbey Theatre with *Birthright,* a version of the Cain-Abel story. *Autumn Fire,* possibly his best play, is a tragedy of quiet despair. He had the ability to create real characters who spoke authentically, but he relied heavily on chance and coincidence in his plotting.

MURRY, KATHLEEN BEAUCHAMP [KATHERINE MANSFIELD] (1888-1923)

Fiction:

In a German Pension, 1911.
Prelude, 1920.
Bliss, 1920.
The Garden Party, 1922.
The Dove's Nest, 1923.
Something Childish and Other Stories, 1924.
And other titles.

Journals and Letters:

Journal of Katherine Mansfield. Ed. J. Middleton Murry. 1927.
The Letters of Katherine Mansfield. Ed. J. Middleton Murry. 2 vols., 1928.
The Scrapbook of Katherine Mansfield. Ed. J. Middleton Murry. 1939.
Katherine Mansfield's Letters to John Middleton Murry 1913-1922. Ed. J. Middleton Murry. 1951.

Bibliographical:

Mantz, Ruth E. *The Critical Bibliography of Katherine Mansfield.* 1931. [Some corrections by Berkman.]

Biographical and Critical:

Alpers, Antony. *Katherine Mansfield,* 1954. [Bib. pp.

367-376; definitive bio.]
Berkman, Sylvia. *Katherine Mansfield: A Critical Study,* 1952. [Bib. pp. 231-236.]
Daly, Saralyn. *Katherine Mansfield,* 1965. [Bib. pp. 133-138; good short study.]
Friis, Anne. *Katherine Mansfield: Life and Stories,* 1946.
Gordon, Ian. *Katherine Mansfield,* 1954.
Mantz, Ruth Elvish, and John Middleton Murry. *The Life of Katherine Mansfield,* 1933.

Murry stands out as a great story teller among the many good ones of the era. Her early life in New Zealand was of major importance to her fiction, providing not only material for many stories in *Bliss* and *Garden Party,* but also forming her habits of close observation and introspection, two striking aspects of her mind. Her work is perfectly undidactic. Typically, her stories deal with some pregnant moment of everyday life which leads to a Joycean epiphany (e.g. "Bliss"). By careful, seemingly intuitive selection of details, she created impressions of startling clarity. Chekhov was an important influence, but her genius transcended obligation to a particular writer or school.

NESBIT, EDITH. [E. NESBIT; MRS. HUBERT BLAND] (1858-1924)

Fiction [juvenile]:

The Story of the Treasure Seekers, 1899.
The Wouldbegoods, 1901.
Five Children and It, 1902.
The Phoenix and the Carpet, 1904.
The Railway Children, 1906.
The Story of the Amulet, 1906.
The Enchanted Castle, 1907.
And other titles.

Edith Nesbit

Poems:

Lays and Legends. 2 ser., 1886, 1892.
Leaves of Life, 1888.
The Rainbow and the Rose, 1905.
Ballads and Verses of the Spiritual Life, 1911.
And other titles.

Autobiography:

Long Ago When I Was Young. Ed. Noel Streatfeild, 1966.

Biographical and Critical:

Moore, Doris Langley. *E. Nesbit: A Biography,* 1933; rvd. ed., 1966.
Streatfeild, Noel. *Magic and the Magician: E. Nesbit and Her Children's Books,* 1958. [Bib. of juvenile wks. pp. 157-160.]

Though Nesbit wrote many adult novels and several volumes of verse, she is remembered only for her children's stories and fairy tales. Realistically and good naturedly, she described the innocent, yet mischievous adventures of happy children (*Treasure Seekers, Wouldbegoods*). Sometimes she added magic, as in *Five Children and It* and *The Story of the Amulet,* which blend fantasy and the everyday world.

NEWBOLT, HENRY JOHN (1862-1938)

Poems:

Admirals All, 1897.
The Island Race, 1898.
The Sailing of the Long-Ships, 1902.
Songs of Memory and Hope, 1909.
Collected Poems, 1897-1907, 1910.
Drake's Drum, and Other Songs of the Sea, 1914.
St. George's Day, 1918.
And other titles.

Henry John Newbolt

Fiction:

The Old Country, 1906.
The New June, 1909.
And other titles.

Autobiography:

My World As in My Time: Memoirs . . . 1862-1932, 1932.
The Later Life and Letters of Sir Henry Newbolt. Ed. Margaret Newbolt. 1942.

Biographical and Critical:

Betjeman, John. "Sir Henry Newbolt After a Hundred Years," *Listener,* LXVII (June 28, 1962), 1114-1115.
Kernahan, Coulson. "Henry Newbolt," *Six Famous Living Poets,* 1926. Pp. 97-110.

Newbolt, champion of imperialism and writer of verse on such action-filled doings of life as war and sports, is a lesser Kipling. He achieved immediate fame with *Admirals All* and *The Island Race,* both of which extolled England's role as law-giver and peacemaker of the world.

NOYES, ALFRED (1880-1958)

Poems:

The Loom of Years, 1902.
Forty Singing Seamen, 1907.
Drake: An English Epic. 2 vols., 1906-1908.
Tales of the Mermaid Tavern, 1913.
The Torchbearers, 1937.
Collected Poems, 1950.
And other titles.

Fiction:

The Hidden Player, 1924.

Alfred Noyes

The Sun Cure, 1929.
No Other Man, 1940.
And other titles.

Autobiography:

Two Worlds for Memory, 1953.

Bibliographical:

Tobin, James E. "Alfred Noyes: A Corrected Bibliography," *Catholic Library World,* XV (March, 1944), 181-184, 189.

Biographical and Critical:

Jerrold, Walter C. *Alfred Noyes,* 1930.
Stanford, Derek. "The Poetic Achievement of Alfred Noyes," *English,* XII (Autumn, 1958), 86-88.

Noyes achieved fame by his songs for the people—tuneful versifications of past heroism and adventure, like *Drake* and *Forty Singing Seamen.* Early in his career, he had considerable skill as narrator and versifier but rarely chose to employ it on serious subject matter. A major dividing line in his life was his conversion to Catholicism in 1925, after which his verse and prose were more earnest and overtly religious, as *The Torch-bearers,* an epic of the advance of science, shows. He wrote creditably in several genres but produced nothing distinguished.

OLIVER, GEORGE. *see* ONIONS, GEORGE OLIVER.

ONIONS, GEORGE OLIVER [OLIVER ONIONS; GEORGE OLIVER] (1873-1961)

Fiction:

The Compleat Bachelor, 1900.
Tales From a Far Riding, 1902.
Back o' the Moon, 1906.
Little Devil Doubt, 1909.
Good Boy Seldom, 1911.
The Debit Account, 1913.
The Tower of Oblivion, 1921.
Cut Flowers, 1927.
The Collected Ghost Stories of Oliver Onions, 1935.
And other titles.

Biographical and Critical:

Swinnerton, Frank Arthur. "The Younger Novelists," *The Georgian Scene,* 1934. Pp. 281-315.

Onions' early works—chats, tales and stories of various kinds—reveal his talent for writing gracious, if unoriginal entertainment *à la* J. M. Barrie or Anthony Hope. *Little Devil Doubt* and *Good Boy Seldom* are semi-autobiographical stories which reveal the author's major virtue and failing: sharp-sighted memory coupled with an inability to make his protagonists more than soulless shadows of himself. Both books show his indignation at the plight of the modern man whose aspirations outrun his capabilities.

ONIONS, OLIVER. *see* ONIONS, GEORGE OLIVER.

OWEN, WILFRED (1893-1918)

Poems:

Poems, 1920.

Wilfred Owen

The Poems of Wilfred Owen. Ed. Edmund Blunden. 1931.
The Collected Poems of Wilfred Owen. Ed. C. Day Lewis. 1963.

Letters:

Wilfred Owen: Collected Letters. Ed. William H. Owen and John Bell. 1967.

Bibliographical:

White, William. "Wilfred Owen (1893-1918): A Bibliography," *Serif,* II (December, 1965), 5-16.

Biographical and Critical:

Cohen, Joseph. "Wilfred Owen: Fresher Fields than Flanders," *English Literature in Transition,* VII: 1 (1964), 1-7.
— "Wilfred Owen's Greater Love," *Tulane Studies in English,* VI (1956), 105-117.
— "Wilfred Owen in America," *Prairie Schooner,* XXXI (Winter, 1957), 339-345.
Hazo, Samuel J. "The Passion of Wilfred Owen," *Renascence,* XI (Summer, 1959), 201-208.
Johnston, John H. "Poetry and Pity: Wilfred Owen," *English Poetry of the First World War,* 1964. Pp. 155-209.
Masson, David I. "Wilfred Owen's Free Phonetic Patterns: Their Style and Function," *Journal of Aesthetics and Art Criticism,* XIII (March, 1955), 360-369.
Owen, Harold. *Journey From Obscurity: Wilfred Owen, 1893-1918. Memoirs of the Owen Family,* 1963-1965 [I, "Childhood"; II, "Youth"; III, "War"].
Spear, Hilda D. "Wilfred Owen and Poetic Truth," *University of Kansas City Review,* XXV (Winter, 1958), 110-116.
Welland, Dennis S. R. *Wilfred Owen: A Critical Study,* 1960.

As man and poet, Owen became a legend almost at the moment of his death. The loss of so gifted and so young a poet in England's most devastating war seemed to symbolize warfare's tragic destruction of talent. Owen was the greatest of the "War Poets," and he avoided the often-indulged extremes of propaganda and sentimentality by using his poems to mirror the reality of war. As he said, he sought to warn mankind about war, but no such simple motive accounts for the power of poems like "Anthem for Doomed Youth" or "Dulce et Decorum Est." Considering the brevity of his life and the smallness of his poetic corpus, Owen has had unusual impact on twentieth-century poetry and the modern consciousness.

PAGET, VIOLET [VERNON LEE] (1856-1935)

Fiction:

Ottilie: An Eighteenth Century Idyl, 1883.
Miss Brown, 1884.
Hauntings: Fantastic Stories, 1890.
Penelope Brandling . . ., 1903.
Pope Jacynth and Other Fantastic Tales, 1904.
For Maurice: Five Unlikely Stories, 1927.
And other titles.

Prose:

Studies of the Eighteenth Century in Italy, 1880.
Belcaro: Being Essays on Sundry Aesthetical Questions, 1883.
Euphorion: Being Studies of the Antique and the Mediaeval in the Renaissance, 1884.
Juvenilia: Being a Second Series of Essays on Sundry Aesthetical Questions, 1887.
Limbo, and Other Essays, 1897.
Genius Loci: Notes on Places, 1899.
The Enchanted Woods, and Other Essays on the Genius of Places, 1905.
The Beautiful: An Introduction to Psychological Aesthetics, 1913.
The Handling of Words, and Other Studies in Literary Psychology, 1923.
And other titles.

Violet Paget

Bibliographical:

"An Interim Bibliography of Vernon Lee," *Colby Library Quarterly,* III (November, 1952), 123-127.

Biographical and Critical:

Brooks, Van Wyck. "Notes on Vernon Lee," *Forum,* XLV (April, 1911), 447-456.

Gunn, Peter. *Vernon Lee: Violet Paget, 1856-1935,* 1964. [Bib. pp. 233-234.]

Wellek, René. "Vernon Lee, Bernard Berenson and Aesthetics," *Friendship's Garland: Essays Presented to Mario Praz on His Seventieth Birthday.* Ed. Vittorio Gabrieli. 1966. II, 233-251.

Paget's best short stories are set in seventeenth and eighteenth-century Italy and use the grotesquely supernormal ("Prince Alberic and the Snake Lady") or the inhumanly cruel ("A Wedding Chest"). The supernatural in these stories deals as often with the psychology of evil, where good and bad war within an individual, as with the fantastically thrilling. Like Pater, Paget explored aesthetic theory in *The Beautiful, The Handling of Words* and other studies.

PAIN, BARRY ERIC ODELL (1864-1928)

Fiction:

In a Canadian Canoe, 1891.
Graeme and Cyril, 1893.
"Eliza," 1900.
Eliza's Husband, 1903.
Eliza Getting On, 1911.
Exit Eliza, 1912.
Mrs. Murphy, 1913.
Futurist Fifteen, 1914.
And other titles.

Barry Eric Odell Pain

Biographical and Critical:

Noyes, Alfred. "Barry Pain," *Bookman* (London), LXXIII (December, 1927), 166-167.

Decidedly a minor novelist, Pain is best remembered for the *Eliza* books—a series relating everyday doings of a bumbling middle-class clerk. Pain's novels abound in similar "characters" (like the charwoman in *Mrs. Murphy*). His works are chiefly comedies of manners.

PATER, WALTER HORATIO (1839-1894)

Prose:

Studies in the History of the Renaissance, 1873; rvd. eds., 1877, 1888.
Appreciations: With an Essay on Style, 1889.
Plato and Platonism, 1893.
Miscellaneous Studies. Ed. C. L. Shadwell. 1895.
Greek Studies. Ed. C. L. Shadwell. 1895.
And other titles.

Fiction:

Marius the Epicurean, 1885.
Imaginary Portraits, 1887.
The Child in the House: An Imaginary Portrait, 1894.
Gaston de Latour. Ed. C. L. Shadwell. 1896. [Unfinished.]

Letters:

Letters of Walter Pater. Ed. Lawrence Evans. 1970.

Bibliographical:

Stonehill, C. A., and H. W. Stonehill. "Walter Pater," *Bibliographies of Modern Authors.* 2nd. ser., 1925. Pp. 129-142.

Walter Horatio Pater

Biographical and Critical:

Bowra, C. M. "Walter Pater," *Sewanee Review,* LVII (Summer, 1949), 378-400.

Brzenk, Eugene J. "The Unique Fictional World of Walter Pater," *Nineteenth-Century Fiction,* XIII (December, 1958), 217-226.

Burgum, Edwin B. "Walter Pater and the Good Life," *Sewanee Review,* XL (July-September, 1932), 276-293.

Child, Ruth C. "Is Walter Pater an Impressionistic Critic?," *Publications of the Modern Language Association of America,* LIII (December, 1938), 1172-1185.

— *The Aesthetic of Walter Pater,* 1940.

Crinkley, Richmond. *Walter Pater: Humanist,* 1970.

DeLaura, David S. "Pater and Newman: The Road to the Nineties," *Victorian Studies,* X (September, 1966), 39-69.

d'Hangest, Germain. *Walter Pater: L'Homme et L'Oeuvre.* 2 vols., 1961. [Bib. II, 311-349.]

Downes, David A. *Victorian Portraits: Hopkins and Pater,* 1965.

Eaker, Jay G. *Walter Pater: A Study in Methods and Effects,* 1933.

Farmer, Albert J. *Walter Pater as a Critic of English Literature,* 1931.

Hafley, James. "Walter Pater's *Marius* and the Technique of Modern Fiction," *Modern Fiction Studies,* III (Summer, 1957), 99-109.

Johnson, R. V. *Walter Pater: A Study of His Critical Outlook and Achievement,* 1961.

Knoepflmacher, U. C. "Historicism as Fiction: Motion and Rest in the Stories of Walter Pater," *Modern Fiction Studies,* IX (Summer, 1963), 139-148.

Lenaghan, R. T. "Pattern in Walter Pater's Fiction," *Studies in Philology,* LVIII (January, 1961), 69-91.

McKenzie, Gordon. *The Literary Character of Walter Pater,* 1967.

Monsman, Gerald C. *Pater's Portraits: Mythic Pattern in the Fiction of Walter Pater,* 1967.

Rosenblatt, Louise M. "The Genesis of Pater's *Marius* . . . ," *Comparative Literature,* XIV (Summer, 1962), 242-260.

Vogeler, Martha Salmon. "The Religious Meaning of *Marius* . . . ," *Nineteenth-Century Fiction,* XIX (December, 1964), 287-299.

Ward, Anthony. *Walter Pater: The Idea in Nature,* 1966.
Wellek, René. "Walter Pater's Literary Theory and Criticism," *Victorian Studies,* I (September, 1957), 29-46.
Wright, Thomas. *The Life of Walter Pater,* 1907.

Pater was a major seminal force for young writers of the 1890's. His essays on literature and art, especially in *The Renaissance* and *Appreciations,* fostered the art for art's sake movement by stressing the superiority of "useless" (i.e. undidactic) art. He felt that the creator of art was superior to common man and, in the "Conclusion" to *The Renaissance,* stressed that beautiful achievements in life and art were possible for the person who managed "to burn always with this hard, gemlike flame, to maintain this ecstasy." Pater's fictional works, like *The Child in The House,* seem attempts at veiled self-explanation and modify some of the doctrines of his essays. *Marius*, for example, suggests that one should show kindness, self-sacrifice and compassion for others, and not live for ecstasy alone.

PHILLIPS, STEPHEN (1864-1915)

Poems:

Poems, 1898.
New Poems, 1908.
And other titles.

Plays:

Paolo & Francesca, 1899.
Herod, 1900.
And other titles.

Biographical and Critical:

Waugh, Arthur. "Stephen Phillips," *Tradition and Change: Studies in Contemporary Literature,* 1919. Pp. 69-88.
Weygandt, Cornelius. "The Rise and Fall of Stephen Phillips,'

Stephen Phillips

Tuesdays at Ten, 1928. Pp. 210-229.

After impressing critics and readers with his early poems and *Paolo & Francesca,* Phillips began publishing over-decorated poetry in monotonous blank verse until, at his death, he was scorned as a poetaster. Later critical consideration showed that his early work had been over-estimated and that his popularity was merely a literary fad.

PINERO, ARTHUR WING (1855-1934)

Plays:

The Money Spinner, 1880.
The Profligate, 1889.
The Second Mrs. Tanqueray, 1893.
The Notorious Mrs. Ebbsmith, 1895.
Trelawny of the "Wells," 1898.
The Gay Lord Quex, 1899.
Iris, 1901.
Mid-Channel, 1909.
And other titles.

Biographical and Critical:

Dunkel, Wilbur Dwight. *Sir Arthur Pinero: A Critical Biography with Letters,* 1941. ["Bib. Note," pp. 137-138, lists plays and wks. about with some annotation.]
Fyfe, Hamilton. *Arthur Wing Pinero, Playwright,* 1902.
— *Sir Arthur Pinero's Plays and Players,* 1930.
Hamilton, Clayton. "General Introduction," *The Social Plays of Arthur Wing Pinero.* 1917-1922, I, 3-33.

Like H. A. Jones, Pinero helped revive English drama by turning to the depiction of actual human problems like the double standard of sex in *The Second Mrs. Tanqueray* and *Mid-Channel.* Pinero had begun writing farces of better than average quality during the 1870's and 1880's, but his subject matter and technique changed markedly under the spell of Ibsen, as *The Profligate* shows. His problem plays were limited in scope: his characters were mainly aristocrats and fell into a few well-worn types. Pinero's lack of invention and vivacity, even in his best plays, made his eclipse by the more brilliant GBS inevitable.

PLUNKETT, EDWARD JOHN MORETON DRAX, LORD DUNSANY [LORD DUNSANY] (1878-1957)

Fiction:

Gods of Pagāna, 1905.
The Sword of Welleran, 1908.
A Dreamer's Tales, 1910.
The Travel Tales of Mr. Joseph Jorkens, 1931.
Jorkens Has a Large Whiskey, 1940.
And other titles.

Poetry:

Fifty Poems, 1929.
While the Sirens Slept, 1944.
And other titles.

Plays:

The Gods of the Mountain, 1911.
A Night at an Inn, 1916.
Plays of Gods and Men, 1917.
Plays of Near and Far, 1922.
And other titles.

Prose:

Unhappy Far-off Things, 1919.
My Ireland, 1937.
Patches of Sunlight, 1938.
And other titles.

Edward John Moreton Drax Plunkett

Biographical and Critical:

Amory, Mark. *Biography of Lord Dunsany,* 1972.
Bierstadt, E. *Dunsany the Dramatist,* 1917.
Price, Nancy. "Lord Dunsany: Migrant to Mystic," *Poetry Review,* XLIX (April-June, 1958), 94-97.
Saul, George Brandon. "Strange Gods and Far Places: The Short Stories of Lord Dunsany," *Arizona Quarterly,* XIX (Autumn, 1963), 197-210.
Sencourt, Robert. "Memories of Lord Dunsany," *Contemporary Review,* CXCIII (January, 1958), 16-18.
Wilson, William. "'Future,' and 'Fortune' in *A Night at an Inn,*" *Papers of the Bibliographical Society of America,* LVIII (Fourth Quarter, 1964), 477-478.

Plunkett's gift of bizarre fantasy is exemplified by *The Sword of Welleran* and *A Dreamer's Tales.* His fantasy fiction largely falls into two classes: tales of pure wonder (e.g. *Time and the Gods*), mostly written before 1919, and tales in which wonder is subdued by the use of a narrator. In some of his later fiction, humor further mitigates the suspension of disbelief, as in *Travel Tales,* in which Mr. Jorkens holds forth under the influence of spirits—liquid variety.

PROBLEM PLAY, THE

Although conceivably any serious drama might be called a "problem play," the term had special significance late in the nineteenth century. It denoted plays written and produced in the 1880's and 1890's which were based on one or more of the problems that certain classes of society were facing at that moment, such as the emancipated or "new" woman, the new standard of sexuality that modified the rigid Victorian double standard, and the plight of the poor. In the 1890's, major creators of problem plays were Arthur Wing Pinero, Henry Arthur Jones and George Bernard Shaw, all of whom owed something to Ibsen's bold treatment of social problems in such plays as *Ghosts* and *A Doll's House*. Varying artistic goals modified the forms which this impulse toward serious realistic drama later assumed, but descendants of the problem play can be found in the work of early twentieth-century English and Irish playwrights.

Q. *see* QUILLER-COUCH, ARTHUR THOMAS.

QUILLER-COUCH, ARTHUR THOMAS [Q.] (1863-1944)

Fiction:

Dead Man's Rock, 1887.
The Splendid Spur, 1889.
Noughts and Crosses, 1891.
The Ship of Stars, 1899.
Old Fires and Profitable Ghosts, 1900.
The Adventures of Harry Revel, 1903.
Major Vigoreaux, 1907.
Corporal Sam, 1910.
Tales and Romances by Q. "Duchy Edition." 30 vols., 1928-1929.
And other titles.

Poems:

Green Bays, 1893.
Poems and Ballads by 'Q', 1896.
And other titles.

Prose:

Adventures in Criticism, 1896.
Poetry, 1914.
Studies in Literature. 3 ser., 1918, 1922, 1929.
Charles Dickens and Other Victorians, 1925.
And other titles.

Arthur Thomas Quiller-Couch

Autobiography:

Memories and Opinions. Ed. S. C. Roberts. 1944.

Biographical and Critical:

Brittain, F. *Arthur Quiller-Couch: A Biographical Study of Q*, 1947. [Bib. pp. 159-166.]
Peschmann, Hermann. "Sir Arthur Quiller-Couch: An Appreciation," *English*, V (Autumn, 1944), 85-86.
Ward, A. C. "Arthur Quiller-Couch: 'Selected Stories,'" *Aspects of the Modern Short Story*, 1924. Pp. 158-166.
Willey, Basil. *The 'Q' Tradition*, 1946.

Known early in his career as a novelist, Quiller-Couch gained renown as editor of *The Oxford Book of English Verse* and other collections. His slight literary reputation is likely to endure because of his gifts as parodist and precise stylist. Of his adventure stories, *The Splendid Spur*, a fictitious memoir of Charles I's time, still appeals as a cleverly plotted, brightly written romance.

RHYMERS' CLUB, THE

The Rhymers were a group of young poets influenced by Walter Pater's prose and D. G. Rossetti's verse. They organized informally in 1891 and met thereafter at the Cheshire Cheese to hear each other's work. Members included Ernest Dowson, Richard Le Gallienne, W. B. Yeats, John Davidson, Arthur Symons and Lionel Johnson. The Rhymers collaborated on two volumes of verse and contributed to *The Yellow Book* and *The Savoy*. They disbanded in 1894.

RICHARDSON, DOROTHY (1873-1957)

Fiction:

Pointed Roofs, 1915.

Dorothy Richardson

Backwater, 1916.
Honeycomb, 1917.
Interim, 1919.
Revolving Lights, 1923.
The Trap, 1925.
Clear Horizon, 1935.
Pilgrimage. 4 vols., 1938. [Richardson's collected wks.; includes all the above and titles not listed here.]
And other titles.

Bibliographical:

Glikin, Gloria. "Dorothy M. Richardson: An Annotated Bibliography of Writings About Her," *English Literature in Transition,* VIII: 1 (1965), 12-35.

Biographical and Critical:

Blake, Caesar R. *Dorothy Richardson,* 1960. [Bib. pp. 201-207.]
Glikin, Gloria. "Dorothy M. Richardson: The Personal 'Pilgrimage,'" *Publications of the Modern Language Association of America,* LXXVIII (December, 1963), 586-600.
Kumar, Shiv K. "Dorothy Richardson," *Bergson and the Stream of Consciousness Novel,* 1963. Pp. 36-63, and passim.
Mais, S. P. B. "Dorothy Richardson," *Books and Their Writers,* 1920. Pp. 75-86.
Powys, John C. *Dorothy M. Richardson,* 1931.

Richardson was one of the early experimenters with stream-of-consciousness fiction. Unlike James Joyce and other exponents of this method, however, she substituted reticence for candidness; every crucial event, as one critic said, "occurs off-stage, between the volumes; she reduces the stream of consciousness to a trickle." All her volumes are parts of one unending novel, *Pilgrimage,* the subject of which is the inner experience of Miriam Henderson, really Richardson herself.

RICHARDSON, HENRIETTA. *see* RICHARDSON, HENRY HANDEL.

RICHARDSON, HENRY HANDEL [ETHEL FLORENCE LINDESAY, HENRIETTA RICHARDSON, ETHEL FLORENCE LINDESAY ROBERTSON] (1870-1946)

Fiction:

Maurice Guest, 1908.
The Getting of Wisdom, 1910.
Australia Felix, 1917.
The Way Home, 1925.
Ultima Thule, 1929. [With two preceding vols. forms *The Fortunes of Richard Mahony.*]
The Young Cosima, 1939.
And other titles.

Autobiography and Letters:

Myself When Young, 1948. [Bib. pp. 211-214.]
Letters of Henry Handel Richardson to Nettie Palmer. Ed. Karl-John Rossing. 1953.

Bibliographical:

Wittrock, Verna D. "Henry Handel Richardson: An Annotated Bibliography of Writings About Her," *English Literature in Transition*, VII: 3 (1964), 146-187.

Biographical and Critical:

Buckley, Vincent. *Henry Handel Richardson*, 1962.
Gibson, Leonie J. *Henry Handel Richardson and Some of Her Sources*, 1954.
Palmer, Nettie. *Henry Handel Richardson: A Study*, 1950.
Purdie, Edna and Olga M. Roncoroni (eds.). *Henry Handel Richardson: Some Personal Impressions*, 1957. [Essays by various hands.]
Robertson, J. G. "The Art of Henry Handel Richardson:

An Essay in Appreciative Criticism," *Myself When Young,* 1948. Pp. 153-210.

As novelist, Richardson looked back to the nineteenth century and lacked a sufficiently personal method to enable her to rise above such influences as Zolaesque realism and Flaubertian psychology. Two motifs in her fiction are music, prominent in *Maurice Guest* and *The Young Cosima,* and Australian local color, as in *The Getting of Wisdom* and *The Fortunes of Richard Mahony.* Her musical studies are marred by lady-novelist clichés and excessive sentiment, although *Maurice* raises valid questions about love and genius. In Australian literature, *Fortunes* is a monument, but its drab realism, unlightened by poetry, enthusiasm or anger, has aroused little more than indifference.

RIDGE, WILLIAM PETT [WARWICK SIMPSON] (1860-1930)

Fiction:

A Clever Wife, 1895.
An Important Man and Others, 1896.
Mord Em'ly, 1898.
A Son of the State, 1899.
Light Refreshment, 1910.
Love at Paddington, 1912.
The Kennedy People, 1915.
And other titles.

Prose and Autobiography:

Speaking Rather Seriously, 1908.
A Story-teller: Forty Years in London, 1923.
I Like to Remember, 1925.

Ridge amused his contemporaries by his humorous fiction which, like that of Barry Pain, exploited the nuances of Cockney dialect. Simply an entertainer, he wrote pleasing, shallow fiction.

RLS, R.L.S. *see* STEVENSON, ROBERT LOUIS.

ROBERTSON, ETHEL FLORENCE LINDESAY. *see* RICHARDSON, HENRY HANDEL.

ROBINSON, AGNES MARY FRANCES. *see* DUCLAUX, MARY.

ROBINSON, ESMÉ STUART LENNOX (1886-1958)

Plays:

The Clancy Name, 1908.
The Cross-Roads, 1909.
Harvest, 1910.
Patriots, 1912.
The Dreamers, 1915.
The Whiteheaded Boy, 1916.
The Lost Leader, 1918.
The Round Table, 1922.
The Portrait, 1925.
The White Blackbird, 1925.
The Big House, 1926.
And other titles.

Fiction:

A Young Man from the South, 1917.
Dark Days, 1918.
Eight Short Stories, 1920.
And other titles.

Prose:

W. B. Yeats: A Study, 1939.
Towards an Appreciation of the Theatre, 1945.
Ireland's Abbey Theatre: A History, 1899-1951, 1951.

Esmé Stuart Lennox Robinson

Autobiography:

Curtain Up, 1941.

Biographical and Critical:

O'Conor, Norreys. "A Dramatist of Changing Ireland," *Sewanee Review,* XXX (July, 1922), 277-285.
O'Neill, Michael J. *Lennox Robinson,* 1964. [Bib. pp. 181-184.]
Phillipson, Wulstan. "Lennox Robinson," *Downside Review*, LXXVII (Summer, 1959), 266-270.
Starkie, Walter. "Lennox Robinson: 1886-1958," *The Theatre Annual,* XVI (1959), 7-19.

Robinson was associated with the Abbey Theatre as manager, director and dramatist from the days of W. B. Yeats and Lady Gregory until his death half a century later. As the unconventional and uncompromising realism of *Clancy Name* and *Harvest* shows, Robinson was more modern in approach than other Abbey realists like Edward Martyn. He often dealt with social-political problems, as in *The Lost Leader* and *The Big House,* but he did not have Ibsen's power of making a personal situation a microcosm for society. His comic-satiric vein produced one play likely to endure, *The Whiteheaded Boy.*

ROLFE, FREDERICK WILLIAM SERAFINO AUSTIN LEWIS MARY [BARON CORVO] (1860-1913)

Fiction:

Stories Toto Told Me, 1898.
In His Own Image, 1901.
Hadrian the Seventh, 1904.
Don Tarquinio, 1905.
The Desire and Pursuit of the Whole, 1934.
Nicholas Crabbe, or The One and The Many, 1958.
Don Renato, An Ideal Content, 1963.
And other titles.

Frederick William Serafino Austin Lewis Mayr Rolfe

Letters:

Letters to C. H. C. Pirie-Gordon. Ed. Cecil Woolf. 1959.
Letters to Leonard Moore. Ed. Cecil Woolf and Bertram W. Korn. 1960.
Letters to R. M. Dawkins. Ed. Cecil Woolf. 1962.

Bibliographical:

Woolf, Cecil. *A Bibliography of Frederick Rolfe, Baron Corvo,* 1957.

Biographical and Critical:

Highet, Gilbert. "The First Deadly Sin," *Talents and Geniuses,* 1957. Pp. 143-150.
Leslie, Shane. "Corvo," *National Review,* X (January 14, 1961), 24-25.
O'Sullivan, Vincent. "Frederick Rolfe," *Opinions,* 1959. Pp. 150-173.
Someren, I. Van. "Baron Corvo's Quarrels," *Life and Letters,* LVII (February, 1947), 104-109.
Symons, A. J. A. *The Quest for Corvo,* 1934. [Somewhat sensational and unsympathetic.]
Vaglio, Carla Marengo. *Frederick Rolfe, Baron Corvo,* 1969. [Bib. pp. 197-202.]

Rolfe was quintessentially *fin de siècle*, a mysterious figure who expressed his unhappiness and feelings of neglect in books which were an odd compound of wild romance and autobiography. His best known novel is *Hadrian the Seventh,* a delineation of the life of an imaginary Pope, none other than Rolfe in disguise. Rolfe went to Venice for a brief visit but remained there, penniless and indignant, bombarding his comfortable friends at home with pleas for money, and few men have written odder or more vitriolic letters than these.

ROSENBERG, ISAAC (1890-1918)

Poems:

Night and Day, 1912.
Youth, 1915.
Moses, 1916. [Poetic drama.]
The Collected Works of Isaac Rosenberg. Ed. Gordon Bottomley and Denys Harding. 1937. [The definitive ed.]

Biographical and Critical:

Bewley, Marius. "The Poetry of Isaac Rosenberg," *Commentary*, VII (January, 1949), 34-44.
Cohen, Joseph. "Isaac Rosenberg: From Romantic to Classic," *Tulane Studies in English*, X (1960), 129-142.
Harding, Denys. "Aspects of the Poetry of Isaac Rosenberg," *Scrutiny*, III (March, 1935), 358-369.
Johnston, John H. "Poetry and Pity: Isaac Rosenberg," *English Poetry of the First World War*, 1964. Pp. 210-249.
Lindeman, Jack. "The 'Trench Poems' of Isaac Rosenberg," *Literary Review*, II (Summer, 1959), 577-585.

Although best known as a war poet, Rosenberg's poetic self was fully established by 1914. He sought not so much to express fully worked out ideas, as to create an elusive richness. His war poetry is somewhat impersonal, but not cold in tone and stresses the significance of a war which called for great strength and suffering. Rosenberg did not sentimentalize, and he was not ironic. The verbal density of his poems makes them seem quite modern.

ROSS, MARTIN. *see* MARTIN, VIOLET FLORENCE; *see also* SOMERVILLE, EDITH OENONE.

RUSSELL, GEORGE WILLIAM [AE] (1867-1935)

Poems:

Homeward: Songs by the Way, 1894.
The Earth Breath, 1897.
The Divine Vision, 1904.
By Still Waters, 1906.
Dark Weeping, 1929.
The House of the Titans, 1934.
And other titles.

Fiction:

The Mask of Apollo, 1904.
The Interpreters, 1920.

Prose:

Some Irish Essays, 1906.
The Hero in Man, 1909.
Imaginations and Reveries, 1915.
The Candle of Vision, 1918.
Song and Its Fountains, 1932.
And other titles.

Letters:

AE's Letters to Mínanlábáin, 1937.
Letters from AE. Ed. Alan Denson. 1961.

Bibliographical:

Denson, Alan. *Printed Writings by George W. Russell (AE): A Bibliography . . .*, 1961.

Biographical and Critical:

Bose, A. C. *Three Mystic Poets: Yeats, AE, and Tagore*, 1945.
Boyd, E. A. "George W. Russell (A. E.)," *Ireland's Literary Renaissance*, 1916. Pp. 219-239.

Figgis, Darrell Edmund. *AE (George W. Russell): A Study of a Man and a Nation,* 1916.
Magee, W. K. *A Memoir of AE: George William Russell,* 1937.

Lyric poet, a founder of the Abbey Theatre, influential journalist, friend of W. B. Yeats and George Moore, Russell was an important figure in the Celtic Renaissance. But his poetry has won little lasting acclaim. Despite a strong poetic inclination and mystical inspiration, his lyrics are repetitious in subject matter, commonplace in treatment and archaic in diction.

RUTHERFORD, MARK. *see* WHITE, WILLIAM HALE.

SAINTSBURY, GEORGE EDWARD BATEMAN (1845-1933)

Prose:

A History of Nineteenth Century Literature: 1780-1895, 1896.
A Short History of English Literature, 1898.
A History of Criticism and Literary Taste in Europe.... 3 vols., 1900-1904.
A History of English Prosody.... 3 vols., 1906-1910.
A History of English Criticism, 1911.
A History of English Prose Rhythm, 1912.
A History of the French Novel.... 2 vols., 1917.
The Collected Essays and Papers, 1875-1920. 4 vols., 1923-1924.
And other titles.

Bibliographical:

Leuba, W. "Bibliography of G. Saintsbury," *Book-Collector's Quarterly,* XII (October, 1933), 43-52.
Danielson, Henry. "Bibliographies of Modern Authors: George Saintsbury," *London Mercury,* I (December, 1919), 238-239.

George Edward Bateman Saintsbury

Biographical and Critical:

Elton, Oliver. "George Saintsbury," *Life and Letters,* IX (June-August, 1933), 181-190.
Leuba, Walter. *George Saintsbury,* 1967. [Bib. pp. 120-126.]
Richardson, Dorothy. "Saintsbury and Art for Art's Sake in England," *Publications of the Modern Language Association of America,* LIX (March, 1944), 243-260.

Saintsbury preferred to judge literature by its "transport"—the work's power to inspire the beholder. He was an appreciator, not an analyst or a pursuer of a definite philosophy of literature. Though important as a critic, he wrote more prolifically as a journalist, contributing essays on social, political and religious topics to a number of periodicals.

SAKI. *see* MUNRO, HECTOR HUGH.

SASSOON, SIEGFRIED LORAINE (1886-1967)

Poems:

Poems, 1906.
The Daffodil Murderer, 1913. [Parody of Masefield's *The Everlasting Mercy.*]
Discoveries, 1915.
The Old Huntsman, 1917.
Counter-Attack, 1918.
The War Poems of Siegfried Sassoon, 1919.
Selected Poems, 1925.
Satirical Poems, 1926.
The Heart's Journey, 1927.
Collected Poems, 1908-1956, 1961.
And other titles.

Siegfried Loraine Sassoon

Autobiography:

Memoirs of a Fox-Hunting Man, 1928.
Memoirs of an Infantry Officer, 1930.
Sherston's Progress, 1936.
Siegfried's Journey, 1945.

Bibliographical:

Keynes, Geoffrey. *A Bibliography of Siegfried Sassoon,* 1962.

Biographical and Critical:

Cohen, Joseph. "The Three Roles of Siegfried Sassoon," *Tulane Studies in English,* VII (1957), 169-185.
Maguire, C. E. "Harmony Unheard: The Poetry of Siegfried Sassoon," *Renascence,* XI (Spring, 1959), 115-124.
Thorpe, Michael. *Siegfried Sassoon: A Critical Study,* 1966.

Sassoon, a minor poetic talent, occupies a permanent place in World War I poetry. Although he entered service with sentiments akin to those of Rupert Brooke, by 1916 he began to tear the romantic mask from war. At his best with colloquial, racy, tuneful, Kiplingesque verse, Sassoon mingled compassion for soldiers with vicious irony directed against perpetrators of the sweet lies about war. A gifted parodist, Sassoon probably absorbed all he needed—except the war experience itself—from poets like Kipling and Brooke to produce verse like "Base Details," which is perilously close to parody. After the war, he wrote no verse of comparable quality. His memoirs are still readable.

SAVOY, THE

Sometimes called "The Beardsley," *The Savoy* was a fortunate side-effect of the Wilde scandal. When Aubrey Beardsley, art editor of *The Yellow Book,* was fired because of a supposed link with Wilde, Leonard Smithers hired him early in 1896 to fill that role on *The Savoy* under the general editorship of Arthur Symons. The consumptive Beardsley contributed some of his finest illustrations to the journal, but neither they nor the writings of such lights of the 1890's as Max Beerbohm, W. B. Yeats, Joseph Conrad and GBS could save the periodical from early demise. *The Savoy* perished in the year of its birth, after eight numbers appeared.

SCHREINER, OLIVE EMILIE ALBERTINA [RALPH IRON] (1855-1920)

Fiction:

The Story of an African Farm, 1883.
Dreams, 1891.
Dream Life and Real Life, 1893.
Trooper Peter Halket of Mashonaland, 1897.
Stories, Dreams, and Allegories, 1923.
From Man To Man; or, Perhaps Only–, 1926.
Undine, 1928.

Letters:

The Letters of Olive Schreiner, 1876-1920. Ed. S. C. Cronwright-Schreiner. 1924.

Bibliographical:

Verster, Evelyn. *Olive Emilie Albertina Schreiner, 1855-1920,* 1946.

Biographical and Critical:

Cronwright-Schreiner, S. C. *The Life of Olive Schreiner,* 1924.
Friedmann, Marion V. *Olive Schreiner: A Study in Latent Meanings,* 1955. [Bib. pp. 65-66.]
Gould, Vera B. *Not Without Honor: The Life and Writing of O. Schreiner,* 1949. [Occasional uncritical evaluation.]
Hobman, D. L. *Olive Schreiner: Her Friends and Times,* 1955.

Olive Emilie Albertina Schreiner

The Story of an African Farm, sometimes termed a second-rate *Wuthering Heights,* is the work for which Schreiner is chiefly known. It deals with a strong-willed girl (Lyndall) and a lonely boy (Waldo), both of whom are sensitive, isolated and tormented by cruel parent figures. Their childhood is confused by contradictory religious experiences. Lyndall's inflexible will makes her choose sexual experience without marriage, since she feels marriage without perfect love would be a sort of prostitution—a choice which points toward the heroine of Grant Allan's inferior *The Woman Who Did* and later fiction concerning the new woman.

SEAMAN, OWEN (1861-1936)

Poems and Parodies:

With Double Pipe, 1888.
Horace at Cambridge, 1895.
The Battle of the Bays, 1896.
In Cap and Bells, 1900.
Borrowed Plumes, 1902.
A Harvest of Chaff, 1904.
Salvage, 1908.
Made in England, 1916.
And other titles.

Biographical and Critical:

Kernahan, Coulson. "Sir Owen Seaman of 'Punch,'" *Five More Famous Living Poets,* 1928. Pp. 177-265.

Seaman caught the poetic nuances and mannerisms of his famous contemporaries, using parody as a form of literary criticism. *The Battle of the Bays* speculated satirically on the best candidate for the vacant post of poet laureate. Seaman also edited *Punch* from 1906 to 1932.

SHARP, WILLIAM [FIONA MACLEOD] (1855-1905)

Poems:

Earth's Voices, 1884.
Romantic Ballads and Poems of Fantasy, 1888.
Sospiri di Roma, 1891.
**From the Hills of Dream*, 1897.[1]
**The Dominion of Dreams*, 1899.
And other titles.

Fiction:

The Children of To-morrow, 1889.
A Fellowe and His Wife [with Blanche Willis Howard], 1892.
**Pharais*, 1894.
**Green Fire*, 1896.
Ecce Puella, 1896.
Silence Farm, 1899.
And other titles.

Plays:
**The House of Usna, 1900*.
And other titles.

Prose:

Dante Gabriel Rossetti: A Record and a Study, 1882.
Life and Letters of Joseph Severn, 1892.
**Where the Forest Murmurs*, 1906.
And other titles.

Collected Works:

Selected Writings of William Sharp. "Uniform Edition." 5 vols., 1912.
**The Works of Fiona Macleod*. "Uniform Edition." 7 vols., 1909-1910.

---

[1]Titles marked with asterisk published under pseudonym Fiona Macleod.

William Sharp

Biographical and Critical:

Garbáty, Thomas Jay. "Fiona Macleod: Defence of Her Views and Her Identity," *Notes and Queries*, VII (December, 1960), 465-467.
Iorio, John J. "A Victorian Controversy: William Sharp's Letters on 'Motherhood,'" *Colby Library Quarterly*, IV (May, 1957), 178-184.
Sharp, Elizabeth A. *William Sharp (Fiona Macleod): A Memoir Compiled by His Wife*, 1910.

Sharp's creation, after 1893, of prose, verse and drama supposedly written by Fiona Macleod was one of the most unusual — and best concealed — pseudonymous literary adventures of the era. Unlike his own romantic but restrained and literal manner, Macleod's was dream-like and shadowy (cf. *Romantic Ballads* and *Hills of Dream* or *Silence Farm* and *Green Fire*). Sharp derives from nineteenth-century English literary tradition; Macleod from the "Celtic Twilight." As author, Sharp certainly had two sides, but neither was able to rise above mannerism, or clever imitation.

SHAW, GEORGE BERNARD [GBS, G.B.S.] (1856-1951)

Plays:

Widowers' Houses, 1892.
Arms and the Man, 1894.
Candida, 1897.
The Devil's Disciple, 1897.
You Never Can Tell, 1900.
Captain Brassbound's Conversion, 1900.
Mrs. Warren's Profession, 1902.
John Bull's Other Island, 1904.
Man and Superman, 1905.
Major Barbara, 1905.
Caesar and Cleopatra, 1906.
The Doctor's Dilemma, 1906.
Getting Married, 1908.

The Shewing-up of Blanco Posnet, 1909.
Misalliance, 1910.
Fanny's First Play, 1912.
Androcles and the Lion, 1912.
Pygmalion, 1913.
Heartbreak House, 1920.
Back to Methuselah, 1922.
Saint Joan, 1923.
The Apple Cart, 1929.
And other titles.

Fiction:

Cashel Byron's Profession, 1886; rvd. ed., 1901.
An Unsocial Socialist, 1887.
Love Among the Artists, 1900.
The Irrational Knot, 1905.

Prose:

The Quintessence of Ibsenism, 1891; rvd. ed., 1913.
The Perfect Wagnerite, 1898.
Dramatic Opinions and Essays . . . , 1907.
The Intelligent Woman's Guide to Socialism and Capitalism, 1928.
Music in London, 1890-1894, 1932.
Our Theatres in the Nineties, 1932.
And other titles.

Collected Works:

Works. "Standard Edition." 36 vols., 1931-1950.
Complete Prefaces, 1938.
Complete Plays, 1950.

Autobiography and Letters:

Ellen Terry and Bernard Shaw: A Correspondence. Ed. Christopher St. John. 1931.
Sixteen Self Sketches, 1949.
Bernard Shaw and Mrs. Patrick Campbell: Their Correspondence. Ed. Alan Dent. 1952.

George Bernard Shaw

Advice to a Young Critic and Other Letters. Ed. J. West. 1955.
Bernard Shaw's Letters to Granville Barker. Ed. C. B. Purdom. 1956.
To a Young Actress: The Letters of Bernard Shaw to Molly Tompkins. Ed. Peter Tompkins. 1960.
Collected Letters, 1874-1897. Ed. Dan H. Laurence. vols., 1965- . [The standard ed. of Shaw's letters; subsequent vols. in preparation.]

Bibliographical:

Broad, C. Lewis, and Violet M. Broad. *Dictionary to the Plays and Novels of Bernard Shaw, with Bibliography of His Works and of the Literature Concerning Him . . .,* 1929.
Holmes, Maurice. *Some Bibliographical Notes on the Novels of George Bernard Shaw,* [1929].
Kerr, Alison. *Bernard Shaw: An Exhibition of Books and Manuscripts . . .,* 1963.
Lowenstein, F. E. *The Rehearsal Copies of Bernard Shaw's Plays: A Bibliographical Study,* 1950.
Wells, Geoffrey H. *A Bibliography of the Books and Pamphlets of George Bernard Shaw,* 1929.

Biographical and Critical:

Bentley, Eric. *Bernard Shaw, 1856-1950.* 1947; rvd. ed., 1957.
Brown, Ivor. *Shaw in His Time,* 1966.
Carpenter, Charles A. *Bernard Shaw & the Art of Destroying Ideals: The Early Plays,* 1969.
Chesterton, G. K. *George Bernard Shaw,* 1909.
Colbourne, Maurice. *The Real Bernard Shaw,* 1931; rvd. ed., 1949.
Dietrich, R. F. *Portrait of the Artist as a Young Superman: A Study of Shaw's Novels,* 1969.
Duffin, Henry. *The Quintessence of Bernard Shaw,* 1939.
Ervine, St. John. *Bernard Shaw: His Life, Work and Friends,* 1956.
Fromm, Harold. *Bernard Shaw and the Theater in the Nineties: A Study of Shaw's Dramatic Criticism,* 1967. [Bib. pp. 227-232.]

Harris, Frank. *Frank Harris on Bernard Shaw: An Unauthorized Biography Based on First Hand Information...*, 1931.
Henderson, Archibald. *George Bernard Shaw: Man of the Century*, 1956.
Irvine, William. *The Universe of G. B. S.*, 1949.
Joad, C. E. M. *Shaw*, 1949.
Kaye, Julian B. *Bernard Shaw and the Nineteenth-Century Tradition*, 1958.
Meisel, Martin. *Shaw and the Nineteenth-Century Theater*, 1963.
Nethercot, Arthur H. *Men and Supermen: The Shavian Portrait Gallery*, 1954.
Pearson, Hesketh. *Bernard Shaw: His Life and Personality*, 1961.
Purdom, C. B. *A Guide to the Plays of Bernard Shaw*, 1963.
Rattray, R. F. *Bernard Shaw: A Chronicle*, 1951.
Ward, A. C. *Bernard Shaw*, 1950; rvd. ed., 1951. [Bib. pp. 204-209.]
Watson, Barbara Bellow. *A Shavian Guide to the Intelligent Woman*, 1964.
Weintraub, Stanley. *Journey to Heartbreak: The Crucible Years of Bernard Shaw 1914-1918*, 1971.
Wilson, Colin. *Bernard Shaw: A Reassessment*, 1969.
Winsten, Stephen. *Jesting Apostle: The Life of Bernard Shaw*, 1956.
— *Shaw's Corner*, 1952.

Shaw is a leading example of the artist as reformer—one who believes in the power of the written word to change man's attitudes and values. In his long, varied career as drama and music critic, prosaist and playwright, Shaw championed such unpopular literary and social causes as Fabianism, the plays of Henrik Ibsen and Richard Wagner's operas. Though his literary reputation rests primarily on his plays, he used prose for his most explicit indictments of man and society, as in the lengthy prefaces he supplied to explicate and expound the ideas of his plays and in *The Quintessence of Ibsenism*. His dramatic and musical criticism shines with erudition, wit and cool objectivity even for such English idols as Shakespeare and G. F. Handel. In their treatment of real social problems such as slum landlords in *Widowers' Houses* and prostitution in *Mrs.*

Warren's Profession, his early plays superficially resemble the problem plays of Pinero and Jones, but Shaw's mind was not narrowly middle class and moral. As dramatist, Shaw was a satirist who sought to purge his countrymen of their pride in such hallowed aspects of English life as the army in *The Devil's Disciple,* class consciousness in *Pygmalion* and benevolent institutions, represented by the Salvation Army, in *Major Barbara.* He also ranged over more "serious" issues such as medical ethics in *The Doctor's Dilemma,* religion in *Saint Joan* and man's place in the evolutionary scheme in *Back to Methuselah.*

SHORTHOUSE, JOSEPH HENRY (1834-1903)

Fiction:

John Inglesant, 1880.
The Countess Eve, 1888.
And other titles.

Biographical and Critical:

Anson, Harold. "The Church in Nineteenth-Century Fiction, II – J. H. Shorthouse," *Listener,* XXI (May 4, 1939), 945-946.
Bishop, Morchard. "*John Inglesant* and Its Author," *Essays by Divers Hands,* XXIX (1958), 73-86.
Gosse, Edmund. "The Author of 'John Inglesant,'" *Portraits and Sketches,* 1912. Pp. 151-162.
More, Paul Elmer. "J. Henry Shorthouse," *Shelburne Essays.* 3rd ser., 1905. Pp. 213-243.
Shorthouse, Sarah (ed.). *Life and Letters of J. H. Shorthouse.* 2 vols., 1905.

Readers bothered by problems of religious doubt welcomed *John Inglesant.* In a vivid, though somewhat inaccurate historical setting, Shorthouse exposed his hero to various religious philosophies in seventeenth-century England and Europe. Inglesant, despite contact with English Civil War and the horrors of the plague, remains calmly pure of heart. The book's religious philosophy and Shorthouse's lavish use of quotations and paraphrases from seventeenth-century authors gave rise to fervid discussion.

SIMPSON, WARWICK. *see* RIDGE, WILLIAM PETT.

SINCLAIR, MAY (1865-1946)

Fiction:

Audrey Craven, 1897.
Mr. and Mrs. Nevil Tyson, 1898.
The Divine Fire, 1904.
The Helpmate, 1907.
The Combined Maze, 1913.
The Tree of Heaven, 1917.
Anne Severn and the Fieldings, 1922.
The Allinghams, 1927.
And other titles.

Prose:

The Three Brontës, 1912.
A Journal of Impressions in Belgium, 1915.
A Defence of Idealism, 1917.
And other titles.

Bibliographical:

Boll, Theophilus M. "On the May Sinclair Collection," *The Library Chronicle* (University of Pennsylvania), XXVII (Winter, 1961), 1-15.

Biographical and Critical:

Brewster, Dorothy, and Angus Burrell. "May Sinclair: New Light on Old Virtues," *Modern Fiction*, 1934. Pp. 110-136.

de Bosschere, Jean. "Charity in the Work of May Sinclair," *Yale Review*, XIV (October, 1924), 82-94.

The novels of Sinclair, in their expression of revolt against Victorian repression and denial, owe much to the example of French naturalism. *The Helpmate* grows out of Anne's determination to raise her husband to her spiritual level, but she denies him love, and, indirectly, causes his death. The theme of love denied is ubiquitous in Sinclair's fiction. Dominating elders, inbred timidity and circumstance conspire—often in highly improbable ways—to prevent the gratification of her characters' sexual needs. Although she was generally regarded as a major female novelist by 1920, her detailed, tedious studies of frustration have won few adherents since.

SOMERVILLE, EDITH OENONE (1858-1949)

Fiction:

Naboth's Vineyard [with Violet Florence Martin], 1891.
The Real Charlotte [with VFM], 1894.
The Silver Fox [with VFM], 1897.
Some Experiences of an Irish R. M. [with VFM], 1899.
Mount Music, 1919.
An Enthusiast, 1921.
The Big House of Inver, 1925.
And other titles.

Prose:

Some Irish Yesterdays [with VFM], 1906.
Irish Memories, 1917.
Stray-Aways, 1920.
Wheel-Tracks, 1923.
And other titles.

Bibliographical:

Hudson, Elizabeth. *A Bibliography of the First Editions of*

the Works of E. OE. Somerville and Martin Ross, 1942.
Vaughan, Robert. *The First Editions of Edith Oenone Somerville and Violet Florence Martin,* 1952.

Biographical and Critical:

Cummins, Geraldine. *Dr. E. OE. Somerville: A Biography,* 1952. [Bib. pp. 243-271.]
Flanagan, Thomas. "The Big House of Ross-Drishane," *Kenyon Review,* XXVIII (January, 1966), 54-78.
Powell, Violet. *The Irish Cousins: The Books and Background of Somerville and Ross,* 1970.
Watson, Cresap S. "Realism, Determinism and Symmetry in *The Real Charlotte,*" *Hermathena,* LXXXIV (November, 1954), 26-44.

Gifted as writer, painter and musician, Somerville is best remembered as collaborator with her cousin Violet Florence Martin (Martin Ross) in a series of novels and essays describing high-born life in Ireland between 1889 and 1915, the time of Miss Martin's death. The troubled times in which the women lived is not reflected in their work, but they achieved distinction, both literary (with *The Real Charlotte*) and popular (with *Irish R. M.*). Somerville's later books also bear the Somerville and Ross by-line, since Somerville believed that death had not removed Miss Martin's inspirational force.

SQUIRE, JOHN COLLINGS [SOLOMON EAGLE] (1884-1958)

Poems:

Poems and Baudelaire Flowers, 1909.
The Three Hills, 1913.
The Lily of Malud, 1917.
Poems: First Series, 1918.
Collected Poems, 1959.
And other titles.

John Collings Squire

Prose:

Books in General. 3 ser., 1919-1921.
Life and Letters, 1920.
Books Reviewed, 1922.
Essays at Large, 1922.
And other titles.

Parodies:

Imaginary Speeches, 1912.
Steps to Parnassus, 1913.
Tricks of the Trade, 1917.
Collected Parodies, 1921.
And other titles.

Autobiography:

The Honeysuckle and the Bee, 1937.
Water-Music, or a Fortnight of Bliss, 1939.

Bibliographical:

Williams, I. A. *John Collings Squire and James Stevens,* 1922.

Biographical and Critical:

Munro, H. "Section V: J. C. Squire," *Some Contemporary Poets,* 1920. Pp. 148-156.
Priestley, J. B. "The Poetry of Mr. J. C. Squire," *Figures in Modern Literature,* 1924. Pp. 188-215.
Swinnerton, F. "J. C. Squire and the Georgians," *The Georgian Literary Scene,* 1935. Pp. 222-227.

Squire, a contributor to *Georgian Poetry,* wrote a fair amount of serious poetry, often experimenting—without notable success—with metrics. A general lack of originality and spontaneity severely limited his achievement in this genre, but proved no handicap when he wrote parody. *Imaginary Speeches* and *Steps to Parnassus* brilliantly capture—and distort—the nuances of Henley, Kipling, Yeats and others.

STEEL, FLORA ANNIE (1847-1929)

Fiction:

From the Five Rivers, 1893.
Miss Stuart's Legacy, 1893.
The Potter's Thumb, 1894.
On the Face of the Waters, 1896.
Voices in the Night, 1900.
The Adventures of Akbar, 1913.
Indian Scene, 1933.
And other titles.

Prose:

India, 1905.
A Sovereign Remedy, 1906.
India through the Ages, 1908.
The Garden of Fidelity, 1929.

Biographical and Critical:

Collins, J. P. "Flora Annie Steel," *Living Age*, CCXCVI (February 2, 1918), 289-293.
Patwardhan, Daya. *A Star of India, Flora Annie Steel: Her Works and Times*, 1963.

In at least one way, Steel is a female counterpart of Rudyard Kipling: both spent significant portions of their lives in India and vividly communicated their impressions of the land and its customs through fiction. But while Kipling outgrew India, Steel never did; from her first books to her last, her subject is India. *On the Face of the Waters* is a fine novel on the Indian Mutiny.

STEPHEN, JAMES KENNETH (1859-1892)

Poems:

Quo Musa Tendis?, 1891.

James Kenneth Stephen

Lapsus Calami, 1891.
Lapsus Calami and Other Verses, 1896.

Biographical and Critical:

Benson, A. C. "J. K. Stephen," *The Leaves of the Tree: Studies in Biography,* 1911. Pp. 78-107.
MacCarthy, Desmond. "J. K. Stephen," *Portraits,* 1931. Pp. 248-254.

Stephen was one of the great parodists of the era, and in *Lapsus Calami,* he made poets such as Browning and Kipling writhe under the humorous-critical strokes of his lash. His original verse has the same deftness as his parodies, but only the latter show Stephen's true gift.

STEVENSON, ROBERT LOUIS [RLS, R.L.S.] (1850-1894)

Fiction:

New Arabian Nights, 1882.
Treasure Island, 1883.
More New Arabian Nights: The Dynamiter [with Fanny Stevenson], 1885.
The Strange Case of Dr. Jekyll and Mr. Hyde, 1886.
Kidnapped, 1886.
The Merry Men, 1887.
The Black Arrow, 1888.
The Wrong Box [with Lloyd Osbourne], 1889.
The Master of Ballantrae, 1889.
The Wrecker [with Lloyd Osbourne], 1892.
Island Nights' Entertainments, 1893.
Catriona, 1893. [Am. ed. titled *David Balfour.*]
Weir of Hermiston, 1896. [Unfinished.]
St. Ives, 1897. [Unfinished; completed by Quiller-Couch.]
And other titles.

Prose:

An Inland Voyage, 1878.

Travels with a Donkey, 1879.
Virginibus Puerisque, 1881.
Familiar Studies of Men and Books, 1882.
The Silverado Squatters, 1883.
Memories & Portraits, 1887.
Across the Plains, 1892.
And other titles.

Poems:

A Child's Garden of Verses, 1885.
Underwoods, 1887.
Ballads, 1890.
Songs of Travel, 1896.
And other titles.

Collected Works:

Works. "Tusitala Edition." 35 vols., 1924.
Works. "South Seas Edition." 32 vols., 1925.
Collected Poems. Ed. Janet Adam Smith. 1950.

Letters:

Letters. Ed. Sidney Colvin. 4 vols., 1911. [Many editorial deletions; use with care.]
Henry James and Robert Louis Stevenson: A Record of Friendship and Criticism. Ed. Janet Adam Smith. 1948.
RLS: Stevenson's Letters to Charles Baxter. Ed. De Lancey Ferguson and Marshall Waingrow. 1956.

Bibliographical:

Ehrsam, Theodore G., and Robert H. Deily. "Robert Louis Stevenson," *Bibliographies of Twelve Victorian Authors*, 1936. Pp. 228-261. [Some inaccuracies; use with caution .
McKay, George L. *A Stevenson Library: Catalogue of a Collection of Writings by and About Robert Louis Stevenson Formed by Edwin J. Beinecke*. 6 vols., 1951-1964. [Super sedes all other bibs.]
Prideaux, W. F. *A Bibliography of the Works of Robert Louis Stevenson*, 1903. [New and rvd. ed. by Mrs. Luther S. Livingston, 1917.]

Robert Louis Stevenson

Biographical and Critical:

Aldington, Richard. *Portrait of a Rebel: The Life and Works of Robert Louis Stevenson,* 1957.
Balfour, Graham. *The Life of Robert Louis Stevenson.* 2 vols., 1901. [Basic source for much bio. material.]
Caldwell, Elsie Noble. *Last Witness for Robert Louis Stevenson,* 1960.
Chesterton, G. K. *Robert Louis Stevenson,* 1927.
Cooper, Lettice. *Robert Louis Stevenson,* 1947.
Cornford, L. Cope. *Robert Louis Stevenson,* 1900.
Cowell, Henry. *Robert Louis Stevenson: An Englishman's Re-Study, After Fifty Years, of R. L. S. the Man,* 1945.
Daiches, David. *Stevenson and the Art of Fiction,* 1951.
Dalglish, Doris N. *Presbyterian Pirate: A Portrait of Stevenson,* 1937.
Dark, Sidney. *Robert Louis Stevenson,* 1931.
Eigner, Edwin M. *Robert Louis Stevenson and Romantic Tradition,* 1967.
Elwin, Malcolm. *The Strange Case of Robert Louis Stevenson,* 1950.
Fisher, Anne B. *No More A Stranger,* 1946.
Furnas, J. C. *Voyage to Windward: The Life of Robert Louis Stevenson,* 1951. [List of "crucial" work about Stevenson, pp. 473-492.]
Hellman, George S. *The True Stevenson: A Study in Clarification,* 1925.
Hinkley, Laura L. *The Stevensons: Louis and Fanny,* 1950.
Kiely, Robert. *Robert Louis Stevenson and the Fiction of Adventure,* 1964.
Osbourne, Lloyd. *An Intimate Portrait of R. L. S.,* 1924.
Smith, Janet Adam. *R. L. Stevenson,* 1937.
Steuart, John A. *Robert Louis Stevenson, Man and Writer: A Critical Biography.* 2 vols., 1924. [Added material missed by previous bios.]
Swinnerton, Frank R. *R. L. Stevenson: A Critical Study,* 1914.

While *Treasure Island* is the essence of all pirate stories and *Kidnapped* sets the pattern followed in all subsequent hunt-and-chase novels, Stevenson's other adventure stories failed to equal these two classics of high adventure. His fiction evolved toward the serious novel, and *The Master of Ballantrae*, though it contains many elements of adventure, shows Stevenson seriously considering the effect of good and evil on two brothers. The unfinished *Weir of Hermiston* probes the influences shaping character. Stevenson's short stories often deal with the strange and the mysterious ("The Pavilion on the Links," "The Sire de Maletroit's Door") or the macabre and the supernatural ("The Body Snatcher," "Thrawn Janet"), sometimes with touches of humorous satire. In "Markheim" and *The Strange Case of Dr. Jekyll and Mr. Hyde,* Stevenson symbolizes the horror of man's secret desires by the appearance of the inner self in flesh and blood form. Though Stevenson was influenced by the aesthetic movement (shown by his love of language and the occasional ornate sentences of his essays and stories), he forged his own aesthetic of adventure and defended staunchly the exhilaration of physical action and escape in romantic fiction. He continued the tradition of the familiar essay in *Virginibus Puerisque* and *Familiar Studies*. Of his poetry, only *A Child's Garden of Verses* is remembered, chiefly because of its eloquently simple expression of the child's view of the world.

STOKER, BRAM (1847-1912)

Fiction:

Dracula, 1897.
The Jewel of Seven Stars, 1903.
The Lair of the White Worm, 1911.
Dracula's Guest, and Other Weird Stories, 1914.
And other titles.

Biographical and Critical:

Kirtley, Bacil F. "Dracula, the Monastic Chronicles and Slavic Folklore," *Midwest Folklore,* VI (Fall, 1956), 133-139.
Ludham, Harry. *A Biography of Dracula: The Life Story of Bram Stoker,* 1962.

Nandris, Grigore. "The Historical Dracula: The Theme of His Legend in the Western and the Eastern Literatures of Europe," *Comparative Literature Studies,* III (1966), 367-396.

Despite its nearly unreadable epistolary style, *Dracula* continues to be popular because Stoker captures in the idea of vampirism a symbolic image of innocence so overcome that it acquires the insatiable, perverted appetites of its seducer. But Stoker's ponderous style and stereotyped characters make his horror novels inferior to the work of Arthur Machen and M. R. James.

STRACHEY, GILES LYTTON (1880-1932)

Prose:

Landmarks in French Literature, 1912.
Eminent Victorians, 1918.
Queen Victoria, 1921.
Books and Characters, French and English, 1922.
Elizabeth and Essex, 1928.
And other titles.

Letters:

Letters: Virginia Woolf and Lytton Strachey. Ed. Leonard Woolf and James Strachey. 1956.

Bibliographical:

Kallich, Martin. "Lytton Strachey: An Annotated Bibliography of Writings About Him," *English Fiction in Transition,* V: 3 (1962), 1-77.

Biographical and Critical:

Bacon, Leonard. "An Eminent Post-Victorian," *Yale Review,* XXX (December, 1940), 310-324.
Clemens, Cyril. *Lytton Strachey,* 1942.

Hartwell, Robert M. "Lytton Strachey," *University of California Chronicle*, XXXIV (October, 1932), 409-441.
Holroyd, Michael. *Lytton Strachey*. 2 vols., 1967-1968. [Bib. II, 721-728; the definitive bio.]
James, Rolfe A. S. *Lytton Strachey*, 1955.
Johnstone, John K. *The Bloomsbury Group*, 1954.
Kallich, Martin. *The Psychological Milieu of Lytton Strachey*, 1961.
Sanders, Charles R. *Lytton Strachey: His Mind and Art*, 1957.

Strachey's importance to the art of biography rivals Conrad's to the art of fiction. He sharply altered at least two aspects of the usual "biographical approach." In his reëvaluations of revered Victorians like Florence Nightingale and Dr. Arnold (in *Eminent Victorians*), Strachey drew frank, sometimes unflattering word-portraits instead of the customary glamorized versions. In place of the usual emphasis on documentary minutiae, Strachey depicted action, dialogue and his "characters'" thoughts, although sometimes, as in *Elizabeth and Essex*, at the expense of credibility. His artistically restrained employment of such techniques makes *Queen Victoria* his noblest achievement.

STREET, GEORGE SLYTHE (1867-1936)

The Autobiography of a Boy, 1894.

Street was a minor essayist, remembered chiefly for his playful satire of decadence *The Autobiography of a Boy*, in which Tubby, a rather ordinary person, attempts to mold his individuality by following the aesthetes. Tubby encounters a *fin de siècle* woman who hardly lives up to his expectations: "I had hoped for a moment to find her a Faustine, or at least with something of Herodias' daughter. She was merely a respectable Cockney playing truant. I wanted her to be wild and wicked and abandoned, and she was nothing of the sort."

SWINNERTON, FRANK (1884-)

Fiction:

The Happy Family, 1912.
On the Staircase, 1914.
Nocturne, 1917.
September, 1919.
Coquette, 1921.
And other titles.

Prose:

George Gissing, 1912.
R. L. Stevenson: A Critical Study, 1914.
Authors and the Book Trade, 1932.
The Georgian Literary Scene, 1935; rvd. eds., 1938, 1950.
Arnold Bennett, 1950.
Background with Chorus: A Footnote to Changes in English Literary Fashion Between 1901 and 1917, 1956.
And other titles.

Autobiography:

Swinnerton: An Autobiography, 1936.

Biographical and Critical:

Bennett, Arnold, *et al. Frank Swinnerton: Personal Sketches,* 1920. [Title, contributors and date of this miscellany vary in different editions; general, pleasant "appreciations."]
Collins, Joseph. "Mr. Frank Swinnerton and His Books," *Taking the Literary Pulse,* 1924. Pp. 190-206.
McKay, Ruth Capers. *George Gissing and His Critic, Frank Swinnerton,* 1933. [Chs. V-VII on Swinnerton's fiction; bib. pp. 109-111.]
Mais, S. P. B. "Frank Swinnerton," *Books and Their Writers,* 1920. Pp. 37-45.

In his most successful novels, Swinnerton followed Gissing by describing the lower middle-class life of women and men, who hindered by such an existence, strove to better their place in society. His depiction of women groping to experience a satisfactory life (*Nocturne, September*) is effective and occasionally involves the problem of sexual standards. However, Swinnerton's view of the lower middle class is much less harsh than that of Gissing. As an essayist, Swinnerton often gives sidelights on the literati and bookmen of the 1880-1920 period, a milieu with which he was particularly familiar.

SYMONDS, JOHN ADDINGTON (1840-1893)

Prose:

Sketches in Italy and Greece, 1874.
The Renaissance in Italy. 7 vols., 1875-1886.
Shelley, 1878.
The Life of Michelangelo Buonarroti, 1892.
In the Key of Blue, 1893.
And other titles.

Poems:

Many Moods, 1878.
New and Old, 1880.
Animi Figura, 1882.
And other titles.

Translations:

The Sonnets of Michael Angelo Buonarroti and Tommaso Campanella, 1878.
Wine, Women and Song, 1884.
And other titles.

Letters:

Letters and Papers of John Addington Symonds. Ed. Horatio F. Brown. 1923.
The Letters of John Addington Symonds. Ed. Herbert L. Schueller and Robert L. Peters. 3 vols., 1967-1969.

John Addington Symonds

Bibliographical:

Babington, Percy L. *Bibliography of the Writings of J. A. Symonds*, 1925.

Biographical and Critical:

Brooks, Van Wyck. *John Addington Symonds: A Biographical Study*, 1914.
Brown, Horatio F. *John Addington Symonds: A Biography*, 1895.
Grosskurth, Phyllis. *John Addington Symonds: A Biography*, 1964.

Like Walter Pater, Symonds drew inspiration for his critical and creative works from the Renaissance. *The Renaissance in Italy,* although comparatively shapeless, was an important factor in awakening interest in that era, dormant since Ruskin's belittling of Renaissance art and culture. Symonds' many prose works reveal deep admiration for—if little deep understanding of—such baffling figures as Shelley and Michaelangelo. His poetry is decadent but undistinguished.

SYMONS, ARTHUR (1865-1945)

Prose:

The Symbolist Movement in Literature, 1899.
Aubrey Beardsley, 1905.
Spiritual Adventures, 1905.
Studies in Seven Arts, 1906.
The Romantic Movement in English Poetry, 1909.
Dramatis Personae, 1923.
A Study of Thomas Hardy, 1927.
A Study of Oscar Wilde, 1930.
A Study of Walter Pater, 1932.
And other titles.

Arthur Symons

Poems:

Days and Nights, 1889.
Silhouettes, 1892.
London Nights, 1895.
Amoris Victima, 1897.
Poems, 1902.
Lesbia, 1920.
And other titles.

Autobiography:

Confessions, 1930.

Collected Works:

The Collected Works. 9 vols., 1924.

Bibliographical:

Danielson, H. "Arthur Symons," *Bibliographies of Modern Authors*, 1921. Pp. 173-198.

Biographical and Critical:

Baugh, Edward. "Arthur Symons, Poet: A Centenary Tribute," *Review of English Literature*, VI (July, 1965), 70-80.
Kermode, Frank. "Arthur Symons," *The Romantic Image*, 1957. Pp. 107-119.
Lhombreaud, Roger. *Arthur Symons: A Critical Biography*, 1963. [The standard bio.]
Munro, John M. *Arthur Symons*, 1969. [Bib. pp. 163-167.]
Stanford, Derek. "Arthur Symons and Modern Poetics," *Southern Review*, II (Spring, 1966), 347-353.
Welby, T. Earle. *Arthur Symons: A Critical Study*, 1925. [Bib. pp. 141-148.]

Symons played prominent parts in the aesthetic movement of the 1880's and 1890's as student and perceptive critic of French literature (*The Symbolist Movement*), member of the Rhymers' Club and editor of *The Savoy*. His poetic subject matter and forms did not differ markedly from those of the other Rhymers, but fastidiousness of phrasing gave them rare finish. He had unusual ability to create images of bittersweet sensuality, as "The Opium Smoker" shows. Symons never regained his mental equilibrium after a breakdown in 1908. He is therefore chiefly important as a critic-interpreter and poet of the "yellow decades."

SYNGE, JOHN MILLINGTON (1871-1909)

Plays:

The Shadow of the Glen, 1904.
Riders to the Sea, 1904.
The Well of the Saints, 1905.
The Playboy of the Western World, 1907.
The Tinker's Wedding, 1909.
Deirdre of the Sorrows, 1910.

Prose:

The Aran Islands, 1907.

Poems:

Poems and Translations, 1909.

Autobiography:

Autobiography. Ed. Alan F. Price. 1963. [Short autobio. ed. from Synge's notebooks.]

Letters:

Letters to Molly: John Millington Synge to Marie O'Neill 1906-1909. Ed. Ann Saddlemyer. 1971.

Collected Works:

Plays. "Revised Collected Edition." 1932.
Collected Works. Ed. Robin Skelton. 4 vols., 1962-1968.

John Millington Synge

The Plays and Poems of J. M. Synge. Ed. T. R. Henn. 1963.

Biographical and Critical:

Bickley, Francis. *J. M. Synge and the Irish Dramatic Movement,* 1912.
Bourgeois, Maurice. *John Millington Synge and the Irish Theatre,* 1913. [Bib. pp. 251-296.]
Corkery, Daniel. *Synge and Anglo-Irish Literature,* 1931.
Coxhead, Elizabeth. *J. M. Synge and Lady Gregory,* 1952.
Estill, A. D. *The Sources of Synge,* 1939.
Gerstenberger, Donna Lorine. *J. M. Synge,* 1964. [Bib. pp. 142-152.]
Greene, David H., and Edward M. Stephens. *J. M. Synge, 1871-1909,* 1959. [Bib. pp. 308-310.]
Howe, Percival. *J. M. Synge: A Critical Study,* 1912.
Johnston, Denis. *John Millington Synge,* 1965.
Price, Alan F. *Synge and Anglo-Irish Drama,* 1961. [Excellent study of the plays.]
Setterquist, Jan. *Ibsen and the Beginnings of Anglo-Irish Drama. I: John Millington Synge,* 1951.
Skelton, Robin. "The Poetry of J. M. Synge," *Poetry Ireland,* I (Autumn, 1962), 32-44.
Strong, L. A. G. *John Millington Synge,* 1941.
Synge, Samuel. *Letters to My Daughter: Memories of John Millington Synge,* 1931.
Yeats, W. B. *J. M. Synge and the Ireland of His Time,* 1911.

Synge's plays now are ranked among the finest of the first decade of the Abbey Theatre, even if, at the time, Irish audiences found them scandalously distorted pictures of Irish life (especially *Playboy*). As poet, Synge was indebted to François Villon and other continental writers, but he forged his own poetic faith. His highly personal lyrics of love, loneliness and death reach heights surpassed by few of his countrymen. One source of Synge's power as poet-playwright is his ability to recreate Irish speech and imagery. *The Aran Islands* helps one understand Synge's deep affection for humble Irish life.

THOMAS, EDWARD [EDWARD EASTAWAY] (1878-1917)

Poems:

Poems, 1917.
Last Poems, 1918.
Collected Poems. Ed. Walter de la Mare. 1920.
Six Poems, 1927.
And other titles.

Prose:

Oxford, 1903.
Light and Twilight, 1911.
Algernon Charles Swinburne, 1912.
The Icknield Way, 1913.
In Pursuit of Spring, 1914.
The Childhood of Edward Thomas, 1938. [Fragment of an autobio.]
And other titles.

Fiction:

Celtic Stories, 1911.
Norse Tales, 1912.
The Happy-Go-Luck Morgans, 1913.
Four-and-Twenty Blackbirds, 1915.

Bibliographical:

Eckert, Robert P. "Edward Thomas, Soldier-Poet of His Race," *American Book Collector,* IV (July-August, 1933), 19-21; 66-69. [Checklist to 1931; incomplete.]

Biographical and Critical:

Cooke, William. *Edward Thomas: A Critical Biography 1878-1917,* 1970. [Bib. pp. 279-287.]
Coombes, H. *Edward Thomas,* 1956. [Bib. pp. 248-249.]
Eckert, Robert P. *Edward Thomas: A Biography and a Bibliography,* 1937.
Farjeon, Eleanor. *Edward Thomas: The Last Four Years,* 1958.

Guthrie, James J. *To the Memory of Edward Thomas,* 1937.
Moore, John C. *The Life and Letters of Edward Thomas,* 1939.
Thomas, Helen. *As It Was,* 1926.
— *World Without End,* 1931.
Thomas, R. George. "Edward Thomas, Poet and Critic," *Essays and Studies,* XXI (1968), 118-136.
Whicher, George F. "Edward Thomas," *The Yale Review,* IX (April, 1920), 556-567.

Thomas' reputation rests almost solely on the poetry which he wrote in the last two and a half years of his life, a genre which he attempted partly because of the example of Robert Frost. His verse has the freshness and rusticity of subject matter and diction that characterize Frost's work, but Thomas' poetic self was tempered by war. He wrote many poems in training and at the front. Much of Thomas' prose was hack work, but his outdoor prose, especially *In Pursuit of Spring,* foreshadows his poetic achievement.

THOMPSON, FRANCIS (1859-1907)

Poems:

Poems, 1893.
Sister Songs . . . , 1895.
New Poems, 1897.
The Works of Francis Thompson. Ed. Wilfrid Meynell. 1913.
Poems of Francis Thompson. Ed. Terence L. Connolly. 1932.
The Man Has Wings: New Poems and Plays by Francis Thompson. Ed. T. L. Connolly. 1957.
And other titles.

Prose:

Shelley, 1909.
Saint Ignatius Loyola, 1909.
A Renegade Poet, 1910.
Essays of Today and Yesterday, 1927.

Francis Thompson

Literary Criticisms by Francis Thompson, Newly Discovered and Collected. Ed. T. L. Connolly. 1948. [Bib. pp. 563-596.]

And other titles.

Letters:

The Letters of Francis Thompson. Ed. John Evangelist Walsh. 1969.

Bibliographical:

Catalogue of the "Francis Thompson" Collection: Presented to the Harris Public Library . . . with Supplementary List of "Thompsoniana" . . . , 1950.

Catalogue of Manuscripts, Letters and Books in the Harris Public Library . . . , 1959.

Connolly, T. L. (ed.). *An Account of Books and Manuscripts of Francis Thompson,* 1937.

Pope, Myrtle Pihlman. *A Critical Bibliography of Works by and about Francis Thompson,* 1959. [Originally pub. in *Bulletin of New York Public Library,* LXII (November, 1958), 571-576; LXIII (January, March, April, 1959), 40-49; 155-161; 195-204.]

Biographical and Critical:

de la Gorce, Agnes. *Francis Thompson,* 1933.

Mégroz, R. L. *Francis Thompson: The Poet of Earth in Heaven,* 1927.

Meynell, Everard. *The Life of Francis Thompson,* 1913.

Meynell, Viola. *Francis Thompson and Wilfrid Meynell: A Memoir,* 1952.

Owlett, F. C. *Francis Thompson,* 1936.

Reid, John Cowie. *Francis Thompson: Man and Poet,* 1959.

Thompson, Paul Van Kuykendall. *Francis Thompson: A Critical Biography,* 1961.

Walsh, John. *Strange Harp, Strange Symphony: The Life of Francis Thompson,* 1967.

Wright, T. H. *Francis Thompson and His Poetry,* 1927.

As in metaphysical poetry, texture is of great importance in Thompson's work, with far-fetched conceits, elaborate epithets and stylized diction combining to produce baroque poetic texture. Essentially an autobiographical poet, Thompson drew passionate inspiration from the agony of his life-long struggle with poverty, drug addiction and illness. His religious fervor, however, was strong despite bodily ills, as "The Kingdom of God" reveals. Many of his poems may seem merely bizarre, but in "The Hound of Heaven," objections to imagery or language are made irrelevant by Thompson's intensity of vision.

TODHUNTER, JOHN (1839-1916)

Poems:

Alcestis: A Dramatic Poem, 1879.
Forest Songs, 1881.
The Banshee, 1888.
Sounds and Sweet Airs, 1900.
From the Land of Dreams, 1918.
Selected Poems. Ed. D. C. Todhunter and Alfred Perceval Graves. 1929.
And other titles.

Plays:

Helena in Troas [with E. W. Godwin], *1886.*
A Sicilian Idyll, 1890.
The Black Cat, 1893.
And other titles.

Prose:

A Riverside Walk: An Easy-going Essay by a Peripatetic Philosopher, 1898.
Essays, 1920.
And other titles.

John Todhunter

Already recognized as an English poet by 1888, Todhunter contributed to *Poems and Ballads of Young Ireland,* and from then until about 1895, made a significant contribution to the Celtic Renaissance in his use of Irish bardic material, as in *The Banshee.* But when the fervor for Irish literature began to wane, Todhunter returned to the poetic tradition that had formed him. He also had some importance as an exponent of "new drama," his *Black Cat* appearing at the Independent Theatre shortly after Shaw's *Widowers' Houses.*

TRENCH, HERBERT (1865-1923)

Poems:

Haileybury Verses, 1882.
Deirdre Wed, 1901.
New Poems, 1907.
Lyrics and Narrative Poems, 1911.
Poems: With Fables in Prose, 1918.
The Collected Works of Herbert Trench. Ed. Harold Williams. 1924.
And other titles.

Biographical and Critical:

Clarke, Austin. "The Poetry of Herbert Trench," *London Mercury,* X (June, 1924), 157-167.

Trench showed promise and enjoyed a brief period of fame between 1900 and 1910 with *Deirdre* and *New Poems.* He was at his best in such personal lyrics as "Come, let us make love deathless, thou and I," which achieve a fusion of form and emotion. More ambitious poems like "Apollo and the Seamen" fail from the over-heavy burden of idea.

TRENCH POETS

None of England's wars had engendered more moving literary appraisals than the poems of the many young Englishmen who wrote about their experiences in the First World War. Chief among them were Wilfred Owen, Rupert Brooke, Isaac Rosenberg and Siegfried Sassoon. To group them as "Trench Poets" or "War Poets" risks blurring the distinctions between them as poets. Brooke was more romantic than the others, Sassoon more didactic and ironic. Their attitudes toward the War ranged from Brooke's shallow celebration, through Sassoon's lectures aimed at complacent stay-at-homes, to Owen's and Rosenberg's stately, realistic, balanced presentations of suffering and death.

TYNAN, KATHARINE [MRS. HINKSON] (1861-1931)

Poems:

Louise de la Vallière, 1885.
Ballads and Lyrics, 1891.
Poems, 1901.
Collected Poems, 1930.
And other titles.

Novels:

The Way of a Maid, 1895.
A Girl of Galway, 1902.
Julia, 1904.
Mary Gray, 1908.
The Man From Australia, 1919.
And other titles.

Tynan was prominent in the Celtic Renaissance as religious poet and popular novelist. She had no literary standard for her novels and annually cooked up several for her circulating-library public. Two major influences on her poetry were D. G. Rossetti, as "The Dead Spring" shows, and Ireland's past, as mirrored in "Waiting." Her poetry is as effortless and ingenuous as her prose.

WALPOLE, HUGH (1884-1941)

Fiction:

The Wooden Horse, 1909.
Fortitude, 1913.
The Duchess of Wrexe, 1914.
The Dark Forest, 1916.
The Green Mirror, 1918.
Jeremy, 1919.
The Captives, 1920.
The Cathedral, 1922.
John Cornelius, 1937.
And other titles.

Prose:

Joseph Conrad, 1916.
The English Novel, 1925.
Anthony Trollope, 1928.
And other titles.

Autobiography:

The Crystal Box, 1924.
My Religious Experience, 1928.
The Apple Trees, 1932.
Roman Fountain, 1940.

Biographical and Critical:

Dane, Clemence. *Tradition and Hugh Walpole*, 1930.
Hart-Davis, Rupert. *Hugh Walpole*, 1952. [Excellent bio.]
Hergesheimer, Joseph. *Hugh Walpole*, 1919.
Priestley, J. B. "Hugh Walpole," *English Journal*, XVII (September, 1928), 529-536.
Steen, M. *Hugh Walpole*, 1933.
West, Anthony. "Hugh Walpole," *Principles and Persuasions*, 1957. Pp. 155-163.

Hugh Walpole

Although a contemporary of many more "modern" writers, Walpole was quite traditional, harkening back (especially in *The Cathedral*) to the ideals of English life of Trollope's time. Counterbalancing this tendency was a fascination with evil and terror, a gothic, Russian side on the reverse of his placid English figure. But, chameleon-like, Walpole turned from one fashion to another throughout his career without taking on a lasting hue—much to the detriment of his achievement.

WARD, MRS. HUMPHRY (1851-1920)

Fiction:

Robert Elsmere, 1888.
The History of David Grieve, 1892.
The Case of Richard Meynell, 1911.
Bessie Costrell, 1912.
Eltham House, 1915.
And other titles.

Autobiography:

A Writer's Recollections, 1918.

Biographical and Critical:

Gosse, Edmund. "Mrs. Humphry Ward," *Silhouettes*, 1925. Pp. 203-210.
Gwynn, S. L. *Mrs. Humphry Ward*, 1917.
Knoepflmacher, U. C. "The Rival Ladies: Mrs. Ward's *Lady Connie* and Lawrence's *Lady Chatterley's Lover*," *Victorian Studies*, IV (December, 1960), 141-158.
Lederer, Clara. "Mary Arnold Ward and the Victorian Ideal," *Nineteenth-Century Fiction*, VI (December, 1951), 201-208.
Trevelyan, Janet Penrose. *Life of Mrs. Humphry Ward*, 1923.
Walters, J. S. *Mrs. Humphry Ward: Her Work and Influence*, 1912.
Willey, Basil. "How *Robert Elsmere* Struck Some Contemporaries," *Essays and Studies*, X (1957), 53-68.

Mrs. Humphry Ward

Ward was a major feminine force in her time. She championed a faith in social mission and helped a variety of causes with her presence as well as her pen. *Robert Elsmere,* a study of a clergyman's loss of faith, shocked people who were accustomed to finding religious reassurance in popular fiction. With the possible exception of *Richard Meynell,* she failed in her later novels to equal even the modest skill of intellectual analysis and characterization she showed in *Elsmere,* but her regularly produced political-didactic-realistic novels, all *romans à clef,* brought her sufficient fame.

WATSON, JOHN [IAN MACLAREN] (1850-1907)

Fiction:

Beside the Bonnie Brier Bush, 1894.
The Days of Auld Langsyne, 1895.
A Doctor of the Old School, 1895.
Kate Carnegie and Those Ministers, 1896.
Afterwards, and Other Stories, 1898.
And other titles.

Autobiography:

Young Barbarians, 1901.

Biographical and Critical:

Nicoll, William Robertson. "*Ian Maclaren,*" 1908.
Pond, J. B. "The Rev. Dr. John Watson ('Ian Maclaren')," *Eccentricities of Genius,* 1900. Pp. 405-452.

When Watson published *Brier Bush,* he exchanged the life of a relatively obscure parson, already the author of several weighty religious tomes, for that of popular novelist. In a few years, he was the best known writer of the Kailyard School. He gave the public harmless, idyllic sketches of Scots life and, even if he could not write, his literary endeavors brought him substantial success.

WATSON, JOHN WILLIAM [WILLIAM WATSON] (1858-1935)

Poems:

Wordsworth's Grave, 1890.
Lachrymae Musarum, 1893.
Odes, 1894.
The Purple East, 1896.
The Year of Shame, 1897.
Ode on the Day of the Coronation of King Edward VII, 1902.
The Muse in Exile, 1913.
Selected Poems, with Notes by the Author, 1928.
The Poems of Sir William Watson, 1878-1935, 1936.
And other titles.

Prose:

Excursions in Criticism, 1893.

Bibliographical:

Woolf, Cecil. "Some Uncollected Authors XII: Sir William Watson," *The Book Collector,* V (Winter, 1956), 375-380. [See additions and corrections in VI, 66-67, 285-286 and 402.]

Biographical and Critical:

Archer, William. "William Watson," *Poets of the Younger Generation,* 1902. Pp. 483-521.
Kernahan, Coulson. "Sir William Watson, An 'Old Contemptible' of Song," *Five More Famous Living Poets,* 1928. Pp. 269-312.
Nelson, James G. *Sir William Watson,* 1966. [Bib. pp. 181-185.]
White, G. "An Agnostic Poet," *Sewanee Review,* VIII (July, 1900), 365-377.
Woodberry, G. E. "William Watson," *Century Magazine,* LXIV (September, 1902), 801-803.

Had Watson received the laureateship at Tennyson's death, the office would have been capably filled, as

Watson's coronation ode shows, and his own professional life would have been sweeter. But he was denied the position on this and two other occasions, largely because he annoyed important people by his indignant poetic attacks on tyranny (*The Purple East*) and his compassionate defense of oppressed peoples like the Boers and the Irish. Today his verse seems craftsmanlike, sincere, but rather dated—a natural product of his bold but limited confrontation of social issues.

WATSON, WILLIAM. *see* WATSON, JOHN WILLIAM.

WEBB, MARY (1881-1927)

Fiction:

The Golden Arrow, 1916.
Gone to Earth, 1917.
The House in Dormer Forest, 1920.
Seven for a Secret, 1922.
Precious Bane, 1924.

Poems:

Poems and The Spring of Joy. Ed. Walter de la Mare, 1929.
Fifty-one Poems, 1946.

Collected Works:

The Novels of Mary Webb. "Sarn Edition." 7 vols., 1942.

Bibliographical:

Sanders, Charles. "Mary Webb: An Annotated Bibliography of Writings about Her," *English Literature in Transition,* IX: 3 (1966), 119-136.

Biographical and Critical:

Addison, Hilda. *Mary Webb,* 1931.
Chappell, W. R. *The Shropshire of Mary Webb,* 1930.
Davis, W. Eugene. "The Poetry of Mary Webb: An Invitation," *English Literature in Transition,* XI: 2 (1968), 95-101.
Moult, Thomas. *Mary Webb: Her Life and Work,* 1932.
Wrenn, Dorothy P. H. *Goodbye to Morning,* 1964.

Webb's novels and poems are saturated with the scenes and the lore of Shropshire, but she was no genteel local colorist. Her novels often deal with suffering, thwarted hopes and violence. *Precious Bane* is best known, but *The Golden Arrow,* with its careful symbolism, may be the more artistic novel. Webb is sometimes called a Georgian because of the bucolic subject matter of her poems, but they are far more personal, sensual and sometimes erotic (e.g. "The Plain in Autumn") than is typical of Georgian verse. In her rather melancholy view of life and her employment of Shropshire material, she may have been influenced by A. E. Housman.

WELLS, HERBERT GEORGE (1866-1946)

Fiction:

The Time Machine, 1895.
The Wheels of Chance, 1896.
The Island of Doctor Moreau, 1896.
The Invisible Man, 1897.
The War of the Worlds, 1898.
When the Sleeper Wakes, 1899. [Rvd. ed. titled *The Sleeper Awakes,* 1911.]
Love and Mr. Lewisham, 1900.
Tales of Space and Time, 1900.
The First Men in the Moon, 1901.
Kipps, 1905.
Tono-Bungay, 1908.
Ann Veronica, 1909.
The History of Mr. Polly, 1910.

The Country of the Blind, 1911.
The New Machiavelli, 1911.
Marriage, 1912.
Joan and Peter, 1918.
The Croquet Player, 1936.
The Desert Daisy. Ed. Gordon N. Ray. 1957. [Story written and illustrated by Wells as a boy.]
And other titles.

Prose:

Anticipations, 1902.
Mankind in the Making, 1903.
A Modern Utopia, 1905.
New Worlds for Old, 1908.
First and Last Things, 1908; rvd. ed., 1917.
The War That Will End War, 1914.
Boon, 1915.
The Outline of History, 1919-1920. [Published serially.]
The Open Conspiracy, 1928.
The Shape of Things to Come, 1933.
The Anatomy of Frustration, 1936.
'42 to '44: A Contemporary Memoir, 1944.
Mind at the End of its Tether, 1945.
H. G. Wells: Journalism & Prophecy, 1893-1946: An Anthology. Ed. W. Warren Wagar. 1965.
And other titles.

Collected Works:

Works. "Atlantic Edition." 26 vols., 1924-1927.
The Short Stories of H. G. Wells, 1927.

Letters and Autobiography:

Experiment in Autobiography, 1934.
Henry James and H. G. Wells: A Record of Their Friendship, Their Debate on the Art of Fiction, and Their Quarrel. Ed. Leon Edel and Gordon N. Ray. 1958.
Arnold Bennett and H. G. Wells: A Record of a Personal and a Literary Friendship. Ed. Harris Wilson. 1960.

George Gissing and H. G. Wells: A Record of Their Friendship and Correspondence. Ed. Royal A. Gettmann. 1961.
"H. G. Wells and Sinclair Lewis: Friendship, Literary Influence, and Letters." Ed. Martin Light. *English Fiction in Transition,* V: 4 (1962), 1-20.

Bibliographical:

Chappell, Fred A. *Bibliography of H. G. Wells,* 1924. [Incomplete; inaccurate.]
H. G. Wells Society. *H. G. Wells: A Comprehensive Bibliography.* 2nd ed., rvd., 1968.
Weeks, Robert P. "Bibliography, News and Notes: H. G. Wells," *English Fiction in Transition,* I: 1 (1957), 37-42. [Bib. of a few wks. about Wells, with occasional annotation.]
Wells, Geoffrey H. *The Works of H. G. Wells 1887-1925: A Bibliography, Dictionary, and Subject-Index,* 1926.

Biographical and Critical:

Belgion, Montgomery. *H. G. Wells,* 1953. [Bib. pp. 37-43.]
Beresford, J. D. *H. G. Wells,* 1915.
Bergonzi, Bernard. *The Early H. G. Wells: A Study of the Scientific Romances,* 1961. [Excellent examination of symbol and myth.]
Brome, Vincent. *H. G. Wells: A Biography,* 1951.
Brooks, Van Wyck. *The World of H. G. Wells,* 1915.
Connes, G. A. *A Dictionary of the Characters and Scenes in the Novels, Romances and Short Stories of H. G. Wells,* 1926.
Dickson, Lovat. *H. G. Wells: His Turbulent Life and Times,* 1969. [Bib. pp. 319-322.]
Doughty, F. H. *H. G. Wells: Educationist,* 1926.
Guyot, Edouard. *H. G. Wells,* 1920.
Hillegas, Mark R. *The Future as Nightmare: H. G. Wells and the Anti-Utopians,* 1968.
Kagarlitski, J. *The Life and Thought of H. G. Wells.* Trans. Moura Budberg. 1966.
Meyer, Mathilde Marie. *H. G. Wells and His Family, As I Have Known Them,* 1956. [Memoir by governess.]
Nicholson, Norman. *H. G. Wells,* 1950.
Parrinder, Patrick. *H. G. Wells,* 1970. [Bib. pp. 110-120.]

Raknem, Ingvald. *H. G. Wells and His Critics,* 1962. [Lack of index makes valuable information inaccessible; extensive list of revs. of Wells wks., pp. 446-459.]
Wagar, W. Warren. *H. G. Wells and the World State,* 1961.
West, Geoffrey [i.e. Geoffrey H. Wells]. *H. G. Wells: A Sketch for a Portrait,* 1930.

Wells, sensing the excitement surrounding scientific experiment, created the scientific romance, now called science fiction. He was the first to write of time travel by a purely mechanical means (*The Time Machine*) and the invasion of earth by extraterrestrial life (*War of the Worlds*). Among his scientific marvels were invisibility, exploration of the moon, medical evolution and the development of supermen. In his science fiction, Wells often added depth to the entertainment of his fantasy with symbolism and myth. Wells turned his attention to social issues, first in a rather light-hearted fashion (*Wheels of Chance*), but increasingly with a serious purpose. In early comedies (*Kipps, Mr. Polly*), he depicted in humorously satiric terms the tribulations of lower middle-class men caught in changing Edwardian society. *Tono-Bungay,* Wells' greatest novel, provides an analysis of the break up of Victorian values. With each succeeding novel, he moved increasingly away from comedy toward pure propaganda. After about 1914, Wells made no pretense at writing imaginative fiction, and turned instead to arguing about history, politics, economics and the condition of man. Wells was primarily a social critic, both in fiction and non-fiction, who grew increasingly cynical about progress, science and man's innate goodness. He saw hope, however, in education for all men, which led him to write encyclopaedic works like *The Outline of History* and to propose vast repositories of cumulative knowledge. Despite so many earnest propaganda novels and much serious non-fiction, Wells' best work is his science fiction and a few social comedies.

WEYMAN, STANLEY JOHN (1855-1928)

Fiction:

The House of the Wolf, 1890.
The New Rector, 1891.
A Gentleman of France, 1893.
The Red Cockade, 1895.
Shrewsbury, 1898.
Count Hannibal, 1901.
Starvecrow Farm, 1905.
And other titles.

Biographical and Critical:

Chapman, Grace. "Stanley Weyman," *London Mercury*, XXVII (April, 1933), 530-538.
Hughes, T. Cann. "Stanley John Weyman," *Manchester Quarterly*, LIX (1933), 283-301.

Weyman wrote fiction of three sorts: English-topical (*The New Rector, Starvecrow Farm*), English-historical (*Shrewsbury*) and foreign-historical (most of the other titles). Although his work is marred by sentimentality, he constructed elaborate plots with all the trappings and happenstance necessary to successful romance. He wrote solely to bring pleasure to his own generation.

WHITE, WILLIAM HALE [MARK RUTHERFORD] (1831-1913)

Fiction:

The Autobiography of Mark Rutherford, Dissenting Minister, 1881.
Mark Rutherford's Deliverance, 1885.
The Revolution in Tanner's Lane, 1887.
Miriam's Schooling, and Other Papers, 1890.
Catharine Furze, 1893.
Clara Hopgood, 1896.

William Hale White

Autobiography, Journals and Letters:

Pages from a Journal, with Other Papers, 1900.
More Pages from a Journal, with Other Papers, 1910.
The Early Life of Mark Rutherford by Himself, 1913.
Last Pages from a Journal with Other Papers. Ed. Dorothy V. White. 1915.
Letters to Three Friends. Ed. Dorothy V. White. 1924.

Bibliographical:

Davis, W. Eugene. "William Hale White ('Mark Rutherford'): An Annotated Bibliography of Writings About Him," *English Literature in Transition,* X: 2, 3 (1967), 97-117; 150-160.
Smith, Simon Nowell. "Mark Rutherford: A Short Bibliography of First Editions," Supplement to *The Bookman's Journal,* XVIII: 14 (1930).

Biographical and Critical:

Maclean, Catherine. *Mark Rutherford: A Biography of William Hale White,* 1955. [Solid study; no notes or index.]
Merton, Stephen. *Mark Rutherford,* 1967.
Stock, Irvin. *William Hale White (Mark Rutherford), A Critical Study,* 1956.
Stone, Wilfred. *Religion and Art of William Hale White . . .,* 1954. [Valuable study.]
White, Dorothy Vernon. *Groombridge Diary,* 1924.

Today White is respected as a sincere, candid chronicler of Victorian dissent and a novelist of considerable insight. To a large extent, his novels are fictionalized autobiography (especially *Autobiography* and *Deliverance*), and while he limited himself to a handful of character types and a few themes (notably the confrontation of simple, passive characters by religious or psychological problems), his economical style and forthright treatment continue to win him scholarly interest.

WHITEING, RICHARD (1840-1928)

Fiction:

The Island, 1888.
No. 5 John Street, 1899.
The Yellow Van, 1903.
All Moonshine, 1907.
And other titles.

Prose:

Living Paris and France, 1886.
The Life of Paris, 1900.
Little People, 1908.
And other titles.

Autobiography:

My Harvest, 1915.

Bibliographical:

Harris, Wendell V. "A Selective Annotated Bibliography of Writings about Richard Whiteing," *English Literature in Transition,* VIII: 1 (1965), 44-48.

Biographical and Critical:

"Fiction and Philanthropy," *Edinburgh Review,* CXCI (April, 1900), 305-333.
MacFall, Haldane. "Literary Portraits: III—Richard Whiteing," *Canadian Magazine,* XXIII (July, 1904), 206-208.
W., C. "Richard Whiteing," *Bookman* (London), XLIX (January, 1916), 124-126.

Were it not for the satire-fantasy in *The Island* and *No. 5 John Street,* Whiteing would probably be forgotten. In *The Island,* Pitcairn Islanders pride themselves on their place in the Empire, of which they know nothing. The later work sends the islanders news of the Diamond Jubilee from the basement of No. 5 John Street. Some of Swift's *saeva indignatio* is present in Whiteing's bitter portrayal of life underground.

WILDE, OSCAR FINGALL O'FLAHERTIE WILLS (1856-1900)

Plays:

Lady Windermere's Fan, 1892.
A Woman of No Importance, 1893.
Salomé, 1894 [Paris]; *1905* [London].
An Ideal Husband, 1895.
The Importance of Being Earnest, 1895.
And other titles.

Poems:

Poems, 1881.
The Sphinx, 1894.
The Ballad of Reading Gaol, 1898.
The Poems of Oscar Wilde, 1906.
And other titles.

Fiction:

The Happy Prince, 1888.
The Picture of Dorian Gray, 1891.
Lord Arthur Savile's Crime, 1891.
A House of Pomegranates, 1891.

Prose:

Intentions, 1891.
The Soul of Man under Socialism, 1895.
Miscellanies, 1908.
A Critic in Pall Mall, 1919.
The Artist as Critic: Critical Writings of Oscar Wilde. Ed. Richard Ellmann. 1969.

Oscar Wilde

Autobiography and Letters:

De Profundis, 1905. [First complete ed., 1949. Ed. V. Holland.]
Wilde vs. Whistler, 1906.
Resurgam: Unpublished Letters, 1917.
Letters to the Sphinx, 1930.
Sixteen Letters from Oscar Wilde, 1930.
The Letters of Oscar Wilde. Ed. Rupert Hart-Davis. 1962.

Collected Works:

Works. Ed. Robert Ross. 14 vols., 1908.
Complete Works, 1966.

Bibliographical:

Finzi, John Charles. *Oscar Wilde and His Literary Circle: A Catalogue of Manuscripts and Letters in the William Andrews Clark Memorial Library*, 1957.
Mason, Stuart. *Bibliography of Oscar Wilde*, 1914. [Some errors, but a mine of information.]

Biographical and Critical:

Agate, James E. *Oscar Wilde and the Theatre*, 1947.
Brasol, Boris. *Oscar Wilde: The Man, the Artist, the Martyr*, 1938.
Beckson, Karl (ed.). *Oscar Wilde: The Critical Heritage*, 1970.
Broad, Lewis. *The Friendships and Follies of Oscar Wilde*, 1954.
Byrne, Patrick. *The Wildes of Merrion Square*, 1953.
Douglas, Alfred Bruce. *Oscar Wilde: A Summing-Up*, 1940.
Ellmann, Richard (ed.). *Oscar Wilde: A Collection of Critical Essays*, 1969.
Ervine, St. John. *Oscar Wilde: A Present Time Appraisal*, 1952.
Harris, Frank. *Oscar Wilde: His Life and Confessions*, 1914.
Holland, Vyvyan. *Oscar Wilde: A Pictorial Biography*, 1961.
Hyde, H. Montgomery. *Oscar Wilde: The Aftermath*, 1963.
Jullian, Phillippe. *Oscar Wilde*. Trans. Violet Wyndham. 1969. [Bib. pp. 411-414.]

Laver, James. *Oscar Wilde,* 1954.
Lewis, Lloyd, and Henry J. Smith. *Oscar Wilde Discovers America (1882),* 1936.
Mason, Stuart. *Oscar Wilde and the Aesthetic Movement,* 1920.
Merle, Robert. *Oscar Wilde,* 1948.
Ojala, Aatos. *Aestheticism and Oscar Wilde: Part I, Life and Letters,* 1954.
Pearson, Hesketh. *The Life of Oscar Wilde,* 1946.
Roditi, Edouard. *Oscar Wilde,* 1947.
San Juan, Epifanio, Jr. *The Art of Oscar Wilde,* 1967.
Winwar, Frances. *Oscar Wilde and the Yellow 'Nineties,'* 1940.
Woodcock, George. *The Paradox of Oscar Wilde,* 1948.

In his life and writings, Wilde was the leading force of the aesthetic-decadent movement. He was a poseur who delighted in extravagant dress and paradoxical, witty conversation—aspects which his contemporaries, like Gilbert and Sullivan in *Patience,* often lampooned. His most durable writings have proved to be his plays, especially the comedies of manners *Lady Windemere's Fan* and *The Importance of Being Earnest.* While they may seem purely art for art's sake, they obliquely criticize the elegant, empty society of the 1890's. Like George Moore, Wilde had an impressionable nature which absorbed influences from different countries, centuries and artistic styles. His poems, for example, are largely products of clever eclecticism rather than genuine poetic inspiration. Although echoes of Baudelaire, Rossetti and Swinburne drown Wilde's own voice in most of his verse, "The Sphinx" and "The Ballad of Reading Gaol" show Wilde might have become a substantial poet. *The Picture of Dorian Gray,* which tells of a portrait that grows old and decays as its eternally youthful subject falls deeper into sin and misery, is a fictionalized version of aesthetic-decadent life.

WRATISLAW, THEODORE WILLIAM GRAF (1871-1933)

Poems:

Some Verses, 1892.

Theodore William Graf Wratislaw

Caprices, 1893.
Orchids, 1896.
Selected Poems. Ed. J. Gawsworth. 1935.

Prose:

Algernon Charles Swinburne: A Study, 1900.

Biographical and Critical:

Ellis, S. M. "Theodore Wratislaw: A Poet of the Nineties," *Mainly Victorian*, 1925. Pp. 378-381.

One of the more minor decadent poets, Wratislaw achieved some fame for his study of Swinburne. As poet, he saw sadness beneath earthly joys and cultivated a pose of wan regret for the evanescence of beauty. Neither in themes nor treatment is there much to distinguish him from other poets of the movement.

YEATS, WILLIAM BUTLER (1865-1939)

Poems:

The Wanderings of Oisin, 1889.
The Countess Kathleen and Various Legends and Lyrics, 1892.
Poems, 1895.
The Wind Among the Reeds, 1899.
In the Seven Woods, 1903.
Poems: Second Series, 1909.
Poems Written in Discouragement 1912-1913, 1913.
Responsibilities, 1914.
The Wild Swans at Coole, 1917.
Michael Robartes and the Dancer, 1920.
The Tower, 1928.
The Winding Stair, 1929.
New Poems, 1938.
Last Poems and Two Plays, 1939.
The Collected Poems of W. B. Yeats, 1950.

The Variorum Edition of the Poems of W. B. Yeats. Ed. P. Allt and R. K. Alspach, 1957.
And other titles.

Plays:

The Land of Heart's Desire, 1894.
The Countess Cathleen, 1899.
Cathleen Ni Houlihan [with Lady Gregory], *1902.*
The Hour-Glass [with Lady Gregory], *1903.* [Versified version, *1912.*]
The King's Threshold [with Lady Gregory], *1903.*
Where There is Nothing [with Lady Gregory], *1904.*
The Shadowy Waters, 1904.
On Baile's Strand [with Lady Gregory], *1904.*
Deirdre [with Lady Gregory], *1906.*
The Unicorn from the Stars [with Lady Gregory], *1907.*
The Golden Helmet, 1908. [Later titled *The Green Helmet, 1910.*]
The Collected Plays of W. B. Yeats, 1952.
The Variorum Edition of the Plays of W. B. Yeats. Ed. R. K. Alspach. 1966.
And other titles.

Prose:

John Sherman, and Dhoya, 1891. [Novels.]
The Celtic Twilight, 1893; rvd. ed., 1902.
The Secret Rose, 1897.
Ideas of Good and Evil, 1903.
Discoveries, 1907.
The Cutting of an Agate, 1912.
A Vision, 1925.
Mythologies, 1959.
The Senate Speeches of William Butler Yeats. Ed. D. R. Pearce. 1960.
Uncollected Prose by W. B. Yeats. Vol. I: First Reviews and Articles 1886-1896. Ed. John P. Frayne. 1970.
And other titles.

William Butler Yeats

Autobiography:

Reveries over Childhood and Youth, 1915.
The Trembling of the Veil, 1922.
Dramatis Personae, 1935.
The Autobiography of William Butler Yeats, 1938. [Rpts. *Reveries, Trembling, Dramatis.*]
Autobiographies, 1955. [1938 ed. plus some new material.]

Letters:

Letters on Poetry from W. B. Yeats to Dorothy Wellesley, 1940.
Letters to Katharine Tynan. Ed. Roger McHugh. 1953.
W. B. Yeats and T. Sturge Moore: Their Correspondence 1901-1937. Ed. Ursula Bridge. 1953.
Some Letters from W. B. Yeats to John O'Leary and His Sister. Ed. Allan Wade. 1953.
The Letters of W. B. Yeats. Ed. Allan Wade. 1954.

Bibliographical:

Parrish, Stephen Maxfield. *A Concordance to the Poems of W. B. Yeats,* 1963.
Stoll, John E. *The Great Deluge: A Yeats Bibliography,* 1971 .
Wade, Allan, and Russell Alspach. *A Bibliography of the Writings of W. B. Yeats,* 1968.

Biographical and Critical:

Berryman, Charles. *W. B. Yeats: Design of Opposites,* 1967.
Bloom, Harold. *Yeats,* 1970.
Bradford, Curtis B. *Yeats at Work,* 1965.
Bushrui, S. B. *Yeats' Verse Plays: The Revisions,* 1966.
Clark, David R. *W. B. Yeats and the Theatre of Desolate Reality,* 1965.
Ellman, Richard. *Eminent Domain: Yeats Among Wilde, Joyce, Pound, Eliot, and Auden,* 1967.
— *The Identity of Yeats,* 1954.
Engleberg, Edward. *The Vast Design,* 1964.
Garab, Arra M. *Beyond Byzantium: The Last Phase of Yeats's Career,* 1969.

Grossman, Allen R. *Poetic Knowledge in the Early Yeats: A Study of "The Wind Among the Reeds,"* 1969.
Henn, T. R. *The Lonely Tower: Studies in the Poetry of W. B. Yeats,* 1950.
Hone, Joseph. *W. B. Yeats 1865-1939,* 1942.
Jeffares, A. Norman. *A Commentary on the Collected Poems of W. B. Yeats,* 1968.
— *The Poetry of W. B. Yeats,* 1961.
— *W. B. Yeats: Man and Poet,* 1966.
Koch, Vivienne. *W. B. Yeats: The Tragic Phase,* 1951.
Levine, Bernard. *The Dissolving Image: The Spiritual-Esthetic Development of W. B. Yeats,* 1970.
MacNeice, Louis. *The Poetry of W. B. Yeats,* 1941.
Maxwell, D. E. S., and S. B. Bushrui (eds.). *W. B. Yeats, 1865-1965: Centenary Essays on the Art of W. B. Yeats,* 1966. [Bib. pp. 227-241.]
Moore, Virginia. *The Unicorn: William Butler Yeats' Search for Reality,* 1954. [Bib. pp. 476-488.]
Nathan, Leonard E. *The Tragic Drama of William Butler Yeats: Figures in a Dance,* 1965.
Orel, Harold. *The Development of William Butler Yeats: 1885-1900,* 1968.
Saul, George Brandon. *Prolegomena to the Study of Yeats's Plays,* 1958.
— *Prolegomena to the Study of Yeats's Poems,* 1957.
Stallworthy, Jon. *Vision and Revision in Yeats's Last Poems,* 1969.
Torchiana, Donald T. *W. B. Yeats and Georgian Ireland,* 1966.
Ure, Peter. *Yeats, the Playwright,* 1963.
— *Towards a Mythology: Studies in the Poetry of W. B. Yeats,* 1946.
Vendler, Helen. *Yeats's "Vision" and the Later Plays,* 1963.
Whitaker, Thomas R. *Swan and Shadow: Yeats' Dialogue with History,* 1966.
Wilson, F. A. C. *W. B. Yeats and Tradition,* 1958.
Zwerdling, Alex. *Yeats and the Heroic Ideal,* 1965.

Yeats' literary, political and philosophical ideals continued to evolve throughout his long, richly productive life. From 1889-1904, he wrote attractive Rhymers' Club verse on Celtic subject matter. After 1904, his involvement in two heart-rending affairs, one with Maud Gonne, the other with the Irish struggle for self-determination, gave his verse greater urgency and concreteness. His greatest period was 1916-1929 when he achieved a rare balance between private torment and public concern in poems like "Sailing to Byzantium" and "Among School Children." In his last decade, his keen awareness of old age and the dream of youth made him write "mad songs." Yeats was a potent force in drama, and while he lived to see his dreams of an Irish verse-drama revival fade, his own achievements in that genre (like *Deirdre*) are superb—both as poetry and drama. His use of obscure symbolism, his frequent changes of poetic fashion and his employment of magic and the occult have proved barriers to understanding and appreciation of his poetic gifts, but he remains pre-eminent among the poets of his generation.

YELLOW BOOK, THE

An illustrated hard-cover quarterly published 1894-1897, *The Yellow Book* was the best of the art-plus-literature periodicals of the 1890's. From the first, it symbolized revolt against Victorian standards of ethics and morals in its contents and in its emphasis on yellow, the color used for covers of shocking French novels. Art editor Aubrey Beardsley supplied drawings and literary editor Henry Harland accepted the work of young dissidents like George Moore, W. B. Yeats, Hubert Crackanthorpe, Max Beerbohm, Arthur Symons, John Davidson and a few more respectable literary lions like Henry James. The editors sought, however, not to shock their readers, but to be modern and to make the journal a thing of beauty. Although the demise of *The Yellow Book* was deferred until 1897, the fatal blow was struck by the Wilde debacle in 1895. Beardsley was forced off the staff, and—although Wilde had not been closely associated with the journal—the outcry against rebellious and unconventional young men doomed what had been from the outset a product of young rebels.

YOUNG, FRANCIS BRETT (1884-1954)

Fiction:

Deep Sea, 1914.
The Dark Tower, 1915.
The Iron Age, 1916.
The Young Physician, 1919.
The Black Diamond, 1921.
And other titles.

Poems:

Five Degrees South, 1917.
Poems: 1916-18, 1919.

Prose:

Robert Bridges: A Critical Study, 1914.
Marching on Tanga, 1917.
And other titles.

Biographical and Critical:

Swinnerton, Frank. *The Georgian Literary Scene,* 1935. Pp. 252-254.
Twitchett, E. G. *Francis Brett Young,* 1935.
Young, Jessica Brett. *Francis Brett Young: A Biography,* 1962.

The lyric impulse in Young's fiction and verse was strong. His fiction, for which he is chiefly remembered, differs sharply from that of other poet-novelists, like Hardy, in its lack of the dramatic element. The pace of the novels is slow, their tone, mellow. His aim was not realism but the presentation of panoramas, picturesque reflections of the life of the English midlands, such as a landscape painter might fashion. Relative stasis has severely limited the appeal of his novels, despite their beautiful descriptions of nature.

ZANGWILL, ISRAEL (1864-1926)

Fiction:

The Bachelors' Club, 1891.
The Big Bow Mystery, 1892.
Children of the Ghetto, 1892.
Ghetto Tragedies, 1893.
The King of Schnorrers, 1894.
Joseph the Dreamer, 1895.
The Master, 1895.
The Mantle of Elijah, 1900.
The Grey Wig, 1903.
Ghetto Comedies, 1907.
The Grandchildren of the Ghetto, 1914.
The Works of Israel Zangwill. Ed. A. A. Walmark. 14 vols., 1925.
And other titles.

Prose:

Italian Fantasies, 1910.
The Voice of Jerusalem, 1920.
Speeches, Articles and Letters. Ed. Maurice Simon. 1937.
And other titles.

Bibliographical:

Adams, Elsie B. "Israel Zangwill: An Annotated Bibliography of Writings About Him," *English Literature in Transition*, XIII: 3 (1970). 209-244.
Peterson, Annamarie. "Israel Zangwill (1864-1926): A Selected Bibliography," *Bulletin of Bibliography*, XXIII (September-December, 1961), 136-140.

Biographical and Critical:

Adams, Elsie Bonita. *Israel Zangwill*, 1971. [Bib. pp. 164-171.]
Bensusan, S. L. "Israel Zangwill," *Quarterly Review*, CCXLVII (October, 1926), 285-303.
Golding, Louis. "Zangwill the Man," *Fortnightly Review*,

CXXI (April, 1927), 519-528.
Leftwitch, Joseph. *Israel Zangwill: A Biography,* 1957. [Weak; short on analysis.]
Wohlgelernter, Maurice. *Israel Zangwill: A Study,* 1964. [Bib. pp. 321-334.]

A man of independent mind, Zangwill enjoyed challenging accepted beliefs and championing unpopular causes like women's suffrage. He actively supported the establishment of Jewish colonies abroad, and his creative work often depicts Jews struggling in a hostile world. *Children of the Ghetto,* Zangwill's best known work, is based on firsthand experience of life in London's East End ghetto and marks him a member of the naturalistic movement of English fiction. While he employed pathetic ghetto subject matter—poverty, illness, oppression—in this and later works, his treatment of it, as in *Ghetto Comedies,* was lightened by humor.

INDEX OF NAMES AND TERMS

Numbers in italics refer to main entries in Part II.

A

Abbey Theatre 53, 55, 56, 57, 58, 113, 118, 145, 164, 233, 254, 258, 285

Abercrombie, Lascelles *79*

AE. See Russell, George

Aesthete, aesthetic, aestheticism 30-31, 32, 35, 41, 69-70, *80*, 128, 156, 174, 176, 277, 283, 306

Allen, Grant i, *80-81*, 262

Anodos. See Coleridge, Mary

Anstey, F. Guthrie. See Guthrie, Thomas

Archer, William 46, 48, *81-82*

Arnold, Matthew 29, 66

Art for art's sake (*l'art pour l'art)* 31, 33, 35, 36, 70, 80, 128, 229, 244, 306

Ashford, Daisy *83*

Auden, W. H. 35

B

Balzac, Honoré de 5, 19, 227

Barker, Harley Granville. See Granville-Barker, Harley

Barlas, John *83-84*

Baron Corvo. See Rolfe, Frederick

Barrie, James 52, *84-86*, 125, 195, 238

Baudelaire, Charles 31, 306

Beardsley, Aubrey *86-87*, 128, 260-261, 311

Beerbohm, Max 72, *88-89*, 261, 311

Belloc, Hilaire 68, 74, *89-91*, 115

Bennett, Arnold 8-9, 10, *91-93*

Benson, Arthur *93-94*, 95

Benson, Edward *94*, 95

Benson, Robert *95*

Bentley, E. C. *96*

Beresford, John *97-98*

Besant, Walter *98-99*

Binyon, Robert *99*

Birrell, Augustine *100*

Blackwood, Algernon *100-101*

Bland, Mrs. Hubert. See Nesbit, Edith

Blunden, Edmund 155

Blunt, Wilfred *101-102*

Bottomley, Gordon *102-103*

Bridges, Robert 40, *103-105*, 130, 179

Brooke, Rupert 41-42, 43, *105-106*, 260, 291

Brooke, Stopford *106*
Brown, George Douglas (George Douglas) *107*, 195, 232
Browne, Thomas 61
Browning, Robert 29, 96, 118
Buchan, John 25-26, *107-109*, 116
Burns, Robert 118
Burton, Richard 60, 62
Butler, Samuel 2-3, 4, 50, 63-64, 67, 68, 98, *109-111*, 221

C

Caine, Hall. See Caine, Thomas
Caine, Thomas *111-112*
Cannan, Gilbert *112-113*
Carlyle, Thomas 66
Celtic Renaissance (Celtic Revival, Irish Literary Renaissance) 34-35, 53-58, *113*, 114, 164, 218, 228, 258, 290, 291
Celtic Revival. See Celtic Renaissance
Celtic Twilight *114*, 264
Chekhov, Anton 22, 234
Chesterton, G. K. 27, 41, 74, *114-116*
Childers, Erskine 25, *116*
Clerihew (verse form) 96n
Clerihew, E. See Bentley, E. C.
Coleridge, Mary *116-117*
Collins, Wilkie 27
Colum, Padraic 54, 55, 56-57, *117-118*
Conrad, Joseph 11-13, 16, 18, 20, 62, *118-122*, 188, 261, 279
Corelli, Marie. See Mackay, Mary
Corvo, Baron. See Rolfe, Frederick
Cory, Vivian 81n
Crackanthorpe, Hubert 17, 19, 20, *122-123*, 311
Craigie, Pearl *123-124*
Crashaw, Richard 40
Crockett, Samuel *125*, 195
Cross, Victoria. See Cory, Vivian
Cunninghame-Graham, R. B. See Graham, Robert Cunninghame
Custance, Olive. See Douglas, Mrs. Alfred

D

Darmesteter, James 141
Darmesteter, Mary. See Duclaux, Mary
Darwin, Charles 60, 63, 64
Davidson, John *126-127*, 249, 311
Davies, William 40, *127-128*
Decadence, decadent 30-31, 32, 33, 34, 41, 80, *128*, 132, 136-137, 146, 156, 174, 194, 279, 282, 306, 307

De la Mare, Walter 155
De Morgan, William *129*
Dickens, Charles 1, 98, 129
Dickinson, Emily 117
Dixon, Richard 40, *130-131*
Dobson, Henry *131-132*
Doughty, Charles 61, *132-133*
Douglas, Alfred *133-134*
Douglas, Mrs. Alfred *134-135*
Douglas, Evelyn. See Barlas, John
Douglas, George. See Brown, George Douglas
Douglas, Olive. See Douglas, Mrs. Alfred
Dowson, Ernest 32, 33, 34, 128, *135-137*, 249
Doyle, Arthur Conan 25, 27, 28, *137-139*
Drinkwater, John 40-41, *139-140*, 156
Duclaux, Mary *140-141*
Du Maurier, George *142-143*
Dunsany, Lord. See Plunkett, Edward

E

Eagle, Solomon. See Squire, John
Eastaway, Edward. See Thomas, Edward
Eliot, T. S. 35, 65, 103, 149
Ellis, Havelock 4, 72-73, *143-144*
English Review 188
Ervine, St. John 55, 58, *144-145*
Estheticism. See Aesthete

F

Fabian, Fabianism 66-68, 66n, 267
Falkner, J. Meade 25, 26, *146*
Fin de siècle 32, 128, 141, *146-147*, 255
Fitzgerald, Edward 29
Flaubert, Gustave 5, 227
Flecker, James *147*
Ford, Ford Madox. See Hueffer, Joseph
Forster, E. M. ii, 15-16, 23, 23n, *148-150*, 205
Fortnightly Review 173
Frazer, James 64-65, *150-151*
Freeman, John *151-152*
Frost, Robert 287
Fry, Christopher 103

G

Galsworthy, John 8, 9-10, 51-52, *152-154*, 163
Gautier, Theophile 31
GBS, G.B.S. See Shaw, George Bernard
George, Walter *155*

Georgian Poetry 30, 40-41, 71, 152, *155-156*, 272, 297
Gilbert, W. S. 45, 306
Gissing, George 5-6, 8, 92, *156-158*, 205, 230, 280, 281
Goncourt, E. L. A. de 5, 19
Goncourt, J. A. H. de 5, 19
Gonne, Maud 35
Gosse, Edmund 74, *158-160*
Graham, Robert Cunninghame (R. B. Cunninghame-Graham), 62, *160-161*
Grahame, Kenneth *161-162*
Granville-Barker, Harley 50-51, *162-163*
Gregory, Isabella (Lady Gregory) 53, 54-55, 113, *163-164*, 254
Grein, J. T. 48, 53
Grossmith, George *164*
Grossmith, Walter *164*
Guthrie, Thomas *165*

H

Haggard, H. Rider 25, 28, 108, 109, *165-167*, 173
Hankin, St. John *167*
Hardy, Thomas 2, 3-4, 8, 14, 35, 37-38, 39, 81, *168-171*, 205, 312
Harland, Henry *171-172*, 311
Harris, Frank *172-173*
Hawkins, Anthony Hope (Anthony Hope) *173*, 238
Henley, W. E. 35, 37, 65, *174*, 208
Hewlett, Maurice *175-176*
Hichens, Robert *176*
Hinkson, Mrs. See Tynan, Katharine
Hobbes, John Oliver. See Craigie, Pearl
Hood, George. See Brown, George Douglas
Hope, Anthony. See Hawkins, Anthony Hope
Hopkins, Gerard Manley 35, 39-40, 130, *177-179*
Hornimann, A. E. F. (Miss) 53
Houghton, Stanley *179-180*
Housman, A. E. 35, 37, 38-39, *180-182*, 297
Housman, Clemence *182*
Housman, Laurence 182, *183-184*
Howells, W. D. 124
Hudson, W. H. 61-62, 63, 161, *184-185*
Hueffer, Joseph (Ford Madox Ford) 13, *185-188*
Huysmans, J. K. 31

I

Ibsen, Henrik 5, 46, 48, 54, 56, 57, 74, 82, 160, 163, 165, 218, 224, 245, 247, 254, 267

Irish Literary Renaissance. See Celtic Renaissance
Iron, Ralph. See Schreiner, Olive

J

Jacobs, W. W. *188-189*
James, Henry 311
James, M. R. 26, 146, *189-190*, 278
Jefferies, Richard 62-63, *190-192*
Jerome, Jerome K. *192-193*
Johnson, Lionel 32, 33-34, *193-194*, 249
Jones, Henry Arthur 46-47, *194-195*, 245, 247, 268
Joyce, James ii, 23n, 65, 149, 250

K

Kailyard School 86, 107, 125, *195*, 294
Kaye-Smith, Sheila *195-196*
Keats, John 80, 207
King, Kennedy. See Brown, George Douglas
Kipling, Rudyard 19-21, 25, 35-37, *197-200*, 236, 260, 273
Korzeniowski, Jozef K. See Conrad, Joseph

L

Lady Gregory. See Gregory, Isabella
Lamb, Charles 60, 210
Lane, John 209
Lang, Andrew 65-66, *201-202*
Lawrence, D. H. ii, 14-15, 16, 17, 21-22, 23n, 41, 149, 155, *202-206*
Ledwidge, Francis *206-207*
Lee, Vernon. See Paget, Violet
Lee-Hamilton, Eugene *207-208*
Le Fanu, J. Sheridan 26
Le Gallienne, Richard *208-209*, 249
Lindesay, Ethel. See Richardson, Henry Handel
Livingstone, David 60
Lord Dunsany. See Plunkett, Edward
Lucas, E. V. *209-210*
Luska, Sidney. See Harland, Henry

M

Macaulay, Rose *211*
Machen, Arthur 26, 146, *212-213*, 278
Mackay, Mary *213-214*
Mackenzie, Compton *214-215*
Maclaren, Ian. See Watson, John
Macleod, Fiona. See Sharp, William

Mallock, W. H. *215-216*
Mansfield, Katherine. See Murry, Kathleen
Marsh, Edward 40-41, 155-156
Martin, Violet (Martin Ross) *217*, 271
Martyn, Edward 53, 54, 55, 113, *218*, 254
Masefield, John 41, 163
Mason, A. E. W. *218-219*
Maugham, Somerset ii, 8, 18, 52, *219-221*
Maupassant, Guy de 19
Meredith, George ii, 224
Merrick, Leonard. See Miller, Leonard
Meynell, Alice *222*
Meynell, Viola 40
Meynell, Wilfred 40
Mill, John Stuart 66
Miller, Leonard *223*
Monkhouse, Allan *223-224*
Montague, C. E. *224-225*
Moore, George 5, 6-8, 54, 68, 92, 128, 141, *225-228*, 258 306, 311
Moore, T. Sturge *228-229*
Morris, William ii
Morrison, Arthur *229-230*
Munro, H. H. *230-231*
Munro, Neil *231-232*
Murray, Thomas C. 54, 56, 57-58, *232-233*
Murry, Kathleen (Katherine Mansfield) 17, 22-23, 23n, *233-234*

N

National Observer 174
Naturalism, naturalist, naturalistic 5, 6, 7, 8, 9, 17, 18-19, 31, 123, 270, 314
Nesbit, Edith *234-235*
Newbolt, Henry *235-236*
Nicoll, William R. 195
Nietzsche, Friedrich 127
Noyes, Alfred *236-237*

O

Oliver, George. See Onions, George Oliver
Onions, George Oliver *238*
Onions, Oliver. See Onions, George Oliver
Owen, Wilfred 42-43, *238-240*, 291

P

Paget, Violet (Vernon Lee) 71-72, *240-241*
Pain, Barry *241-242*, 252
Pater, Walter ii, 31, 39, 69-70, 71, 73, 74, 80, 241, *242-244*, 249, 282

Phillips, Stephen *244-245*
Pinero, Arthur 47, 52, 57, *245-246*, 247, 268
Plunkett, Edward, Lord Dunsany 206, *246-247*
Poe, Edgar Allan 26, 27
Pre-Raphaelites 130, 188
Problem Play 46, 47, 49, 52, 57, 245-246, *247-248*
Punch 165, 262

Q

Q. See Quiller-Couch, Arthur
Quiller-Couch, Arthur *248-249*

R

Rhymers' Club 32-33, 34, 41, *249*, 283-284, 310
Rhys, Ernest 32
Richardson, Dorothy 13, *249-250*
Richardson, Henrietta. See Richardson, Henry Handel
Richardson, Henry Handel *251-252*
Ridge, Pett *252*
Rimbaud, Arthur 136
RLS, R.L.S. See Stevenson, Robert Louis
Robertson, Ethel. See Richardson, Henry Handel
Robertson, Thomas 45
Robinson, A. Mary F. See Duclaux, Mary
Robinson, Lennox 54, 55, 57, *253-254*
Rolfe, Frederick *254-255*
Rolleston, T. W. 32
Rosenberg, Isaac 43, *256*, 291
Ross, Martin. See Martin, Violet; see also Somerville, Edith
Rossetti, Dante Gabriel 29, 80, 112, 249, 291, 306
Ruskin, John 66, 282
Russell, George 53, 113, *257-258*
Rutherford, Mark. See White, William Hale

S

Saki. See Munro, H. H.
Saintsbury, George 73-74, *258-259*
Sassoon, Siegfried *259-260*, 291
Saturday Review 173
Savoy 19, 32, 87, 249, *260-261*, 283
Schreiner, Olive *261-262*
Seaman, Owen *262*
Sharp, William (Fiona Macleod) 113, *263-264*
Shaw, George Bernard ii, 3, 46, 48-50, 51, 52, 62, 66-67, 68, 74, 128, 163, 167, 180, 224, 246, 247, 261, *264-268*, 290

Shorthouse, J. Henry *268-269*
Simpson, Warwick. See Ridge, Pett
Sinclair, May *269-270*
Smithers, Leonard 260
Snow, C. P. 63
Somerville, Edith 217, *270-271*
Squire, John *271-272*
Steel, Flora Annie *273*
Stephen, J. K. *273-274*
Stevenson, Robert Louis 17-18, 24-25, 26, 28, 59-60, 61, 108, 146, *274-277*
Stoker, Bram 26-27, *277-278*
Strachey, Lytton 68-69, *278-279*
Street, George *279*
Sullivan, Arthur 45, 306
Swift, Jonathan 303-304
Swinburne, Algernon 29-30, 31, 306
Swinnerton, Frank *280-281*
Symonds, John Addington 71, 141, *281-282*
Symons, Arthur 32, 71, 249, 261, *282-284*, 311
Synge, J. M. 53, 55, 56, 113, 164, *284-285*

T

Tennyson, Alfred 29, 295
Thackeray, William 1, 16
Thomas, Edward *286-287*
Thompson, Francis 35, 39, 40, *287-289*
Thoreau, Henry 60
Todhunter, John *289-290*
Transatlantic Review 188
Trench, Herbert *290*
Trench Poets 30, 41-43, *291*
Trollope, Anthony 293
Tynan, Katharine *291-292*

V

Vanity Fair 173
Verlaine, Paul 136
Verne, Jules 27
Villon, Francois 285
Vizetelly, Henry 5, 7

W

Wagner, Richard 267
Walpole, Hugh *292-293*
Ward, Mrs. Humphry *293-294*
Watson, John 125, 195, *294*
Watson, John William *295-296*
Watson, William. See Watson, John William
Webb, Mary *296-297*
Wells, H. G. 8, 10-11, 27-28, 67-68, 74, 96, 157, 164, *297-300*
Weyman, Stanley *301*
White, William Hale 2, 4, *301-302*
Whiteing, Richard *303-304*

Wilde, Oscar 31-32, 47-48, 52, 70-71, 80, 87, 128, 134, 176, 231, 260, *304-306*, 311
Woolf, Virginia 92
Wordsworth, William 62-63
Wratislaw, Theodore 32, *306-307*
Wynne-Tyson, Esmé 97

Y

Yeats, W. B. ii, 32, 33, 34-35, 39, 53, 54, 55, 56, 65, 71, 113, 114, 164, 229, 249, 254, 258, 261, *307-311*
Yellow Book 19, 32, 87, 135, 172, 249, 260, *311*
Young, Francis Brett *312*

Z

Zangwill, Israel *313-314*
Zola, Émile 5, 6, 8, 19, 73, 227